To Charles
With Best Wishes

Patrick Gutti
CEO Eagle Star

A HOUSE IN TOWN

22

ARLINGTON
STREET

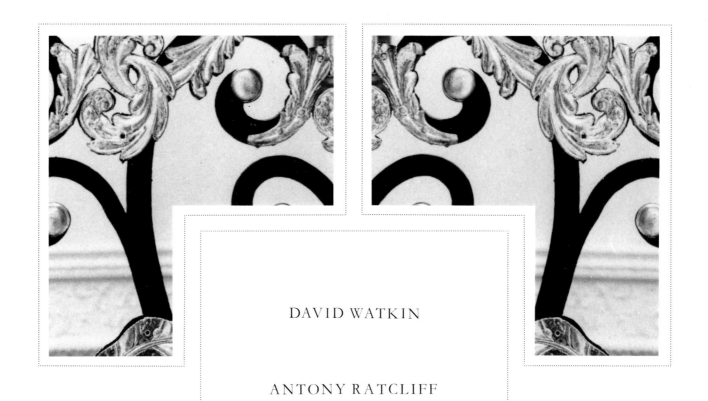

DAVID WATKIN

ANTONY RATCLIFF

NICHOLAS THOMPSON

JOHN MILLS

EDITED BY PETER CAMPBELL

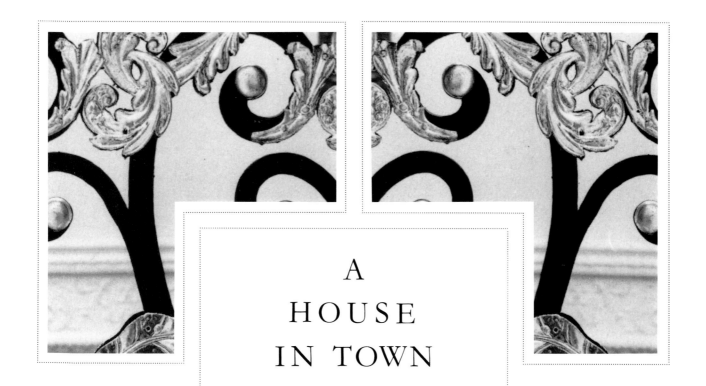

A
HOUSE
IN TOWN

22 ARLINGTON STREET
ITS OWNERS AND
BUILDERS

B.T. BATSFORD LTD, LONDON
in association with
EAGLE STAR HOLDINGS PLC

FIRST PUBLISHED 1984

© EAGLE STAR HOLDINGS PLC

REPRINTED 1997

ALL RIGHTS RESERVED. NO PART OF THIS PUBLICATION

MAY BE REPRODUCED IN ANY FORM OR BY ANY MEANS

WITHOUT PERMISSION FROM THE PUBLISHERS

ISBN 0 7134 4563 7

PRINTED IN HONG KONG THROUGH WORLD PRINT LTD

FOR THE PUBLISHERS, B.T. BATSFORD LTD

583 FULHAM ROAD, LONDON SW6 5BY

IN ASSOCIATION WITH

EAGLE STAR HOLDINGS PLC

60 ST. MARY AXE, LONDON EC3A 8JQ

CONTENTS

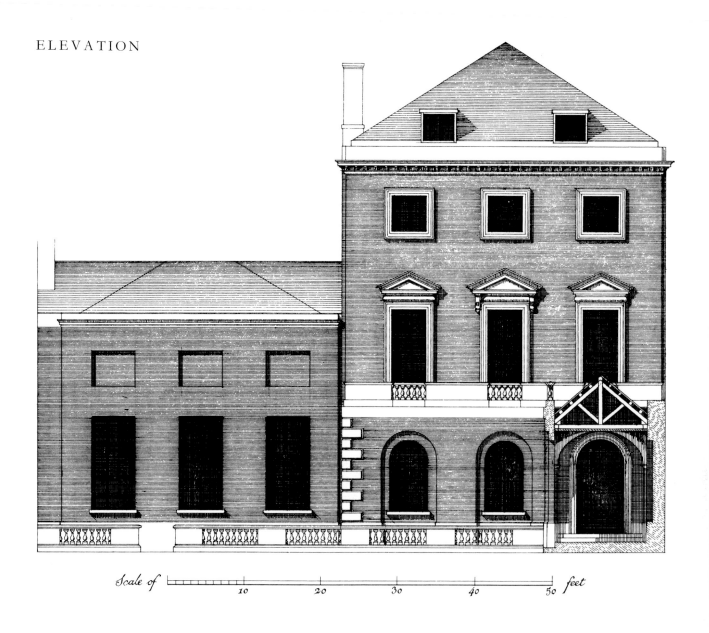

Scale of ⊢—————————————⊣ feet
          10   20   30   40   50

PLANS AND PRINCIPAL ELEVATION OF WILLIAM KENT HOUSE, 22 ARLINGTON STREET, IN 1983

A Arcade	F Great Room	K Saloon
B Entrance Lobby	G Blue Drawing Room	M Octagonal Room
C Entrance Hall	H Green Drawing Room	N Henry Pelham's Room
D Music Room	I Back stairs and lift	O Boudoir
E Oval Room	J Staircase Hall	Q space over Music Room

In the restoration of William Kent House the architects were Stone Toms and Partners.

Historical advice was provided by Donald W Insall and Associates who also acted as architectural consultants for the restoration of the arcade and the main front of William Kent House. Ian Bristow advised on colour schemes for the interior.

The professional team was completed by Watkins Pool Partnership, Quantity Surveyors; Alan Marshall and Partners, Structural Engineers; the Air Conditioning Design Partnership, Services Engineers.

Scarisbrick and Bate Limited were the interior design consultants and the main contractor was Bernard Sunley and Sons Limited.

GROUND FLOOR

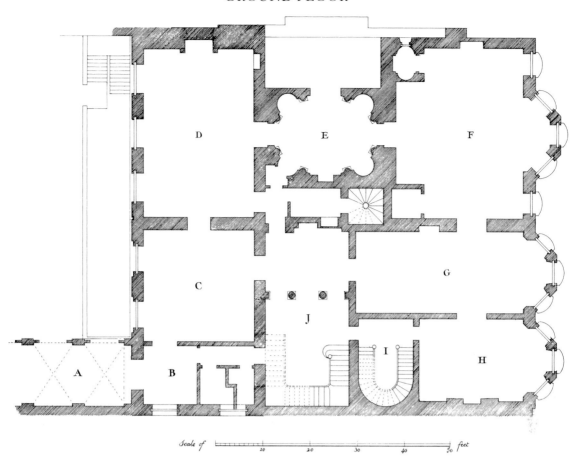

Scale of 10 20 30 40 50 feet

FIRST FLOOR

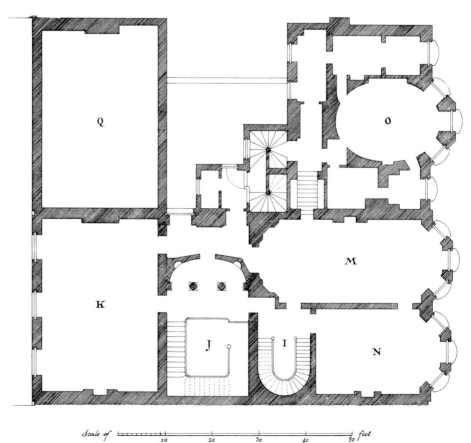

Scale of 10 20 30 40 50 feet

The illustrations are reproduced by permission of the following:
BLACK AND WHITE
P. 10, Devonshire Collection, Chatsworth, reproduced by permission of the Trustees of the Chatsworth Settlement/photo Courtauld Institute; p. 11, Edwin Smith; pp. 12–13, 1 National Portrait Gallery, 2 Country Life, 3 Edwin Smith, 4 A. F. Kersting, 5 Joseph C. Farber; pp. 14–15, 1 The Trustees of Sir John Soane's Museum, 2 & 3 A. F. Kersting, 4 Edwin Smith; p. 16, 1 BBC Hulton Picture Library, 2 Devonshire Collection, Chatsworth reproduced by permission of the Trustees of the Chatsworth Settlement/photo Courtauld Institute; p. 17, 1 & 2 RIBA; pp. 18–19, 1 & 5 Edwin Smith, 2, 3 & 4 A. F. Kersting, 6 & 7 RIBA, 8 National Monuments Record; pp. 20–21, 1 Mansell Collection, 2 National Trust, 3 Edwin Smith, 4 Country Life; pp. 22–23, 1 Centro Internazionale di Studi di Architettura 'Andrea Palladio', Vicenza, 2 & 3 RIBA, 4 A. F. Kersting; pp. 24–25, 1 Country Life, 2 J.-J. Hautefeuille, 3 Jeremy Whitaker; p. 26, Courtauld Institute; p. 27, British Museum; pp. 28–29, 1 Guildhall Library, 2 Aerofilms, 3 Courtauld Institute, 4 Edwin Smith; pp. 30–31, 1 Mansell Collection, 2 American Academy in Rome, 3 & 4 Edwin Smith; p. 32, Roger-Viollet; p.33, Christie's; p. 34, Courtauld Institute; p. 35, Country Life; p. 37, 1 BBC Hulton Picture Library, 2 A. F. Kersting; p. 38, National Monuments Record; p. 39, Country Life; pp. 40–41, 1 & 2 GLC; pp. 42–43, 1 Geoff Goode/Weidenfeld and Nicolson, 2 Courtauld Institute, 3 National Monuments Record; p. 44, National Gallery; p. 45, National Gallery; p. 46, Bildarchiv Foto Marburg; p. 47, Country Life; p. 48, 1 Country Life, 2 GLC; p. 49, 1 Victoria and Albert Museum, 2 A. F. Kersting; pp. 50–51, 1 National Maritime Museum, 2 Victoria and Albert Museum, 3 RIBA, 4 Edwin Smith; p.53 Country Life; pp. 54–55, 1 BBC Hulton Picture Library, 2 Jeremy Whitaker, 3 RIBA; pp. 56–57, 1 Peter Campbell, 2 The Trustees of Sir John Soane's Museum, 3 A. F. Kersting; pp. 58–59, 1 & 2 A. F. Kersting, 3 National Monuments Record, 4 Country Life; p. 60, GLC; p. 62, British Museum; p. 63, Edwin Smith; p. 64, Edwin Smith; p. 65, Courtauld Institute; p. 66, Lord Chichester; pp. 70–71, 1 Lord Chichester, 2 Country Life, 3 Mansell Collection; pp. 72–73, 1 By Gracious Permission of Her Majesty The Queen, 2 & 3 Victoria and Albert Museum, 4 National Portrait Gallery; pp. 74–75, 1 British Library, 2 Victoria and Albert Museum, 3 National Trust; pp. 76–77, 1 National Portrait Gallery, 2 & 3 Country Life, 4 Lord Chichester; pp. 78–79, 1 A. C. Cooper Ltd., 2 RIBA, 3 & 4 Courtauld Institute, 5 British Library; pp. 82–83, 1, 2 & 3 RIBA, 4 GLC; pp. 84–85, 1 Peter Campbell, 2 GLC, 3 British Library; pp. 86–87, 1 National Portrait Gallery, 2 & 4 The Trustees of Sir John Soane's Museum, 3 RIBA, 5 Guildhall Library; pp. 88–89, 1 British Library, 2 RIBA; pp. 90–91, 1 British Library, 2, 3 & 4 Merton Public Library, 5 Lord Chichester, 6 National Monuments Record; pp. 92–93, 1 RIBA, 2 & 3 British Museum; p. 94, National Trust; p. 95, Country Life; p. 97, 1 & 2 National Portrait Gallery; pp. 98–99, 1 Edwin Smith, 2, 3 & 4 British Library; p. 101, Bridgeman Art Library/Private Collection; p. 102, 1, 2 & 3 GLC; p. 104 GLC; p. 105, GLC; pp. 106–107, 1, 2 & 3 British Library, 4 GLC; pp. 108–109, 1 RIBA, 2 & 3 GLC, 4 Colin Westwood; pp. 110–111, 1 RIBA, 2 Bridgeman Art Library/Private Collection; p. 114, 1 Avery Architectural Library, Columbia University, 2 Peter Campbell; p. 115, National Portrait Gallery; p. 116, Private Collection; p. 117, 1 The Marquess of Zetland, 2 Country Life; p. 118, British Museum; p. 119, 1 National Portrait Gallery, 2 National Portrait Gallery/Private Collection; p. 121, 1 The Marquess of Lothian, 2 Everard Studley Miller Bequest, National Gallery of Victoria, Melbourne; pp. 122–123, 1 National Portrait Gallery, 2 The Architectural Press, 3 British Museum; p. 124, Trinity College, Cambridge; p. 126, the Duke of Beaufort/photo Courtauld Institute; p. 127, National Monuments Record; p. 129, Private Collection; pp. 130–131, 1 Private Collection, 2 & 3 RIBA; p. 132 RIBA; p. 133 RIBA; pp. 134–135, 1 & 2 RIBA, 3 Private Collection; p. 137, British Library; pp. 138–139, 1 BSC Dowlais, 3 BBC Hulton Picture Library, 4 National Monuments Record; pp. 140–141, National Monuments Record; pp. 142–143, 1 National Monuments Record, 2 British Library, 3 Sydney W. Newbery, 4 National Monuments Record; p. 144, 1 National Monuments Record, 2 & 3 British Library; p. 145, Press Association; p. 147, Viscount Wimborne; p. 148, 1 GLC, 2 Donald Insall and Associates; p. 149, Savills; pp. 150–151, 1, 2 & 3 Savills; pp. 152–153, 1 GLC, 2 RIBA, 3 Country Life; p. 155, 1 Antony Wysard, 2 Sotheby's; p. 156, Fox Photos; p. 157, Savills; p. 158, Savills; p. 159; Aerofilms; p. 160, Sydney W. Newbery; p. 161, Stone Toms and Partners; p. 163, 1 & 2 Colin Westwood; p. 164, Sydney W. Newbery; p. 165, Simon Mills; p. 166, GLC; p. 167, Simon Mills; pp. 168–169, 1, 2, 3 & 4 Simon Mills; p. 170, GLC; p. 171, 1 & 2 Simon Mills; p. 172, Simon Mills; p. 173, Simon Mills; pp. 174–175, 1, 2 & 3 Simon Mills; pp. 178–179, 1 British Library, 2, 3 & 4 Simon Mills; pp. 180–181, 1 GLC, 2, 3, & 5 Simon Mills; p. 182, Sydney W. Newbery; pp. 184–185, 1, 2, 3, 4 & 5 Simon Mills; pp. 186–187, 1 & 2 GLC, 3 Simon Mills; p. 188, Simon Mills; pp. 189–193 RIBA.

COLOUR
Facing p. 16, London Borough of Redbridge Libraries; facing p.17, Angelo Hornak; facing p. 32, Courtesy of Viscount Coke D.L./photo Jarrold Colour Publications, Norwich; facing p. 33, Franco Cisterna/Foto Techniche, Rome: facing p. 48, By Gracious Permission of Her Majesty the Queen; facing p. 49, By Gracious Permission of Her Majesty the Queen; facing p. 64, Charles Cottrell-Dormer; facing p. 65, Nicholas Meyjes and (top left) Antony Ratcliff; facing p. 80, Bridgeman Art Library/House of Commons; facing page 81, Bridgeman Art Library/Private Collection; facing p. 96, National Portrait Gallery; facing p. 97, Lee Fine Arts; facing p. 112, Jeremy Whitaker; facing p. 113, Jeremy Whitaker; facing p. 128, 1 & 2 British Museum; facing p. 129, the Duke of Beaufort; facing p. 144, Jeremy Whitaker; facing p. 145, Viscount Wimborne; pp. 160–161, Jeremy Whitaker; pp. 176–177, Jeremy Whitaker.

The fire-mark on the front of this book was issued by the original Eagle Star Insurance Company during the first half of the nineteenth century.

PREFACE

This book is the history of a house. It is intended as a memento for our friends, and as a record of the past history and recent restoration of 22 Arlington Street. Peter Campbell, who originally took on the task of designing the book, quickly realised that the series of jottings which we enthusiastically presented to him would only come together as a book under the hammer of inspired and devoted editorial leadership. This he provided. Ann Usborne found pictures for us which we did not know existed; more than that, she conjured them up where they did not, and this book contains a number of 'firsts' for example the Kent ceilings for the Church of S. Giuliano de' Fiamminghi in Rome and for Chicheley Hall.

The Book is in part a memorial to the architect, William Kent, after whom we have renamed the house, and we are grateful to David Watkin for his introductory essay on the place of Kent in the history of English architecture. We are grateful also to Nicholas Thompson, of Donald W. Insall & Associates, who advised on the restoration and who has traced the history of the house and its owners. In so doing he has illuminated the connection between the architectural and social history of the past two hundred and fifty years.

In his foreword to the BBC publication 'Spirit of the Age', to which this book may be regarded as complementary, John Drummond pays tribute to the late Sir Nikolaus Pevsner 'who has taught us all more about British architecture than we thought there was to know', an assertion we respectfully repeat.

If it is not to be a museum, a house must be a changing, and hence a living, thing. In its time this house has been a centre of political power, the scene of high ambitions, and of a concert series which played some part in our musical life. Our book records the changes that have occurred over the past two and a half centuries.

DENIS MOUNTAIN
Chairman & Managing Director
Eagle Star Group

Young William Kent, painted in Rome, in 1718, by his master, Benedetto Luti. Below the title: part of the staircase at 44 Berkeley Square.

DAVID WATKIN

WILLIAM KENT

(*c.* 1685–1748)

Kent is undoubtedly one of the two or three most important architects and designers at work in eighteenth-century England: as Horace Walpole observed, he was 'bold and opinionative enough to dare to dictate, and born with a genius to strike out a system from the twilight of imperfect essays'. The extraordinary richness and diversity of his talent give him a status that is unique: he was not only a prolific and gifted architect but also a painter, book illustrator and distinguished designer of gardens, garden buildings, furniture, interior decoration, sculpture and silverware. He can be seen as a Renaissance *uomo universale* set down in the midst of Whiggish Augustan England. His styles were as diverse as his commissions were varied: despite his role as a pioneer of neo-Palladianism, his work has strong Baroque and even neo-Classical elements, while he was also one of the principal inventors of the Gothic Revival. His fecundity and versatility in so many spheres of artistic endeavour have made him a daunting subject for the modern biographer, so that there is as yet no entirely adequate full-length study of him.

He is too complex a figure to be summarised simply as a protégé of Lord Burlington who consolidated and popularised the new Palladian style which had originally been invented by Burlington and Colen Campbell. There were many conflicting currents of taste circulating in England during the first half of the eighteenth century, and the progress from Baroque to Palladianism in architecture and from formality to naturalism in garden design was as complex as Kent's own artistic personality.

The adoption in England of the principles of Classical architecture and design characteristic of the Italian

1 The Earl of Arundel by Daniel Mytens, 1618. 2 The hall of Inigo Jones's Queen's House, Greenwich. 3 The Whitehall Banqueting House.

Renaissance had been halted by the cultural and religious break with Rome occasioned by the Reformation. The threads were taken up again under King James I and King Charles I who both employed Inigo Jones (1573–1652) as Surveyor-General of the King's Works. Jones's Italian journey of 1613–14 in the company of a great collector and patron, the Earl of Arundel, was important for helping to establish the Grand Tour as a necessary part of an architect's training. From humble beginnings Jones became someone who could mingle freely with patrons and courtiers: again, a pattern which was to be followed in the eighteenth century by architects like Kent, Chambers and Adam. Jones's chaste, refined and almost understated Classical style

4

4 *South front of the Queen's House, Greenwich.* 5 *The Villa Pisani by Palladio. Centrally accented Palladian and neo-Palladian villa façades.*

can be appreciated in his principal surviving buildings: the Queen's House, Greenwich (1616–35), the Banqueting House, Whitehall (1619–22), the Queen's Chapel, St James's (1623–25) and St Paul's, Covent Garden (1631–33). Jones took for his model the classic balance of the High Renaissance especially as exemplified in the buildings and published designs of the great Andrea Palladio (1508–1580) and his extremely conservative follower Vincenzo Scamozzi (1552–1616). It is perhaps curious that Jones should thus have been inspired by a style that was already sixty years out of date at the time of his visit to Italy. The style of seventeenth-century Italy was the Baroque, a style of massive exuberance far removed from the chaste linear-

The beginnings, and maturity, of English Baroque. 1 Wren's 1694 scheme for Greenwich. 2 The north front of Vanbrugh's Blenheim Palace.

ity of Jones. It is not surprising that Baroque elements should begin to appear in English architecture in the course of the seventeenth century, for example in the work of Sir Christopher Wren. Wren's unfinished Winchester Palace and first scheme for Greenwich Hospital provided his successors – Talman, Archer, Hawksmoor and especially Vanbrugh – with hints with which they developed a Baroque language combining monu-

mentality of scale with marked originality of detail. A building like Archer's St John, Smith Square, Westminster (1713–28) may stand as typical of the dynamic sculptural effects which Baroque architects aimed at: forms are moulded in a plastic way so that the elements of the Classical language, especially the column, are seen as essentially decorative rather than functional.

It should thus be appreciated that when the twenty-

3 St John, Smith Square, by Thomas Archer. 4 S. Carlo alle Quattro Fontane, Rome, by Borromini. Campbell thought it 'affected'.

four-year-old William Kent set off for Italy for the first time in 1709, English architecture was dominated by the powerful Baroque genius of architects like Vanbrugh and Archer whose respective designs for Blenheim Palace and the north wing of Chatsworth had been in process of execution from 1704. By contrast, the aim of the immensely influential 3rd Earl of Burlington (1694–1753) and the neo-Palladians was to correct what they felt to be impurities of this kind of design and to return to the strict and truthful canons of antique architecture, especially as interpreted in Renaissance Italy by Andrea Palladio. In suggesting that this ambition embodied Whig, nationalist and Protestant ideals it is necessary to introduce the 3rd Earl of Shaftesbury (1671–1713), whose moral and aesthetic philosophy underpinned the whole Palladian movement. The

1 *Burlington House.* 2 *Lord Burlington by Knapton.* COLOUR: *Wanstead, one of Colen Campbell's influential Palladian country house designs.*

political coup which brought about the Hanoverian succession in 1714 and was followed by the long supremacy of the Whigs was accompanied by the final establishment of Protestanism as the national orthodoxy. To Shaftesbury this represented a new and specifically English freedom in society, politics, and religious organisation which would inevitably be reflected in a new national style in architecture and the arts. Attacking revealed religion, he replaced it with a moralising emphasis on the role of culture and politics, and claimed of the English libertarian state in his *Letter Concerning Design* (1712) that 'Everything tends in such a state towards the improvement of art and science [and architecture]. The taste of one kind brings necessarily that of the others along with it. When the free spirit of a nation turns itself this way . . . the public eye and ear improve: a right taste prevails and in a manner forces its way'.

It was inevitable that Shaftesbury's new national style would differ from the current Baroque style, formed in the shadow of Wren, since Baroque could be seen as a modern Italianate style associated with Catholic church architecture and, in France, with absolute monarchy. Apart from stating his anti-Baroque position, Shaftesbury did not make any positive stylistic recommendations, and it was left to Lord Burlington to propose that the new national style should be founded on a return to Inigo Jones. The fact that a celebrated Englishman such as Jones had already adopted a refined Palladian classicism enabled Burlington and his circle to claim that in following his example they were returning to a truly national source. The creation of the new style was seen as involving the three following tasks: the translation of Palladio's great work of propaganda, *I Quattro Libri dell' Architettura* (1570), the publication of Inigo Jones's architectural designs, and the erection of public buildings in the new national style so as to form taste.

The Venetian architect Giacomo Leoni (*c.* 1686–1746), who settled in England early in the eighteenth century, published a translation (by Nicholas Dubois) of Palladio in five instalments between 1715 and 1720, while Colen Campbell (1676–1729) produced the three celebrated volumes of his *Vitruvius Britannicus* between

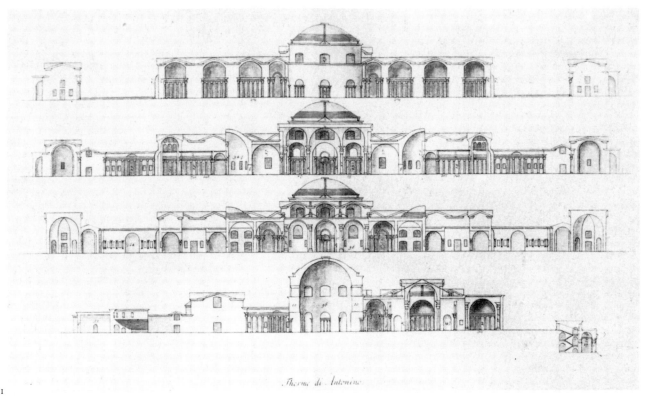

1715 and 1725 which illustrated recent English architecture and argued for the triumph of 'Antique Simplicity' over the 'affected and licentious' method of composition supposedly characteristic of the Baroque. Equally importantly, Campbell designed a group of houses in 1715–1725 which influenced architecture for the rest of the century: Wanstead, Essex, with its immense temple portico; Newby, Yorkshire, the typical five-bay Palladian villa; and Mereworth, Kent, the domed villa inspired by Palladio's Villa Rotonda near Vicenza.

It seems to have been the compelling visual and intellectual documentation assembled by Leoni, Dubois and Campbell which first stimulated Lord Burlington's interest in architecture. In 1719 he dropped the Baroque architect James Gibbs in favour of Colen Campbell as architect for Burlington House, Piccadilly, and in 1720–21 purchased from John Talman an important collection of drawings by Inigo Jones and John Webb. In 1727 he arranged for William Kent to publish these drawings in two volumes under the title *Designs of Inigo Jones . . . with some Additional Designs* [by Burlington and Kent]. Whilst in Italy Burlington had also acquired Palladio's own drawings of the Roman Baths which he published in 1730 as *Fabbriche Antiche disegnate da Andrea Palladio*. Burlington deliberately set

1 The Villa Rotonda by Palladio. 2 Colen Campbell's Mereworth Castle, Kent – a variation on the theme. 3 The Gallery, Mereworth Castle.

out to be the principal arbiter of taste in the England of his day, an ambition which he had fully achieved by the early 1730s. His own buildings, like Chiswick House, Tottenham Park, the Dormitory at Westminster School and the Assembly Rooms at York, brought together for the first time the motifs from the antique, from Palladio and from Inigo Jones which were to be so characteristic of eighteenth-century Anglo-Palladianism: semicircular windows from the Baths of Diocletian, coffered ceilings from the Roman temples, rooms with

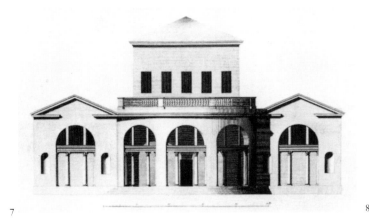

4,5 Chiswick House, by Lord Burlington. Burlington's designs for the dormitory, Westminster School (6) and the Assembly Rooms, York (7,8).

apses and screens of columns from the Roman baths, Venetian windows set in arched recesses, and columnar halls inspired by Palladio's reconstruction of the so-called 'Egyptian' hall described in the 1st century BC by Vitruvius in his celebrated treatise on architecture.

This preliminary survey has been necessary in order that we may understand the individual contribution of William Kent who enjoyed the special patronage of Lord Burlington throughout his career and, indeed, lived with him at Burlington House from 1719 until his

1 The Vatican Logge: *Raphael arabesques. 2 'The Marchese Pallavicini and the artist' by Carlo Maratta – the master of Kent's master.*

death. Burlington, as we have seen, had helped devise the purified style of Classical architecture in which he assumed that his protégé, William Kent, would work. Most of Burlington's own buildings had been designed either for himself or for the circle of his friends so that the next task was to ensure that Burlingtonian Palladianism replaced Baroque as the official style for royal and governmental buildings. An important step in this process was Kent's appointment in 1726, through Burlington's patronage, to a seat on the Board of Works and to the post of Master Mason and Deputy Surveyor in 1735. The most significant buildings that Kent designed in that capacity were his unexecuted Houses of Parliament (1730–40), Royal Mews, Charing Cross (1731–33, demolished 1830), and, in Whitehall, Treasury Buildings (1733–37) and Horse Guards (1748–59).

Lord Burlington had first met Kent in Rome in the winter of 1714–15 and brought him back to England with him in 1719. Kent was born in modest circumstances at Bridlington, Yorkshire, in *c.* 1685 and was

probably apprenticed to a coach-painter in Hull. Showing unusual promise as an artist, he was taken up by three connoisseurs: Sir William Wentworth of Bretton Park in Yorkshire, Burrell Massingberd of Ormsby Hall in Lincolnshire, and Sir John Chester, Bart., of Chicheley Hall in Buckinghamshire. These gentlemen supported him financially during his stay in Italy from 1709. In return, Kent shipped back to them packing-cases of architectural books, copies of Baroque paintings, prints, busts, fans and even soap and treacle. He was taught painting by Benedetto Luti and Giuseppe Chiari who were both disciples of the prolific and influential artist Carlo Maratta (1625–1713). Maratta and his followers were in some sense resistant to the flowing forms of the Baroque and maintained a more static classicising style. The tension between Baroque and anti-Baroque elements in Kent's own architectural work can perhaps be seen as a parallel to this. In 1713 Kent was awarded a medal by the celebrated Roman Accademia di San Luca in a competition for a painting of a miracle, and by 1717 he had sufficiently mastered the art of fresco

3 The Palazzo del Té, Mantua, by Giulio Romano. Kent used similar coffered ceilings at Berkeley Square (4) and Arlington Street.

painting to paint the ceiling of the church of S. Giuliano dei Fiamminghi in the Via del Sudario, Rome, an unimpressive work which can still be seen today.

It was as a decorative painter that Kent primarily regarded himself and it was his skill in that capacity that especially commended him to Lord Burlington. Following his return to England with Burlington in December 1719 he painted ceilings at Burlington House, at Cannons, Middlesex, for the Duke of Chandos and at Wanstead House, Essex, which had been designed for the Earl of Tylney by Colen Campbell. More importantly he was able, through Burlington's patronage, to displace Sir James Thornhill in 1722 in the prestigious commission for decorating Kensington Palace for King George I. Kent's ceiling in the Presence Chamber at Kensington Palace is a brightly coloured neo-antique design of the arabesque type already imitated in the Renaissance by Raphael and Giovanni da Udine in the Vatican *logge* and the Villa Madama and by Vasari in the Palazzo Vecchio in Florence. Kent repeated this type of ceiling in his charming Parlour at Rousham, Oxfordshire. His King's Staircase at Kensington is a characteristic exercise in Baroque illusion, but in general terms his contribution to eighteenth-century interior decoration was his move away from flowing Baroque wall and ceiling paintings towards a kind of ornament that was more subordinated to the architectural elements. This was felt to be more in keeping with the rich but ordered sobriety of Palladian architecture and interiors. Kent's interiors are full of the kind of incident that can be provided by coffered semidomes, niches and broken pediments. Decorative painting tends to be confined to ceilings divided firmly into compartments, and to walls with pictures set in architectural frames: examples of Kent's work in this vein can be seen at Chiswick House for Lord Burlington, at Ditchley House, Oxfordshire, for the Earl of Lichfield, at Houghton Hall, Norfolk, for Sir Robert Walpole, and at Badminton House, Gloucestershire, for the Duke of Beaufort. Most of these date from the 1720s but towards the end of his career Kent devised a sumptuous type of ceiling decor-

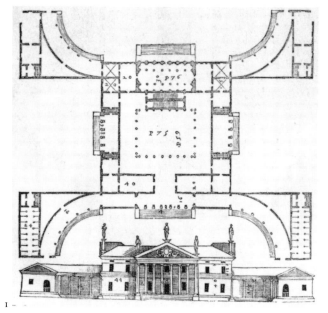

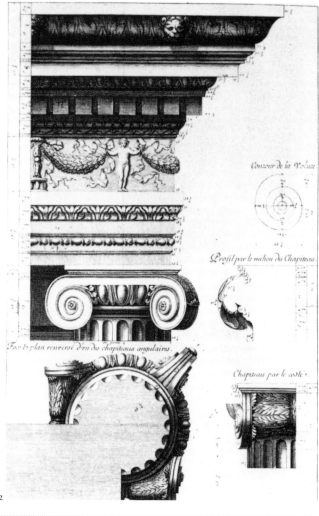

1 Palladio's plan for the Villa Mocenigo, from the 'Four Books on Architecture'. Holkham Hall, with its pavilion wings, derived from it.

ation at 44 Berkeley Square and at 22 Arlington Street which, again, had a firmer architectural organisation and dominance than had been customary in the High Baroque period. Whereas Baroque artists tended to treat the whole ceiling above the cove as a single painted composition, Kent now created a great architectural honeycomb of lozenges and octagons divided by gilded ribs and containing cameo-like grisaille paintings of mythological figures on blue and red grounds. Kent's magnificent but today almost totally unknown saloon at 22 Arlington Street, probably designed in the last year of his life and executed by Stephen Wright, is one of the finest domestic interiors in London. It is astonishing that it should be illustrated for the first time in the present book. Possible pre-Baroque precedents for it which Kent would have known can be seen at the Villa Madama, Rome, and the Doge's Palace in Venice.

One of Kent's most striking contributions to the history of interior design is his concern to integrate decoration and furnishings. In this he was the true precursor of Robert Adam: indeed, he was one of the first English architects to make designs for furniture and, as Cunningham wrote of him in 1820, he 'could plan bookcases, cabinets, and chimney pieces, hang curtains with grace; in short do all and more than all the upholsterer aspires to now'. In the Saloon at Houghton the gilded seat furniture in a massive Italianate style was designed by Kent as part of the architecture of the room, and was originally disposed round the edge of the room in the French manner. The walls and the seat furniture were covered with the same crimson cut wool velvet from Utrecht, while even the tops of the tables were made from the same green *porto venere* marble as the chimney piece. This hotly coloured room of parade forms a deliberate contrast with the white tones of the entrance hall. In the State Bedroom the walls, bed and chairs were originally all covered with the same green silk velvet. Though the wall hangings have been altered, the bed and chairs survive. The massively architectural bed, dominated by an immense fluted

2,3 Plates from Desgodetz's 'Edifices Antiques de Rome', 1682. 4 Palladio's Il Redentore, Venice, a source for the entrance hall at Holkham.

shell with spines picked out in gold braid, is one of the most striking objects Kent ever designed. Architectural is always the adjective which first comes to mind when one is describing Kent's furniture. His monumental mahogany and gilt side tables, sofas and mirrors make emphatic use of ancient Roman motifs like acanthus foliage, consoles, demi-figures, lion supports, Vitruvian scrolls and fret friezes, which would originally have been executed in marble.

In the early 1730s Kent turned his attention from decorative painting to architecture, a field in which he was to show himself greatly more skilled. His finest architectural work is doubtless Holkham Hall, Norfolk, designed in collaboration with its owner, the Earl of Leicester, and with Lord Burlington. It was executed from 1734–65 under the direction of Matthew Brettingham who had made some important and influential designs for it as early as 1726. This chaste but princely palace survives unaltered with its original contents as the finest memorial in the country to that passion for

Italy and the antique which was given expression in the Grand Tour of the eighteenth-century nobleman. One especially telling indication of Holkham's role as a temple of the arts is that no family portraits were originally included amongst the many fine paintings displayed in its principal rooms.

The initial idea for the plan of Holkham with its four pavilion wings was derived from Palladio's design for the Villa Mocenigo. Kent handles the various parts in what has been described as a 'staccato' way which emphasises their autonomy, as opposed to Baroque design with its imposition of an overall fluid unity. Work on the interiors continued long after Kent's death and the only ones which he is known to have designed are in the private wing and the entrance hall. However, we can describe the decoration of the whole interior as Kentian, with its plasterwork, columns and coffered ceilings deriving from Palladio, Jones and the temples of ancient Rome as illustrated in Desgodetz's *Edifices Antiques de Rome* (1682). The cool sculpture gallery with its chaste

1 Wakefield Lodge. Kent anticipated sparsely decorated European Neo-Classical buildings like M.-J. Peyre's Hôtel de Neubourg (2)

sculpture-filled niches anticipates later interiors by Robert Adam such as the gallery at Croome Court and the dining room at Lansdowne House. The great entrance hall is a spectacular tour de force produced by a painterly imagination which can only be described as Baroque. Designed on two levels united by a boldly flowing staircase, this breath-taking space combines elements from Vitruvius' 'Egyptian' Hall, the colonnaded basilicas of ancient Rome and the beautiful curved screen inside Palladio's Il Redentore, Venice.

The only equal in Kent's work to the Holkham staircase is the theatrical staircase at 44 Berkeley Square with its dramatic curved screen of columns on the first-floor landing. The splendour of this staircase and the coffered saloon to which it gives access provide a deliberate contrast with the extraordinarily modest three-bay exterior of the house. Exactly the same is true of the contemporary 22 Arlington Street. Here the understated façade is a close parallel to that of 44 Berkeley Square though the singularly graceless plan is perhaps an echo of the earlier house on the site. In 1734–35 Kent tried to apply this virtually featureless exterior style to the eleven-bay entrance front of the new mansion he was building in Piccadilly for the Duke of Devonshire. The exteriors of Devonshire House

(demolished in 1924–25) were never considered a success but the interiors, especially the high coved Saloon, were amongst Kent's most magnificent. More successful as a composition than Devonshire House was Wakefield Lodge, Northamptonshire, which Kent built in c.1748–50 as a hunting-box for his friend the Duke of Grafton. Its seven-bay entrance front is arrestingly punctuated with five segmental Diocletian windows, and sports an unpedimented Doric portico. Inside, the spacious two-storeyed hall with its gallery supported on consoles is inspired by Inigo Jones's at the Queen's House, Greenwich.

Kent's unexecuted designs of the 1730s for new Houses of Parliament and for an immense royal palace in Hyde Park were imposing if not very lively applications of Burlingtonian-Palladian façades to plans and sections boasting screens, domes and apses inspired by the great baths of Imperial Rome. Neo-antique splendour on such a scale was unique in Europe at that moment. These programmatic examples of the new national style remained unbuilt, and amongst Kent's most brilliant executed designs are the domed temples he built in the mid 1740s in the parks at Badminton, Gloucestershire, and Euston, Suffolk. These compact little masterpieces have a sense of energy just held in

3 *Worcester Lodge, Badminton, Gloucestershire. Kent's domed temples, here and at Euston, Suffolk, combine Baroque and Palladian elements.*

restraint and seem to embody a perfect balance between the opposing tensions of Baroque and Palladianism.

It is possible to see the Classical boldness of Kent and English Palladian architecture as in some sense anticipating the European neo-Classical movement later in the century. In France the frivolously fluttering forms of Rococo ornament survived right into the 1740s and when in *c.* 1750 reaction set in, it took the form of a style not dissimilar to that employed during the previous quarter of a century by designers like Kent and Burlington. Thus the austerity of M.-J. Peyre's Hôtel de Neubourg caused a stir when it was built in 1762 on the outskirts of Paris which it would scarcely have done in England where its bold and largely unadorned wall surfaces had been anticipated in works such as Wakefield Lodge. Kent's Temple of Venus at Stowe of 1731, with its Roman baths motif of an open screen of columns in front of an apsed and coffered niche, affords the closest parallel to a building of forty years later like the Hôtel Guimard in Paris designed by the leading neo-Classical architect C.-N. Ledoux. Similarly the robust massiveness of Kent's furniture design with its prominent use of antique forms such as the Vitruvian scroll and Greek key pattern anticipates the so-called *goût grec* of French furniture design as, for example, in

the furniture designed in *c.* 1756–57 for Lalive de Jully by L.-J. Le Lorrain. Also, the arabesque ceilings which Kent painted at Kensington Palace and Rousham adopted a neo-antique cum neo-Renaissance style which was not revived in France until Clérisseau's decoration of the salon of the Hôtel Grimod de Reynière in Paris in the 1770s.

One of the fields in which Kent's contribution was most innovatory was, perhaps surprisingly, the Gothic Revival. His work in this style undoubtedly influenced later designers in Rococo Gothick such as Daniel Garrett, Batty Langley, Sanderson Miller and Horace Walpole. The story began at Hampton Court in 1731 when Kent was commissioned to rebuild the east side of Clock Court which had become ruinous. He originally proposed a Classical scheme but this was turned down by Sir Robert Walpole, First Lord of the Treasury, on the grounds that the new work should be in harmony with the old. Kent's neo-Tudor Gatehouse is dated 1732. At about the same time, he was extensively rebuilding the fifteenth-century Esher Place, Surrey, for Henry Pelham, for whom he was later to build 22 Arlington Street. Though the Gothick wings Kent added at Esher have been demolished, the gate tower still retains his fanciful ogee-headed and quatre-

A drawing by Kent of Rousham showing how the existing Jacobean house was to be Gothicised. The wings to left and right are Kent additions.

foil windows. In the later 1730s he made designs for Gothicising two Jacobean-style houses, Honingham Hall, Norfolk, and Rousham, Oxfordshire. The former was not carried out but at Rousham his Gothic wings survive today together with a number of important garden buildings to which we shall return shortly. His Gothick interior fittings at York Minster, Gloucester Cathedral and Westminster Hall have all disappeared save for the York pulpit which can be seen in the parish church at his birth place, Bridlington in Yorkshire. The ambitious Gothick folly at Aske Hall, Yorkshire, has also been attributed to Kent on the strength of a drawing, possibly in his hand, showing an octagonal centre flanked by semi-circular projecting bows: the kind of vigorous geometrical composition which Robert Adam was later to deploy in the design of his remarkable Scottish castles.

It is significant that Kent only used Gothic forms when he was adding to or altering buildings that were already in earlier styles, Gothic, Tudor or Jacobean: in other words the essentially Picturesque notion of associationism already played a major part in his approach to architectural design. The sensitivity to the genius loci and to the past helps account for the special imaginative quality of his garden designs which date

from the years 1731–41. To Horace Walpole, Kent was 'the father of modern gardening' and the inventor of 'an art that realizes painting and improves nature'. Kent, so Walpole argued, 'leaped the fence and saw that all nature was a garden. He felt the delicious contrast of hill and valley changing imperceptibly into each other, tasted the beauty of the gentle swell, or concave scoop, and remarked how loose groves crowned an easy eminence with happy ornament . . . By selecting favourite objects, and veiling deformities by screens of plantation; sometimes allowing the rudest waste to add its foil to the richest theatre, he realised the compositions of the great masters in painting'. As early as December 1734 we find Sir Thomas Robinson explaining in a letter to Lord Carlisle the precise nature of the revolution which he felt Kent had effected:

There is a new taste in gardening just arisen, which has been practised with so great success at the Prince's garden in Town [i.e. at Carlton House, acquired by Frederick, Prince of Wales in 1733], that a general alteration of some of the most considerable gardens in the Kingdom is begun, after Mr Kent's notion of gardening, viz., to lay them out, and work without either level or line. By this means I really think the 12 acres the Prince's garden consists of, is more diversified and of greater variety than anything of that compass I ever saw, and this method of gardening is the more agreeable, as, when finished, it has the appearance of beautiful nature, and with-

A fanciful drawing by Kent with Hampton Court on the left, Esher Place on the right, and a domed Palladian temple between them.

out being told, one would imagine art had no part in the finishing, and is, according to what one hears of the Chinese, entirely after their models for works of this nature, where they never plant straight lines or make regular designs. The celebrated gardens of Claremont, Chiswick, and Stowe are now full of labourers, to modernise the extensive works finished in them, even since every one's memory.

Robinson was right in identifying as one of the most striking aspects of Kent's gardening career the fact that he was so often called in to modernise gardens which had only recently been laid out at great expense in a different style. The gardener whom Kent supplanted was Charles Bridgeman (*c.* 1680–1738), Master Gardener to King George II from 1728. The surviving elements of Bridgeman's Kensington Gardens of 1726–33 are a characteristic example of his large-scale planning with three avenues radiating out through the woodland in front of the Palace from the Round Pond which was originally flanked by two artificial mounts capped by circular temples. Further east is Bridgeman's celebrated Serpentine, formed in 1730–32 as one of the first of the irregular sheets of water which were to be such a feature of the later parks of 'Capability' Brown and Humphry Repton. Kensington Gardens thus shows the survival of Baroque planning with radiating avenues

as well as Bridgeman's fondness for garden buildings and his approaches to the 'natural' landscaping movement which succeeded him. He worked at Claremont for the Duke of Newcastle, at Rousham for Colonel Robert Dormer, at Stowe for Lord Cobham and probably at Chiswick for Lord Burlington. In all of these gardens Kent succeeded him in the 1730s, dissolving the almost architectural way in which temples and statues were linked by avenues, terraces and hedges. Kent blurred the transition between these elements and loosened the rather dense planting so as to open a sequence of shifting perspectives in a painterly and three-dimensional way.

The first hints of Kent's own ideas on garden design are given in his book illustrations, notably for Gay's *Poems on Several Occasions* (1720), Pope's *Odyssey* (1725–6), Gay's *Fables* (1727), Thomson's *Seasons* (1730) and Spenser's *Faerie Queen*, published posthumously in 1751. Palladian mansions, Italianate farms, lakes and wild landscapes are mingled in these engraved views in a way which anticipates Kent's drawings for landscape buildings of the 1730s: indeed his first interest in landscape design seems to have been as a setting for his own buildings. His training in Rome had enabled him to acquire a first-hand knowledge of Italian Renaissance

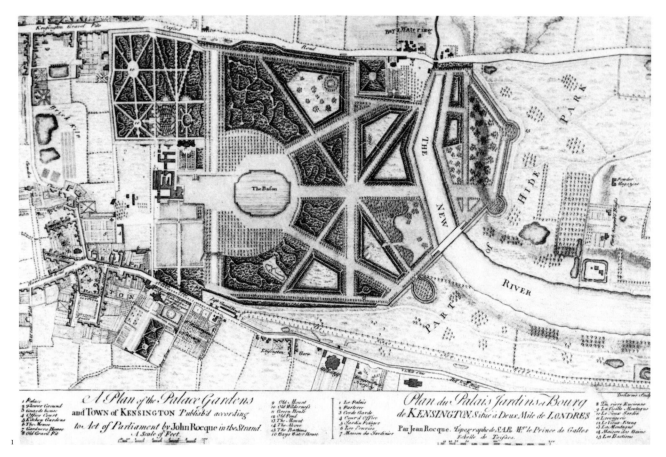

1 *Kensington Gardens. Rocque's plan shows Bridgeman's original design. In the photograph (2) the softening effect of later planting can be seen.*

gardens which had often included secluded and rather wild sections set apart for the maunderings of poets and philosophers. His Elysian Fields at Stowe can in part be seen as an attempt to recreate a similarly suggestive setting for poetic and romantic reflection. The Temple of British Worthies on one side of the river in the Elysian Fields is inspired by buildings in Italian sixteenth- and seventeenth-century gardens such as the now de-

stroyed circus in the grounds of the Villa Mattei in Rome. The circular Temple of Ancient Virtue on the other side of the river echoes an ancient Roman building, the so-called Temple of the Sybil set above the gorge at Tivoli. Even here the continuing influence of Inigo Jones should not be forgotten, for he or one of his circle had drawn just such a temple in a landscaped setting as part of the scenery for a masque. It is certainly

3 The Villa Mattei, Rome. The circus, to the right, is the kind of building which inspired Kent's Temple of British Worthies at Stowe (4).

possible to argue for a theatrical origin in stage and masque design of much of Kent's repertoire.

Another prestigious commission, though one that remained unexecuted, was for the 3rd Duke of Devonshire at Chatsworth where Kent made plans for remodelling the gardens in *c.* 1735–40. The Duke was a great friend of Lord Burlington whose daughter married his son in 1748. Kent proposed an astonishing remodelling of the great hill immediately behind the house at Chatsworth in a manner reminiscent of Tivoli with a circular temple at the top, cascades descending to grottoes and two flanking temples with pyramidal roofs. His sketches for this project show his feeling for light and shade, his management of water and reflection, and his use of contrast and perspective. He uses tall spiky trees like larches, pines and birches to contrast with

1 The Temple of the Sybil, Tivoli. 2 Fontana Rustica, Villa Aldobrandini, Frascati. 3 Fountains in the garden of the Villa d'Este, Tivoli.

bushes and to form screens with which to frame views. This technique appears again in his drawings for Claremont at Esher in Surrey where in the mid 1730s he was remodelling and softening Bridgeman's and Vanbrugh's garden of 1716–25. He retained Vanbrugh's Belvedere, built in 1715 for the Duke of Newcastle as one of the first romantically sited garden ornaments in England, but turned the artificial water into an irregular lake with a cascade and grotto on its bank and a temple on an island. All this survives and has recently been restored after years of neglect. More extensive and equally well preserved is the complete remodelling of Bridgeman's garden at Rousham, Oxfordshire, which Kent carried out in 1730–41 for Alexander Pope's friend General James Dormer. Like the Elysian Fields at Stowe, Rousham represents the creation of a pastoral dream-

4 *The Temple of Ancient Virtue in the gardens at Stowe. Kent, working for Lord Cobham, softened and 'naturalised' Bridgeman's design.*

world dotted with temples and statues in which a confluence of Classical souvenirs from the ancient world and from Renaissance and Baroque Italy provokes a variety of literary and philosophical reflections. The garden at Rousham is bordered by the river Cherwell and the contrived Arcadian vistas are thus piquantly juxtaposed with views of cultivated fields across the water, the whole valley forming a perfect picture of what Shaftesbury called 'Nature's genuine order'.

Claremont and Rousham were still half-Rococo gardens, but at Holkham and at Euston, designed for Burlington's son-in-law, the Duke of Grafton, Kent was beginning to think in terms of parks in a way which anticipated the later practice of 'Capability' Brown: in particular, Kent's device of planting rather bare hillsides with widely spaced clumps of trees. The various features of Holkham and Euston such as temples, pavilions, obelisks, arches and ponds were still centred more or less axially on the house. However, one of the drawings for Holkham seems to represent, interestingly, a view from a window in the house showing in a scenic fashion the apparently asymmetrical relation across the landscape of the temple on the mount and one of the pavilions at the end of the lawn in front of the house.

We have mentioned that Kent anticipated later developments in English garden and park design. His influence on Picturesque taste in eighteenth-century France, especially on the so-called *jardin anglo-chinois*, should also be appreciated. In the 1770s the leading garden designer Louis Carrogis, known as Carmontelle, laid out the Parc Monceau in Paris along lines that were in part inspired by Stowe. Kent's work is included in the first *cahier* of G.-L. Le Rouge's celebrated *Nouveaux Jardins à la mode* (*c.* 1776) and he is hailed as a pioneer in C. C. L. Hirschfeld's five-volumed work, *Theorie der Gartenkunst* (Leipzig, 1779–85).

It is perhaps a suggestive comment on Kent's pictorial approach to garden design that so far no plan for a garden in his own hand has come to light. It may thus not be fanciful to see late in his career an echo of his early training as a decorative painter. We know from at least one contemporary, Lord Harley in 1732, that Kent even saw his own role as essentially that of one who 'decorates'. Moreover, his friends always knew him as the 'signior', that is to say as a colourful but attractive figure who had picked up picturesque Italianate ways in foreign parts. He had a sweet, loving and cheerful nature which endeared him, above all, to Lord Burlington but also to Alexander Pope and Henry Pelham; his undoctrinaire approach also enabled him to work both for Queen Caroline and the son from whom she became estranged, Frederick, Prince of Wales. Kent undoubtedly had a charmed career in which he extended his comparatively slender talents to their utmost limits: non-doctrinal and non-intellectual, he was dominated by a desire to please both socially and artistically – not in the end a bad ambition.

Parc Monceau, Paris. Kent's influence can be seen in Louis Carrogis's design. COLOUR: *Kent's apsed staircase hall at Holkham Hall.*

ANTONY RATCLIFF

THE WORK OF
WILLIAM KENT

During the eighteenth century the antique ruins of classical Rome and the achievements of Renaissance Italy attracted young travellers of two kinds: artists wishing to complete their education and wealthy dilettanti collecting pictures and sculptures for the embellishment of their houses. Some of the latter, unable to undertake the Grand Tour themselves, resorted to patronising a student who could collect or copy works of art for them and it was, as we have seen, under the patronage of Sir William Wentworth, Burrell Massingberd and other English country gentlemen that in 1709, at the age of 25, William Kent travelled to Italy. Kent had shown some talent as a painter whilst apprenticed to a coach painter in Hull about 1700 and in Italy he copied the pictures then fashionable with English collectors. Massingberd asked him, for example, for copies of Guido Reni's Aurora and Guercino's Vesper as well as copies of Poussin and Claude Lorrain and we know that he copied the 'Bath of Diana' by Domenichino, a forerunner of Poussin, for Sir John Chester.

Kent joined the school of Benedetto Luti in Rome and the portrait of Kent painted by Luti in 1718 can be seen at Chatsworth. Whilst in Rome he was admitted to the Duke of Tuscany's Academy in 1713 and subsequently learned the art of ceiling painting, sending home paintings on canvas for the ceilings of his patrons. At this time Kent decorated the ceiling of the Church of S. Giuliano dei Fiamminghi in Rome with a fresco painting of the apotheosis of its patron Saint,

COLOUR: *William Kent's decoration for the ceiling of the church of S. Giuliano dei Fiamminghi, Rome. Below title: a Canaletto Capriccio.*

Drawing by Kent for the ceiling decoration in the church of S. Giuliano dei Fiamminghi, showing the apotheosis of Saint Julian. (See page 33).

Julian. This church then, as now, was consecrated to the needs of the Flemish speaking congregation in Rome.

When, in 1714, Thomas Coke, then only 17, arrived in Rome he and Kent became close friends. Kent advised him on his art purchases and travelled with him, or on his behalf, to Venice, Sicily, Naples, and Florence; that the friendship lasted is witnessed, on Kent's side, by his bequest to Coke (he became Lord Lovel and Earl of Leicester) of busts of Inigo Jones and Palladio. It was the patronage of Lord Burlington, however, whom Kent first met in Rome in 1716, which was to have the greatest influence on his career. Burlington revisited Rome in 1719 – to continue his study of architecture, and, in particular, the work of Palladio. It was at this time that he bought the drawings by Palladio which he published in 1730 and which are now in the library of the RIBA. When he returned to England, Kent travelled with him. Back in London Burlington immediately commissioned him to undertake decoration at Burlington House. The Saloon

which is today the least altered room in this much altered building has a ceiling painting of 'The wedding feast of Cupid and Psyche' attributed by Professor Wittkower to Kent. Other commissions for decorative work for Lord Chandos, at Cannons, and for Lord Castlemaine, at Wanstead, followed. In 1720 Kent was a pupil at the Academy in St Martin's Lane under John Vanderbank and Louis Cheron and amongst his fellow students that year was William Hogarth – soon to become his great antagonist.

The advent of the Hanoverian George I in 1714 had led to a swift change in the balance of power. The ascendant Whigs under Sir Robert Walpole dominated not only the political, but also the artistic and philosophical scene. A key to the politico-artistic philosophy of the times is contained in the *Characteristicks* published by the Earl of Shaftesbury in 1711. He postulated a unity of approach in ethics and aesthetics based on good taste and dignity; his models of art and behaviour are drawn from ancient Rome. In his *Advice to an Author* he sums up this philosophy:

Burlington House, Piccadilly. One of the rooms which still show work in Kent's style. The building was much altered in the 19th century.

Thus are the arts and virtues mutually friends; and thus the science of virtuosos and that of virtue itself, become, in a manner, one and the same. One who aspires to the character of a man of breeding and politeness is careful to form his judgement of arts and sciences upon right models of perfection . . . It were to be wished that we had the same regard to a right taste in life and manners . . . Who would not endeavour to force nature as well in this respect?

This philosophy exactly suited the mood of the Whig aristocracy; in architecture, the Palladian style was to be its visible expression.

The Baroque of Wren, Vanbrugh and Hawksmoor, had already come under political attack. In Shaftesbury's letter to Lord Somers, the Lord Chancellor, written in 1712, he criticised the conduct of Queen Anne's Board of Works and the 'miscarriage' of its public buildings, placing the responsibility on Wren as the Court Architect 'through several reigns'. Shaftesbury's aim was to see the completion, in the Palladian style, of Inigo Jones's scheme for Whitehall, of which only the Banqueting House had been built. He concluded, 'Hardly indeed, as the public now stands, should we bear to see a Whitehall treated like a Hampton Court or even a new cathedral like St Paul's'.

Leaders of Whig opinion in the persons of Lord Burlington, Lord Pembroke, Henry Pelham and Sir Robert Walpole himself, brought their influence to bear and in 1718 Wren was replaced as Surveyor-General by William Benson, who supported the return to the neo-Palladian style of Inigo Jones.

This did not prevent the appointment of Sir James Thornhill as Serjeant Painter to the Crown in 1720 but, although his greatest work, the Painted Hall at Greenwich, was not completed until 1728, his star was on the wane. Already in 1722, designs of his for the Cupola Room in Wren's rebuilt Kensington Palace had been rejected. That commission was given to Burlington's protégé, Kent, by a Board of Works whose members included Sir Thomas Hewett, who, like Burlington, had known Kent in Italy.

This, Kent's earliest public work in England, was followed by commissions to decorate the other main rooms of the Palace and the King's Grand Staircase. In 1726 Kent was appointed Master Carpenter and a member of the Board of Works, and in 1728, Surveyor of Paintings in the Royal Palaces. In 1735 he succeeded Nicholas Dubois as Master Mason and Deputy Surveyor and, in 1739, Charles Jervas as Principal Painter to the Crown and a Commissioner of the Board of Works. During the tenure of these offices Kent restored the two great staircases at Windsor Castle and Rubens's ceiling of the Banqueting House in Whitehall.

King George II commissioned him to undertake some alterations at Hampton Court. Kent's gateway leading out of Clock Court bears the date 1732, and he was responsible for painting the walls and ceiling of the Queen's Staircase and the decoration of the Music Room, the Queen's presence chamber and the state-rooms of the Cumberland Suite.

The focal point in the Green Room of the Cumberland Suite is an arch supported by four Ionic columns giving onto an alcove, which forms the setting for a large picture of St Agnes by Domenichino. The Blue Room which has a fine ribbed ceiling with bosses, contains three of the very few easel paintings by Kent now on public display: 'Henry V and Princess Katherine' at their first meeting and 'The Marriage of Henry V' dated 1729. The contemporary frame of the third picture is inscribed 'The Battle of Crescy' but, on the assumption that the three form a historical trilogy, the Department of the Environment have added a label suggesting, with a degree of hesitation, 'Battle of Agincourt?'

Large-scale paintings by Kent depicting episodes from the story of Aeneas, hang in the Hall at Ditchley and an architectural painting, depicting the interior of a temple hangs at Chiswick Villa. Even in his lifetime, Kent's reputation as a painter was at best second-rate and few of his portraits have survived. It is known that he painted a picture of Lord Burlington's two daughters, Lady Hartington and Lady Euston. His self-portrait which used to hang at Nuneham was included in the collection sold in the nineteen-forties; its present whereabouts appears to be unknown and the only record of it is a photograph in the files of the National Portrait Gallery.

Following his appointment as Principal Painter to the Crown in 1739 Kent painted a number of official portraits and there is a full length portrait of King George II dated 1741 and signed by Kent at Rokeby in Yorkshire. It is known that Henry Pelham had full length portraits of the King and of Queen Caroline in the Great Room at 22 Arlington Street which may well have been by Kent. Kent's advancement was based as much on political patronage as on artistic ability. When the clash of styles, between the high Baroque of Wren and Thornhill and the Palladianism of Burlington and Kent, was emphatically resolved in favour of the latter, it inevitably gave rise to great personal animosity. By 1729, the year in which Hogarth married Thornhill's daughter Jane, Thornhill himself was out of work.

Hogarth was the pre-eminent caricaturist of his time and, in his general attack on Whiggery, Kent did not escape. Two particular cartoons, 'Masquerades and Operas, Burlington House' published in 1724 and 'The Man of Taste' published in 1731 found in him their mark. Hogarth's 'Burlesque on Kent's Altar-piece at St Clement's' is the only surviving record of that unfortunate work, in which Kent allowed his Italianate leanings to overcome his sensibility for the Protestant tradition. It represented St Cecilia with a group of musician angels and the Bishop of London considered it unsuitable to be set up as an altar-piece. The painting was in fact removed to the vestry of the church and Pevsner records that it was destroyed with the church in the second world war.

At St George's Hanover Square the reredos displays a large painting of the Last Supper by William Kent which Pevsner describes as: 'Hot colours, Baroque composition diagonalling into depth but the figures of a French type ultimately derived from Poussin'. Kent also designed the two fine sanctuary chairs in the church.

A number of Kent's architectural drawings have survived in various collections and museums. Apart from these he also illustrated a number of books for writers in Burlington's circle, the first being John Gay's *Poems on Several Occasions*, 1720, followed, in collaboration with John Wootton, the animal and landscape painter, by Gay's *Fables* in 1727. Kent's drawings for James Thomson's *The Seasons* begun in 1726 and completed in 1730, are reminiscent of Italian landscapes and coincide with the start of his career as a landscape gardener, and his 32 copper plate illustrations for Edmund Spenser's *The Faerie Queen*, published in 1751 after Kent's death, are of interest by reason of his own admission that he had been drawn to gardening by Spenser's graphic descriptions.

His lack of much real ability as a painter did not in any way lessen Kent's standing as the most sought-after decorator of his day and his study of ceiling painting in Rome had acquainted him with a wide variety of styles. At Raynham Hall, which he re-modelled for Lord Townshend in 1731, the central oval medallion of the ribbed Hall ceiling displays the coat of arms of the owner, and in the Belisarius room Kent used the magnificent ribbing dating from 1650, and attributed to Inigo Jones, to frame an allegorical picture of Fame recording the name of Alexander Pope,

1 Hogarth's parody of Kent's altarpiece for St Clement's Church. 2 Kent's ceiling painting at Raynham Hall confirms his inadequacies.

the Poet Laureate of the Burlington Circle.

In his decoration of the state rooms in Kensington Palace, which he commenced in 1722, Kent had been less restrained. In the ceiling of the King's Drawing Room, the massive oval ribbing frames a painting of Jupiter and Semele and in the Privy Chamber the central painting represents Mars and Minerva, a compliment to George I and his Queen.

In the King's Gallery, the ceiling without coving or ribbing is given over to paintings of seven scenes from the Legends of Ulysses surrounded by grisaille decoration. In Renaissance decoration ornamental motifs were frequently based on plant forms, particularly acanthus, directly derived from Roman wall decoration. Kent readily adopted these for his scheme of decoration in this Gallery, executed by his Spanish assistant Francisco de Valentia, as a chalked inscription on the back of one of the canvasses witnesses.

During his time in Rome, Kent had struck up a friendship with John Talman, the son of Wren's pupil the architect William Talman. According to Kent, Talman was 'continually preaching to me that I may be

a great painter' and he suggested that a ceiling Kent was designing for Burrell Massingberd who was building a summer-house at Ormsby should be done 'after the grotesk manner'. Kent was however reluctant to use this style out of context and this, his first ceiling piece, which he painted on canvas to be sent home, portrayed the Muses of Music and Poetry.

This was soon followed by another canvas executed in Rome of 'Herse and her Sisters' from Ovid. This had been commissioned by Sir John Chester for the ceiling in the entrance hall at Chicheley Hall, which he was rebuilding in place of the original Tudor Hall which had been sacked during the Civil War. Whilst the entrance hall was designed by Burlington's assistant, Henry Flitcroft, in the Palladian style, the magnificent garden front built between 1719 and 1723 by Francis Smith of Warwick is in the Baroque style of Archer, so much so that for many years the house was attributed to him and dated twenty years earlier.

That Sir John's back-sliding to this now despised style was not accidental is evidenced by a letter from his friend Burrell Massingberd to Lady Chester in 1722.

1 Kent's ceiling at Ditchley Park. 2 The Saloon at 44 Berkeley Square in the 1950s – the coffered ceiling resembles that at 22 Arlington Street.

'When I came to Chicheley I was so fretted to see such havoc made in the architecture, especially in the garden front, which was at first all laid out by my direction, that if Sir John had been home when I first saw it, I should not have forborne the rudeness of exposing all the faults to the utmost'.

The idea of a ceiling in the 'grotesk manner' that Talman had suggested to Kent when they were together in Rome must have struck a chord. This style had been developed at the beginning of the sixteenth century by Raphael from his study of ancient Roman painting. His decoration of the Villa Madama in Rome was based on that of the remains of Nero's Golden House which had been uncovered as a subterranean grotto, giving the name 'Grottesche' to the style. The outstanding example is perhaps the ceiling in the

Palazzo del Té in Mantua by Raphael's pupil Giulio Romano and Kent turned to 'the grotesk manner' for the decoration of the ceiling in the Presence Chamber of Kensington Palace where the central medallion depicting Apollo in his chariot is surrounded by an arabesque design.

This was the earliest use of such designs in England and they were only later to be popularised by the Adam brothers. They found expression years later in the decoration of the long corridor in 22 Arlington Street as photographs taken about 1890 show (see page 127). These had, however, disappeared before Eagle Star purchased the building in 1947.

Kent returned to this Italian style for the ceiling of the drawing room at Houghton and again in 1738, when he remodelled Rousham Park, the Jacobean

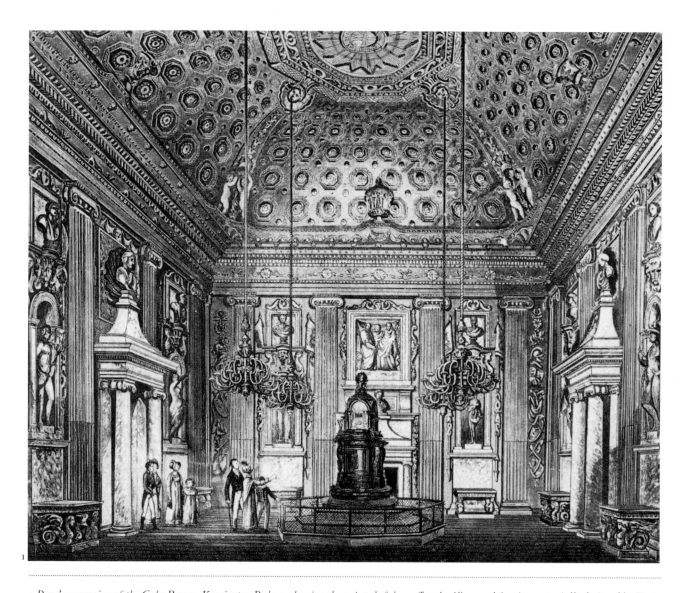

1 Pyne's engraving of the Cube Room, Kensington Palace, showing the painted, false-coffered ceiling, and furniture specially designed by Kent.

house of his friend, General Sir James Dormer. The Painted Parlour at Rousham, described by Pevsner as one of the most beautiful small rooms of its date, was decorated by Kent in the grand manner but in miniature. Its ceiling consists of a central medallion portraying Ceres, Venus and Bacchus, surrounded by arabesques and two landscapes.

By contrast the ceiling in the Great Parlour, originally General Dormer's library, is a rare exercise in Kentian Gothic, its ribs supporting a central hexagonal vault with a central pendant. The frieze and the chimney piece in this room also contain Gothic motifs. The Rococo plasterwork frames of the portraits and the doorcase were executed by Thomas Roberts of Oxford in 1764 when the room was converted into a drawing-room.

In 1726, in the King's Staircase at Kensington Palace, Kent attempted to fill the whole ceiling with painting in the Italian style. Baroque ceiling painting had developed to open up the roof space by means of architectural perspective; such use of *trompe l'oeil* is exemplified by Andrea Pozzo's Church of S. Ignazio in Rome (1691–1694) and this style was perfected on a smaller scale in numerous village churches in Bavaria and Austria. Thornhill used such effects in the grand manner for the ceiling of the Painted Hall in Greenwich but this could never be equalled by Kent.

On the King's Grand Staircase in Kensington Palace the decoration of the lower part consists of trophies and similar emblems whilst the upper part of the walls, on two sides, is given over to a *trompe l'oeil* vaulted gallery with balustraded arcades with giant Ionic columns. The gallery is peopled by a motley crowd of personalities drawn from the Court of the day, apparently observing those approaching up the staircase. The group includes Yeomen of the Guard, pages, Turkish servants and

2 *Pyne's engraving of The King's Drawing Room (see page 37). The ceiling painting, by Kent, shows the story of Jupiter and Semele.*

Peter the Wild Boy, a Mowgli of his day, discovered in the woods near Hanover.

The ceiling is painted with a feigned dome with four lunettes, from each of which more figures look down. These include Kent himself holding palette and pencils as well as his mistress Elizabeth Butler, an actress, and two pupils who worked with him on the decorations. Whilst the perspective can be better appreciated from the staircase than from the landing from which the passing visitor now sees it, neither here, nor elsewhere, does Kent achieve mastery in the style. His best work of this sort was the oval 'Assembly of the Gods' filling the centre of the ceiling in the large Hall of James Gibbs's Ditchley Park, described by Horace Walpole, who admired Kent's architectural work, as 'not so bad as his common'.

Another gathering of gods and goddesses appeared on the ceiling Kent painted for Lord Castlemaine in the Saloon of the mansion at Wanstead which had been built by Campbell and Burlington in 1715. Castlemaine was evidently one of Kent's admirers and a portrait of Kent by Aikman was hung 'in the hall of my Lord Castlemaine's in Essex where he had painted much for his Lordship'. Wanstead House was demolished in 1824 and Kent's work there is only known to us from the detail in Hogarth's 'The Assembly at Wanstead House', painted in 1729, and from Horace Walpole's strictures on Kent's 'flame coloured gods and goddesses' which he considered represented the artist at his worst.

Horace Walpole tells us that when his father, Sir Robert Walpole, commissioned Kent to decorate Houghton Hall he insisted on the work being executed in chiaroscuro as he knew what Kent was capable of in colour, but, even in its composition, the 'Aurora', on the ceiling in the State Bedroom there, is a poor shadow

1 Ditchley Park: one of Kent's doorcases flanked by Kent pictures (see page 36). 2 Kent's drawing for a chimney piece at Houghton.

of the subject popularised at the time by copies of Guido Reni's masterpiece. Another of Kent's influential patrons was Frederick, Prince of Wales. He had leased the White House at Kew in 1730 and engaged Kent to design the ceilings of the two drawing rooms and also new façades. Kew Palace, as it was then called, was demolished in 1802–3 and little is known of Kent's work there.

Massive ceiling ribbing and coffered ceilings had been introduced in England as a feature of decoration by Inigo Jones. In the Great Hall of the Banqueting House in Whitehall, he had divided the ceiling into a 'Frett made of Great Cornishes inriched with carvings' and the introduction of this Venetian style there, in the Queen's House at Greenwich and in Ashburnham House, were bold departures from the elaborate plasterwork of the great Jacobean houses. A number of Jones's designs for coffered ceilings had been collected

by Lord Burlington and these were available to Kent when in 1722 he successfully essayed the use of feigned coffering in the painting of the four great coves forming the Cupola in the Cube Room of Kensington Palace. The octagonal coffers in blue and gold diminish in size to create an illusion of extra height. The Cupola Room was decorated in the Roman manner to reflect the glory of the Hanoverian monarchy and Kent designed a suite of marble-topped side tables supported on sphinxes to furnish it.

Some of Kent's most important decorative work, albeit on a smaller scale, is to be seen in Burlington's Chiswick Villa which has been skilfully restored by the Department of the Environment. In the dome of the octagonal central saloon Kent adopted a similar effect to that in the Cube Room of Kensington Palace. His work at Chiswick can be dated 1729 from the inscriptions on the chimney piece in the Red Velvet Room, the

3 *The drawing room at Houghton. The ceiling was decorated in monochrome: Horace Walpole said his father did not trust Kent with colour.*

ceiling of which is divided into nine panels, with a portrayal of Mercury, in the centre, presiding over representations of Architecture, Painting and Sculpture. The surrounding panels Kent decorated with Roman heads, cherubs and signs of the zodiac.

The rectangular Gallery along the garden front is linked by apses, with open archways surmounted by gilded coffered half-domes, to a circular cabinet at one end and an octagonal cabinet at the other. The central panel of the Gallery ceiling contains a painting of warriors resting in an Italian landscape, attributed to Veronese, and the surrounding panels are decorated by Kent in a conventional manner. The Blue Velvet Room contains Kent's most elaborate ceiling in the villa supported by splendidly ornamented console brackets. Its central feature is an allegorical representation of Architecture surrounded by cherubs carrying drawing instruments. The ceiling is richly decorated in blue and

gold. Above one of the doors in this room is a round panel containing a portrait of Pope by Kent.

At Holkham the Gallery is a twice-scale version of the plan Burlington had used at Chiswick. In the Hall Kent used plain coffering to great effect in the coves and ceiling and both this and the coffered ceiling of the Saloon were based on Inigo Jones's designs. In the restoration of William Kent House a fine original ribbed ceiling has been uncovered in Henry Pelham's room above a false ceiling which had been installed later. Two other ribbed ceilings in the house are also preserved in Kent's original form, in the Saloon on the first floor and in the Octagonal Room.

Kent's most individual use of coffering however, is in the rectangular ceiling and coving of the great first floor Saloon at No. 44 Berkeley Square, dating from 1743. There, rectangular, hexagonal and octagonal panels, decorated with cameos representing the Loves

The second scene in Hogarth's sequence of paintings 'Marriage à la Mode'. The room is based on one in Walpole's house, 5 Arlington Street.

of the Gods and Goddesses, are executed in *grisaille* on red and blue backgrounds. The cruciform ceiling in the Great Room of William Kent House is very similar; here, too, *grisaille* cameos depict classical figures.

KENT INTERIORS

Kent's studies, first in feigned coffering and then in ceiling construction as a feature of interior decoration, inevitably led him to consider the architectural elements of the room as a whole, in particular the chimney pieces and doorcases.

In Southern Europe in the seventeenth century, room heaters often took the form of enclosed stoves, and in the Baroque period these developed into very elegant ceramic decorations. In England, however, interior decorators had to incorporate the customary open fireplace into their designs and Inigo Jones developed monumental chimney pieces, frequently with overmantels framing mirrors or paintings,

harmonising with the doorcases to produce a unity of style.

Doorcases themselves in the Renaissance style were frequently surmounted by pediments and one can trace the development in Kent's work from the severely Classical, as in the early Cupola Room at Kensington Palace and also at Raynham Hall where he completed Inigo Jones's earlier work, to the richer decoration employed in a number of rooms at Houghton Hall, notably the Stone Hall with its massive marble chimney piece carved by Rysbrack to Kent's design.

Hogarth's painting 'Breakfast', Scene II of Marriage à la Mode is set in a Kent interior, the drawing room of Horace Walpole's house at No. 5 Arlington Street. Although exception can be taken to the girandole, the wall sconce which holds two candles and incorporates a clock, a Rococo embellishment here perhaps invented by Hogarth, the unity of style of the chimney piece, picture frames and ceiling is evident. Eagle Star have been fortunate in securing a chimney piece very similar

The fourth scene of William Hogarth's 'Marriage à la Mode', the Countess's levée; a daily scene in the private houses Kent designed.

to that depicted by Hogarth. It is now installed in the Great Room in William Kent House.

Mirror and picture frames were conceived as integral parts of the whole design. A striking example of this unity can be seen in the Music Room at Stourhead where the overmantel of the fireplace, which frames a view of the interior of St Peter's after Pannini, is reflected in a pier-glass set above a heavily carved gilt side table. A similar frame by William Kent, above the chimney piece in the green drawing-room of William Kent House, is of particular interest as it frames a painting of Sir Francis Bacon, copied in 1730 from a painting by Van Somer by John Vanderbank, at whose academy Kent had studied.

Kent's original decorations have survived substantially intact only in the Saloon of William Kent House. In the other principal rooms, mouldings, doorcases and chimney pieces based on known examples of his work, on his published designs or, in some cases, on our records of the house itself, have been re-introduced

where necessary. When one compares the house today with photographs of it taken around 1890 (pages 139–43) it looks sparsely furnished, but early eighteenth-century rooms were not crowded with furniture, as the inventory of the contents of the house taken on Pelham's death in 1754 proves.

The bedroom of the lady of the house was similarly spacious and the overall effect of a grand eighteenth century bedroom is well conveyed in 'The Countess's levée', Scene IV of Hogarth's 'Marriage à la Mode'. The scene in the first Act of Hofmannsthal's *Rosenkavalier*, which takes place in the first decade of the reign of Maria Theresia (1740–50) is set in a room such as this with the Feldmarschallin sitting at her dressing table during her levée. In Hogarth's picture the Countess sits at a dressing table of the kind Chippendale would later show in his *Gentleman and Cabinet Maker's Director* of 1754. She is attended by her coiffeur whilst the lawyer, Silvertongue is engaging her in conversation. The Italian castrato and the flautist are

The palace at Brühl by Balthasar Neumann. Kent's grandest stairs were at Holkham (facing p. 32) and 44 Berkeley Square (right).

making music and even the little negro boy is present. Richard Strauss was obliged to replace the castrato by a tenor but otherwise the cast is, with few additions, the same. His scene is set in Baroque Vienna but it might just as well be Arlington Street.

That Kent's Baroque overtones were not an invention of Hogarth can be seen from his painting of 'The Assembly at Wanstead House' showing Kent's ceiling, doorcase and chimney piece there in a unity of style that can only be described as Baroque and complemented by Kentian furniture on a Baroque scale. Baroque was, above all, a statement of power; its exponents were not antagonistic to the Renaissance forms, they incorporated these into their work not for their aesthetic value but to support weightier superstructures. In this expression, stairs had an important and symbolic significance perhaps nowhere more evident than in Jakob Prandtauer's stairway leading to the imperial apartments at the monastery of St Florian.

Designs for internal staircases developed by Francisco di Giorgio as early as the 1470s fitted the Baroque style and were adopted by later generations of architects. One of these designs, based on a T-plan with a central flight forking at right angles at an intermediate landing into two flights leading on the left and the right to the upper storey, had been used by Bramante in the outer staircase of the Belvedere Court in the Vatican and was subsequently developed into its most elegant form, the Imperial staircase, with a central flight rising to an intermediate landing from which it turns back on itself in two parallel flights to the upper storey. This design was foreshadowed in some of Leonardo's sketches and reached its full expression in the Baroque palaces and monasteries of Southern Europe. Balthasar Neumann, the great Baroque builder, took over the surveyorship of the Residenz in Würzburg in 1720 and it was there, and in the Palaces at Bruchsal and Brühl, that he developed Imperial staircases to their most splendid form.

Inigo Jones at Greenwich had in 1635 developed the form of the spiral staircase around an open well. The 'Tulip Stair' in white marble is cantilevered from the wall

44 Berkeley Square. 1 The staircase vault. 2 The first floor landing. COLOUR: *Kensington Palace: Presence Chamber ceiling and King's staircase.*

without any central support and is embellished with an elegant balustrade in a wrought-iron *fleur-de-lis* design. At Ashburnham House, in Little Dean's Yard at Westminster, Giorgio's design for a square newel staircase was elaborated into one consisting of three straight flights of stairs round three sides of a square open well with the landing on the fourth side and square quarter landings at each corner of the opposite flight. This plan was later adopted by Wren for his grand staircase in Hampton Court Palace and Kensington Palace and it was impossible for the Palladians to escape the Baroque notion of stairs as a central feature of design.

There are a number of examples of the grand use of stairways by Kent. At Holkham the internal stairway leading to the *piano nobile* dominates the main hall. Leading from the ground floor, a monumental flight of stairs ascends to the 'Tribune' and the first floor level is surrounded by a Baroque wrought-iron railing incorporating an enriched 'S' scroll. Most elegant of all, however, in relation to the size of the building is the great stairway at No. 44 Berkeley Square; as Pevsner says: 'There is no other eighteenth-century staircase in England which can so convincingly be compared with those of the great German and Austrian Baroque

architects'. A single flight leads to a half-landing and divides into two to ascend to the first floor from which a single flight again leads to the second floor. The balustrade of the second flight is of a simple wrought-iron S design but the flight to the first floor uses an enriched 'S' scroll-work identical to that at Holkham. By contrast, in William Kent House we have a square cantilevered staircase, the three flights of which ascend to the first floor round three sides of the square central well, but here again, the identical enriched 'S' scroll-work design is incorporated in the balustrade.

The S curve and the serpentine line were indeed themselves Baroque developments, idealised by Hogarth in his *Analysis* as 'the line of beauty', and it was Kent's extensive use of them in his decorative work, his furniture and his gardens which led to their general acceptance within the Palladian style.

On a smaller scale, the Baroque style abounds in Kent's minor works. A delightful example is the Royal Barge which he designed and decorated for Frederick the Prince of Wales in 1732, the drawings for which are in the Victoria and Albert Museum. The carving was executed by James Richards and the barge itself, which was in use on royal occasions until 1849, is now in the

COLOUR: *Hampton Court (see p. 36). Cumberland suite. Kent monuments in Westminster Abbey: 1 Lord Stanhope, 2 William Skaespeare.*

National Maritime Museum at Greenwich.

His collaboration with the sculptor, J. M. Rysbrack, began in 1722 with the bas-relief of a Roman marriage above the fireplace in the Cupola Room at Kensington and reached a high point of Baroque artistry in their chimney piece for the Dining Room at Houghton where the relief depicts a Sacrifice to Bacchus. These achievements resulted in the 1730s in commissions to design and execute the memorial to Marlborough in the chapel at Blenheim and the memorials to Isaac Newton and Lord Stanhope for Westminster Abbey. Kent collaborated with Scheemakers in the memorial to General George Monk, Duke of Albemarle and in his best known sculpture, the memorial to Shakespeare in Poet's Corner, Westminster Abbey.

On a domestic scale, Kent designed a number of pieces of plate and other table decoration. Thirteen illustrations in Vardy's *Some Designs of Mr Inigo Jones and Mr Wm. Kent,* 1744 are devoted to these. Amongst them is the design for the pair of silver chandeliers,

ordered by King George II in 1736 for his palace at Herrenhausen, and now at Anglesey Abbey.

Two of the illustrations are of Baroque designs for cups, one of which Vardy described as 'a gold cup for Colonel Pelham' which was executed by George Wickes in 1736. The finial of the cup, which weighs 58oz, bears the plumes of the Prince of Wales and marked the Hon. James Pelham's appointment as Private Secretary to Frederick, Prince of Wales; this design was subsequently copied by a number of other smiths. The second illustration is of an alternative design for the same purpose which was eventually executed as a pair by George Wickes in 1745 for Sir Charles Hanbury-Williams.

Other designs of Kent's illustrated by Vardy included a Baroque 'surtoute', a design for an epergne commissioned by the Prince of Wales in 1745 and the 'terrine & cover for Lord Mountford'; a pair of these fine soup tureens with horses heads for handles were executed by Wickes for Lord Mountford of Horseheath.

1

2   3

50   A HOUSE IN TOWN

4

1 *Prince Frederick's barge.* 2,3 *A gold cup for Colonel Pelham and the engraved design.* 4 *A Kentian settee at Wilton House.*

KENT'S FURNITURE

Kent's reputation as a furniture designer is based, not on items of 'occasional' furniture for everyday use, but on semi-permanent pieces designed to form part of the architectural context in which they were placed. Designs for such pieces are illustrated in Vardy's collection; following Venetian Baroque models, they are massive and ornate with much carving and gilding. Hogarth's 'The Assembly at Wanstead House' depicts a massive marble-topped gilt table, a gilt settee and gilt chairs, which could all come straight out of Vardy's publication. Other formal items designed by Kent included torchères (candle stands) and terms designed to display the classical busts he had helped his Patrons collect.

Examples of Kent furniture are to be found in various museums but, out of the context for which they were designed, they may seem ponderous and artificial. Pieces from the sets of furniture designed by Kent for Chiswick Villa and for Devonshire House are now to be seen at Chatsworth; in the restoration of William Kent House Eagle Star has been able to place a small number of Kentian pieces in a suitable setting. Perhaps the finest display of William Kent furniture is to be seen at Wilton House. Inigo Jones, at the time of his death in 1652, had been advising the Earl of Pembroke on the reconstruction of part of the house, which had been damaged by fire in 1647 and John Webb, his nephew, completed this work to Jones's designs. The Double Cube room was designed to display family portraits by Van Dyck, and with its ceiling, painted by Edward Pierce, can be regarded as the first English Baroque interior of a private house. It was enhanced much later by a superb collection of Kentian furniture.

In England the limited availability of large pictures for wall decoration led to a greater dependence on the wall coverings and their patterns. At this time the colours used were predominantly red, blue and green, in Chiswick Villa, for example, there is a red velvet room, a blue velvet room, and a green velvet room, so called from the original wall coverings now replaced by similarly coloured flock papers. The walls of the Saloon at Houghton were covered in a bold-patterned cut velvet in crimson as the convention of the day dictated for a great stateroom. The furniture designed by Kent to be placed around the sides of this room was in keeping, the chairs being covered with the same crimson velvet whilst the tables were topped with *porto venere* marble matching that of the fire place.

The drawing room and the state bedroom were furnished in a strong green velvet of which only the hangings of the great bed and the covering of the walnut and parcel gilt chairs now remain. The great bed itself is hung with curtains embellished with gold braid. The broken pediment of the bed head is surmounted by a huge scallop shell. The conception is one of Kent's most striking.

KENT AND THE NEO-PALLADIANS

Reference has already been made to Lord Shaftesbury's attack in 1712 on Queen Anne's Board of Works and on Wren in particular who had been favoured by the Stuart monarchs after the Restoration. Vanbrugh, Hawksmoor and Archer had all collaborated with him in the Queen's Commission of 1711 to undertake fifty new London churches. Nicholas Hawksmoor built his six East End churches over the period 1712–23 and Thomas Archer was responsible for the highly individual design of St John's, Smith Square, 1713.

James Gibbs, a Scot, a Catholic, a Tory and a supporter of the Stuart cause from childhood, had studied in Rome with Bernini's pupil Carlo Fontana. Whilst there, he no doubt made the acquaintance of Tory aristocrats on the Grand Tour and on his return to London in 1709 he attached himself to Wren's circle. In 1713 he was appointed Surveyor to the Queen's Commission, jointly with Hawksmoor (in place of William Dickinson), and took over the responsibility for St Mary-le-Strand.

In the political purge which followed the '15 uprising in Scotland, Gibbs lost his Surveyorship and his career as a public architect was finished. His background had not prevented Burlington engaging him to work on Burlington House but he was dismissed when Campbell appeared in Burlington's circle. The popular acclaim accorded to Gibbs for St Mary-le-Strand when it was completed in 1717, and his standing in Tory party circles, provided him nevertheless with a continuous flow of further commissions; the steeple for St Clement Danes, the Octagon of Orleans House, the church of St Martin-in-the-Fields, Sudbrook Park for the Duke of Argyll, St Bartholomew's Hospital, the Radcliffe Camera in Oxford and in 1736 a house for the Duchess of Norfolk at 16 Arlington Street which now forms part of the building of the Royal Over-Seas League.

Just as the Whig ascendancy in 1714 did not succeed in totally banishing the Baroque style set by Wren and his followers which had determined the course of public building and of the palaces of the mighty from the restoration of the monarchy until 1714, so that style in its time had not totally obliterated the earlier Classical styles. A number of English architects, competitors of Wren, working on a domestic scale, were designing country houses of Palladian proportions for the nobility and wealthy who regarded these as their real homes as opposed to their London town houses. Eltham Lodge, in Kent, designed by Hugh May in 1663 is generally regarded as the prototype of these houses, built in brick with stone quoins and with a large pediment of Britannia crowning the centre of the house. In 1665 May undertook a larger mansion for Lord Berkeley on the site of Hay Hill farm in Piccadilly. John Evelyn wrote of it in his diary that 'The porticos are in imitation of an house described by Palladio, but it happens to be the worst in his booke'; he nevertheless regarded it as 'one of the most magnificent palaces of the Towne'.

Colen Campbell, a young Scottish architect, had worked with Wren at Greenwich and was in fact responsible for carrying out Queen Mary's commission to design the matching block to Webb's King Charles block. When studying at the University of Padua in 1697 he had been deeply impressed by the Palladian style and on his return set to work on his series of volumes *Vitruvius Britannicus*. Each of Campbell's three folio volumes, the first of which appeared in 1715 and was dedicated to King George I, contained 100 plates illustrating British buildings, public and private, with a commentary on their design. The works of Inigo Jones were particularly favoured and Campbell also included a number of his own designs. Apart from this modest

The double cube room, Wilton House. The Kentian furniture would originally have been placed round the walls, not grouped.

1 *Hogarth's 'The Man of Taste'. Kent, on the pediment, looks down on Raphael and Michelangelo. Pope (A) bespatters passers-by.*

self-advertising, the book struck a blow in favour of Palladian architecture at the time when Wren and his followers were losing ground politically. Lord Burlington, then aged twenty, and in Italy on the Grand Tour, was one of the subscribers to Campbell's publication and on his return he appointed him to complete the alterations he was making to Burlington House in Piccadilly.

In the same year, 1715, Giacomo Leoni, a Venetian architect who had settled in London, commenced the publication of the first version in English of Palladio's *I Quattro Libri dell' Architettura*. Originally printed in 1570, this was now, and for many years to come, a definitive work on Classical architecture and introduced Palladio's principles not only to those architects and designers who had kept alive the earlier Classical style in the country, but also to gentlemen throughout the land who were interested in architecture.

Burlington worked with Campbell on the designs for a palatial mansion in the Palladian style at Wanstead in 1715 for Sir Richard Child (later Lord Castlemaine)

and two years later on a Bagno for his own gardens at Chiswick. Campbell, who despised the Baroque style as 'extravagant, affected and licentious', designed Houghton for Sir Robert Walpole in 1722, borrowing Inigo Jones's design for the Hall in the Queen's House, a cube with coffered ceiling and cantilevered gallery, for its Stone Hall. In the same year, he completed Mereworth Castle, in the style of Palladio's Villa Rotonda and one of the finest examples of the Palladian revival in England.

Following his return from his second visit to Italy, Burlington felt sufficiently confident of his mastery of the Palladian style to dispense with Campbell's assistance and to undertake in 1725 the villa, also in the style of the Rotonda, in the grounds of his house at Chiswick which he commissioned Kent to decorate. In 1727 Burlington encouraged Kent to publish by private subscription, *The Designs of Inigo Jones*, based on the drawings and sketches by Jones and Webb that Burlington had collected, together with a few of Burlington's own designs and some by Kent himself. The subscribers

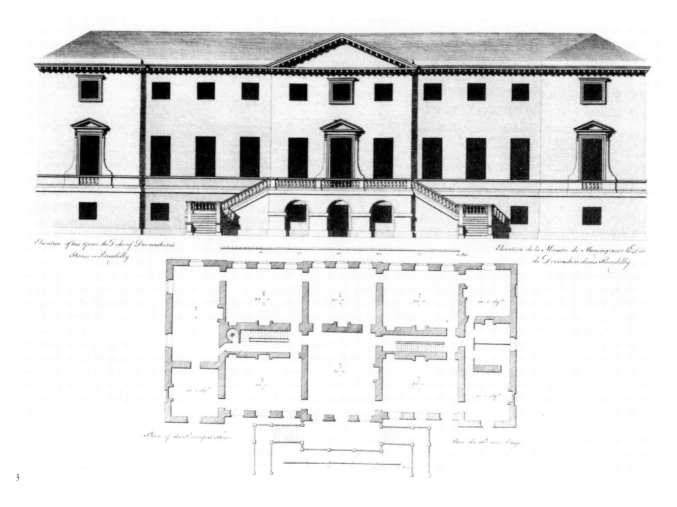

3

2 Badminton House, a house enlarged by Kent. 3 The elevation and plan of the principal floor of Devonshire House, Piccadilly, built in 1735.

included not only Kent's old patrons but also many leading members of the Whig aristocracy. Later, in 1730, Burlington published, at his own expense, previously unknown drawings by Palladio, which he had collected in Italy. These books were further moves in the campaign to woo public taste away from the Baroque of Wren and his followers, and to substitute Palladian propriety. In the same vein the style of Vanbrugh's Blenheim was attacked by the poet Alexander Pope whilst Lord Carlisle, for whom Vanbrugh and Hawksmoor had designed Castle Howard, still not completed when Hawksmoor died in 1736, had his confidence in their work undermined by his son-in-law, Sir Thomas Robinson, whose letters to his father-in-law are full of admiration for each of Kent's newest creations.

WILLIAM KENT THE ARCHITECT

The Palladian style came to dominate the design of English country houses for the next half a century – in provincial Ireland and in North America for considerably longer. The style was not only politically and

socially acceptable but clearly fitted Kent's own inclinations and he now found himself increasingly concerned with problems of architectural design, as opposed to decoration.

Burlington had already steered Kent firmly in the true path of Palladianism during their travels together in Italy and only rarely did Kent allow Baroque elements to creep into his architectural style. At Badminton however Kent did draw on Baroque forms. Here, in 1682 the first Duke of Beaufort added the Great Hall between the wings of the original sixteenth-century house. In 1740 Kent was engaged to add a third storey and the pediment and cupolas on the north façade as well as pavilions at each corner and wings joining them to the central building. Canaletto depicted the new great north front of Badminton House in 1750 on his tour of England. Kent followed this with Worcester Lodge, a great gatehouse at the entrance to the Park at Badminton with an upper storey containing a 'grand room which commands a most glorious prospect where the Duke often dined in summer' and could view the

1 *North front of Kent's Treasury building, Whitehall. 2 Detail of Hogarth's 'Canvassing for Votes' showing Kent's Horse Guards building.*

north façade of his house three miles distant.

A final essay in Baroque, Wakefield Lodge, Northamptonshire, completed around 1750, after Kent's death, for the Duke of Grafton, has a Baroque curved stairway leading up to the entrance. Inevitably it did not please the arbiters of Palladian taste and Horace Walpole commented in 1751 that 'The design is Kent's but as was his manner too heavy'.

Kent's Devonshire House in Piccadilly, commissioned by the third Duke of Devonshire in 1735 to replace Hugh May's Berkeley House which had been destroyed by fire in October 1733, contained no deviation from Palladian principles. Its most elegant feature was the outside double staircase leading to the *piano nobile*. The building, with its fine saloon, enriched by a typical Kent ceiling, was finally demolished in 1925 to make way for the block of apartments still known as Devonshire House.

What would have been Kent's greatest public commission never came to fruition. Attention had, for a considerable time, been focused on the site of the old Palace of Westminster as the suitable centre of government for the now emerging Empire. Inigo Jones's Banqueting House had been designed as part of a palace at Whitehall and John Webb had continued to work on plans for it after Jones's death. Some of their drawings had found their way into Lord Burlington's collection and had been included in Kent's 1727 publication. Between 1732 and 1739, Kent prepared a series of schemes for an imposing Houses of Parliament in the Palladian style on the Whitehall site which would have crowned his architectural career. The collapse of Walpole's peace policy, signalled by the outbreak of the war with Spain in 1739, which then drifted into the war of the Austrian Succession, firmly put paid to monumental public building on such a scale, although Kent's scheme for the new Courts of Justice facing the east end of Westminster Abbey was carried out between 1758

3 The Horseguards – Kent's best-known London building, and (4) Pearwood model of a palace designed by Kent for George II

and 1770 by John Vardy. This building was unfortunately damaged by fire in 1834 and demolished in 1850.

The Royal Mews Stables were built at Charing Cross in 1732 to Kent's designs but were demolished to make way for the National Gallery in 1838. Of his plans for the Treasury building, the central part, overlooking the Horse Guards Parade, was completed in 1734 although the wings and pavilions at each end which were an integral part of the composition were never built. His design for the Horse Guards building itself, which is his best-known building in London, was also carried out after his death, by Vardy 1750–9. Here Palladian proportions were fully realised and it is a fitting memorial to Kent's style and achievement. The Wellington room above the archway with its Venetian window was for many years the office of the Commander-in-Chief of the Army and was occupied by the Duke of Wellington himself for ten years. Even after his death, Kent did not escape Hogarth's derision and the painting 'Canvassing

for Votes' depicts, in the banner hung from the inn-sign, the Royal coach passing under the central arch which has just decapitated the coachman.

One particularly intriguing and strictly Palladian concept was Kent's plan for a country palace for King George II to replace the Royal Lodge in the Old Deer Park at Richmond. This is known only from the very beautiful model in pearwood (*c.* 1735) which can be seen in the Dutch House at Kew.

Kent's greatest completed work is Holkham in Norfolk, perhaps the most perfect of the English eighteenth-century country houses and one that happily survives intact today. Following his return from Italy Thomas Coke had determined to build a house of Classical design which would be a suitable home for the pictures and sculpture he had collected there. The project was the subject of discussion between Coke, Burlington and Kent over a period of fifteen years. Eventually, in 1729, an obelisk by Kent was set up in

Holkham Hall, designed by Kent, and completed after his death. 1 The south front. 2 From the south west showing the disposition of the pavilions.

the centre of the park and the building was started. The inscription above the front door, on the inner side, proclaims that 'This seat on an open barren estate, was planned, built, decorated and inhabited in the middle of the XVIIIth century by Thos. Coke, Earl of Leicester'. The execution of the house was carried out by Matthew Brettingham to Kent's designs and the original draw-

ings are preserved at Holkham. Undoubtedly, however, Coke exercised a controlling influence over the design and execution. According to Brettingham, it was his idea to model the Marble Hall on a Roman basilica. Kent's design incorporates great Ionic columns of Derbyshire alabaster.

Coke's insistence on 'commodiousness' is also seen

3 *The gallery: a twice scale version of a room in Lord Burlington's Villa at Chiswick. 4 A temple in the park at Holkham.*

in the Sculpture Gallery and the Long Library which contains his famous collection of books. The south façade of the house with its great portico, and the placing of the windows, reflect both Palladio's Classical principles and the spaciousness of the interior design. The columns of the portico are in stone but the rest of the building (apart from some of the dressings) is carried out in narrow yellowish brick similar to that used by Roman builders.

THE TOWN HOUSE

Although the Palladian style was well suited to town palaces of the nobility, standing in their own grounds, such as Devonshire House and Burlington House, its insistence on symmetry made its application impracticable in the case of the narrow-fronted town houses built in rows or terraces which sprang up in the seventeenth and eighteenth centuries.

During the second half of the seventeenth century a general plan for the smaller London town house developed. This plan, with an entrance on one side giving onto the staircase, with front and back rooms on each floor and the service rooms in the basement, served for terrace houses until the beginning of the twentieth century and indeed, subject to the intrusion of the garage, for the 'town houses' of the post-war period.

When Inigo Jones designed St Paul's Church in Covent Garden in 1631–33 for the Earl of Bedford who was developing the area, he planned the layout of the surrounding houses in the form of a piazza. This was the forerunner of the London Square, the tall houses themselves and the open colonnades on the ground floor emphasised the Italianate origins. Jones's houses have disappeared over the years but that part of the north side which is still known as 'The Piazza' has retained the general style of the original.

In 1638 Jones designed a row of houses in Lincoln's Inn Fields for William Newton, the first of London's speculative builders. These were on an altogether larger scale which permitted symmetrical double fronts. Of these, Lindsay House (No. 59–60) has survived. With its rusticated ground floor and the Ionic pilasters above supporting the entablature and top balustrade, this set the style for the greater formal London town house of the noble and the wealthy and served as a model for future generations of architects.

Heightened by the similarity of the unusual colour of the brickwork and of the giant pilasters, Lindsay House of 1638 and Archer's Russell House in Covent Garden, finished eighty years later, make a fascinating contrast. Both masterpieces of style, the first showing the adoption of the Renaissance proportions at its most successful, the second showing the disciplined use Archer made of the gift of Baroque, freedom of expression.

Palladian concepts gave little guidance on town house design. Although providing some elegant façades, their proportions occasioned similar difficulties to those noted by Horace Walpole in Burlington's Chiswick Villa: 'too strict adherence to rules and symmetry . . . too many correspondent doors in spaces so contracted'. A case in point was the town house Burlington designed in 1723, on strict Palladian principles, at 30 Old Burlington Street, for General Wade. It was characterised

by Walpole as 'worse contrived on the inside than is conceivable, all to humour the beauty of the front'. The front elevation, based on one drawn by Palladio himself in Burlington's collection, was however much admired and Walpole suggested that 'As the General could not live in it to his ease, he had better take a house over against it and look at it'.

In the 1720s, Burlington developed Savile Row and the adjoining streets behind Burlington House and no doubt Campbell advised on the general scheme. Many of the houses were designed by architects associated with the Palladian revival – Giacomo Leoni, Colen Campbell, and Henry Flitcroft, as well as Kent himself who may well have undertaken the pedimented terminal building demolished in 1937. 1 Savile Row, designed by Kent in 1731–33, still has its original ceilings and staircase behind Edmaston's 1870 alterations.

In 1732 Kent was entrusted with the project for turning 10 Downing Street into a suitable residence for the First Lord of the Treasury. Downing Street itself consisted of a terrace of fifteen houses built as a speculative development by George Downing in 1682. Behind No. 10 was a larger mansion facing Horse Guards built during the reign of Charles II for his illegitimate son the Earl of Lichfield and this building was presented to Walpole by George II. Under the direction of Kent, and with Flitcroft as the Clerk of Works, it was substantially reconstructed and joined by a long narrow room to the smaller front house at number 10. Apart from the renewal of the Downing Street frontage by Kenton Couse between 1766 and 1774, the Prime Minister's residence with its interior decoration remains today very much as Kent and Flitcroft left it.

The most successful of Kent's town houses was that which he designed for Lady Isabella Finch, Burlington's sister-in-law, at 44 Berkeley Square. (This house, one of his later works, resembles William Kent House in a number of respects.) The brick façade has stone quoins, and a rusticated arch framing the doorway, which support a band of masonry, broken with balusters, below the three first-floor windows which are surmounted by triangular pediments; at the second floor level the square windows are blind. The fact that Lady Isabella was unmarried no doubt accounted for the modest bedroom accommodation. The greater part of the interior of the house is given over to the magnificent Saloon, already mentioned, and to the highly dramatic staircase, both of which Kent was able to accommodate within his Palladian scheme.

The façade of 44 Berkeley Square, a town house built on Palladian principles. Many of its features are matched in 22 Arlington Street.

A drawing by Kent of Pope's garden. Its planning was a forerunner of the style of informal landscape gardening Kent practised.

LANDSCAPE GARDENING

The Palladian style was best suited to country mansions and their Classical architecture was set off by their surrounding parks. It was Kent's creation of the natural style in gardening, as a revolt against the formality of the French style that has turned out to be his most lasting contribution to English, and indeed European, culture.

Already during his stay in Italy Kent had been deeply impressed by the landscape paintings of Poussin and Claude Lorrain and he conceived the idea of creating such landscapes in reality, as opposed to the formally patterned gardens which, until then, had been the accepted form. In the new style of gardening, boundary walls were dispensed with in favour of sunken ha-has which integrated the garden into the surrounding countryside and created vistas in the landscape. Woodlands, grass and water were so placed in relation to each other as to create 'pictures' in the style of Claude Lorrain.

Shaftesbury writing his *The Moralists* in 1709 in dialogue form had already pointed the way for this development.

Your Genius, the Genius of the Place and the Great Genius have at last prevailed. I shall no longer resist the passion in me for things of a natural kind; where neither Art, nor the Conceit or Caprice of Man has spoil'd their genuine order, by breaking in upon that primitive state. Even the rude Rocks, the mossy Caverns, the irregular unwrought Grotto's and broken Falls of Waters, with all the horrid Graces of the Wilderness itself, as representing Nature more, will be the more engaging, and appear with the Magnificence beyond the formal Mockery of princely Gardens.

Alexander Pope was one of the first to put these notions into practice in his riverside garden at Twickenham. He remarked to Kent that 'All gardening is landscape painting' and there is, in the British Museum, a sketch of ornamental buildings Kent designed for Pope's garden. Already in 1716 Charles Bridgeman was working on Lord Burlington's gardens at Chiswick and in 1729 Burlington commissioned Kent to replan the grounds around his newly-completed villa. Kent's

Chiswick House: The vista from the house ends with a semi-circular exedra which frames Burlington's statues from Hadrian's villa at Tivoli.

design was an important break with the established tradition, and Chiswick was the forerunner of the new English garden. In its restored form many of Kent's original features can be seen and comparison made with his drawings of the villa itself and of the semi-circular exedra, originally of cut myrtle but now replaced by yew, framing Burlington's statues of Caesar, Pompey and Cicero from Hadrian's villa at Tivoli.

Bridgeman, who was appointed Royal Gardener in 1728, was also developing these new ideas. He was responsible for laying out Kensington Gardens for George II and his design included the Round Pond from which three great tree-lined avenues stretched out into the distance. He also joined up a number of ponds lying to the east to form the lake called, in his plan, 'The New River' and known today as the Serpentine. Bridgeman designed a ha-ha along the boundary with Hyde Park over which the views extended and the work was completed in 1731.

It was Charles Bridgeman who broke up the formality

of the enclosed garden at Stowe and he had also worked on the Duke of Newcastle's gardens at Claremont. In all these gardens, Kensington, Claremont and Stowe his work was extended by Kent. An interesting contemporary insight into their respective talents is provided in Horace Walpole's *The History of the Modern Taste in Gardening*. Bridgeman, he writes,

banished verdant sculpture and did not even revert to the square precision of the foregoing age. He disdained to make every division tally to its opposite, and though he still adhered to strait walks with high clipped hedges, they were only his great lines; the rest he diversified by wildernesses, and with loose groves of oak, though still within surrounding hedges. But the capital stroke . . . was the destruction of walls for boundaries, and the invention of fosses – an attempt then deemed so astonishing, that the common people called them Ha! Ha's! to express their surprize at finding a sudden and unperceived check to their walk. – The contiguous ground of the park without the sunk fence was to be harmonised with the lawn within; and the garden in its turn was to be set free from its prim regularity, that it might assort with the wilder country without. At that moment appeared Kent, painter enough to taste the charms of landscape, bold and opinionative enough to dare to dictate, and born with a genius to strike out a great system from the twilight of

Stowe: the Oxford Bridge and Boycott Pavilions. COLOUR: *The Great Parlour at Rousham and the ceiling at Chicheley Hall*

imperfect essays. He leaped the fence, and saw that all nature was a garden, – his ruling principle was that Nature abhors a straight line'.

In Walpole's view, another of Kent's talents lay in his management of water. At Stowe his major alteration to Bridgeman's layout was the division of one large boating lagoon into two more natural irregular lakes and he enclosed the spring which fed them in a grotto. The larger of the two lakes was overlooked by a Temple of Venus and, according to a letter from 1724, 'The garden of Venus is delightful; you see her standing in her Temple at the head of a noble basin of water and opposite to her is an Amphitheatre with statues of gods and goddesses'. Kent also incorporated a number of other temples including the Temple of Concord and Victory based on the Maison Carrée at Nimes and the Temple of British Worthies as a repository for busts of twelve 'gallant countrymen; Heroes, Patriots and Wits'.

Lancelot Brown ('Capability' Brown) who had been head gardener at Stowe at this time and whose own style was developed from that of Kent, subsequently replanned the grounds but did not interfere with Kent's temples and other buildings. The garden at Stowe was open to the public but, important as Kent's work there was, his most influential commission was the design of the gardens at Carlton House which Frederick, Prince of Wales, had purchased in 1733. His treatment of this 12-acre garden, in the area where Lower Regent Street now runs, firmly established the 'new taste in gardening' noted by Sir Thomas Robinson (see page 106).

In 1729 Henry Pelham had purchased Esher Lodge, an early Tudor Palace, close by Claremont, the estate of his brother, the Duke of Newcastle, and engaged Kent to carry out the extensive alterations and the decoration of the building. In 1735 Kent laid out the grounds to such effect that Pope could write of the place as one 'where Kent and Nature vie for Pelham's love', and in

COLOUR: *Kent's work at Rousham: garden buildings, water, statues, and open asymmetrical planting. 1 A drawing for the cascade in the gardens.*

1748, the year of Kent's death, when the gardens at Claremont and Esher had matured, Walpole wrote of 'the trees, lawns and concaves all in the perfection in which the ghost of Kent would joy to see them'. Nothing remains of the grounds at Esher but an idea of Kent's creation is furnished by the plan published in *Jardins Anglo-chinois* by Le Rouge who saw in the serpentine paths a Chinese influence. The Claremont garden, originally laid out by Vanbrugh and Bridgeman in 1720, and subsequently extended and naturalised by Kent has recently been restored by the National Trust who claim that it is the earliest surviving English landscape garden.

The best surviving example of Kent's landscaping, and perhaps indeed his finest work, is the garden at Rousham, dating from 1738. It is laid out in three landscape sections, each opening up a view of the next, and with a seven arched portico (Praeneste) overlooking the River Cherwell. The result was an organic yet disciplined design in which a natural free-flowing sense of order was imposed on a delightful corner of the English countryside. For Horace Walpole 'the garden is Daphne in little, the sweetest little groves, streams, glades, porticos, cascades and river imaginable; all the scenes are perfectly classic'. The garden today is little changed from that shown in Kent's original sketches displayed in the Hall. The trees, some of which were already 15ft high when planted are fully mature; the elms have unhappily succumbed, and vandals have taken their toll, but a walk round the garden today can give as much pleasure as it afforded Walpole, whose verdict was that Rousham was 'the most engaging of Kent's works. It is Kentissimo'.

Kent broke down the barriers which until then had constrained the art of gardening. His new style was adopted not only throughout England but also in the 'English' gardens throughout Europe. Perhaps the earliest was that laid out by the anglophile Fürst Leopold Franz von Anhalt-Dessau in his park at Wörlitz following his journey to England in 1767, and extolled by Goethe in his letter to Charlotte von Stein of 14 May 1778. Fürst Franz was a close friend of Goethe's patron Duke Carl August of Weimar and on a visit there in 1777 advised them on a new layout for the Weimar Park. The English Garden in Munich dates from 1789 and (the writer's favourite) the gardens of the Laxenburg Palace in Lower Austria were laid out in 1801. Even the formal gardens of Schönbrunn, commenced in the 1770s in the French style, merge into 'the clear landscape of an English park'. Kent's gardens were his most original work – his contribution to gardening his most enduring.

Baron Pelham of Laughton (1653–1711/12), father of two Prime Ministers–Henry Pelham and Thomas Pelham-Holles, Duke of Newcastle.

NICHOLAS THOMPSON

THE PELHAMS: POLITICAL AND ARCHITECTURAL PATRONAGE

A Fishing Temple at Esher Place by Kent

In his *Anecdotes of Painting in England* Horace Walpole, that indefatigable chronicler of his age and son of the great Prime Minister, refers to 'the patronage of the Queen, of the Dukes of Grafton and Newcastle, and Mr Pelham, and the interest of his constant friend', by which William Kent 'was made master carpenter, architect, keeper of the pictures, and after the death of Jervas, principal painter to the Crown'. In alluding to the interest of his constant friend, Walpole inevitably refers to Lord Burlington, who has always been accredited as the man most responsible for Kent's meteoric rise and successful career. The other names are perhaps less obviously connected with Kent, and deserve further investigation.

William Kent worked for Queen Caroline in the 1730s on the gardens and garden buildings at Richmond; at St James's Palace he designed an elaborate library for her just before her death in 1737; and it was no doubt at her request in 1729, during the King's absence in Hanover, that Kent restored the decorative paintings on the two great staircases at Windsor. Kent's work for the Duke of Grafton seems to have been confined to the gardens of Euston Hall in Suffolk (*c.* 1746) and to the design of the hunting lodge at Wakefield in Northamptonshire (*c.* 1748–50), although the Duke's influence may well have led to commissions from others.

Certainly influence was a force in the patronage of the Duke of Newcastle and Henry Pelham, for in addition to the extensive private commissions for which these two brothers employed Kent, their powerful public positions (both ultimately became Prime Ministers) at a period when the structure of the Office of Works was open to political manoeuvre, meant that

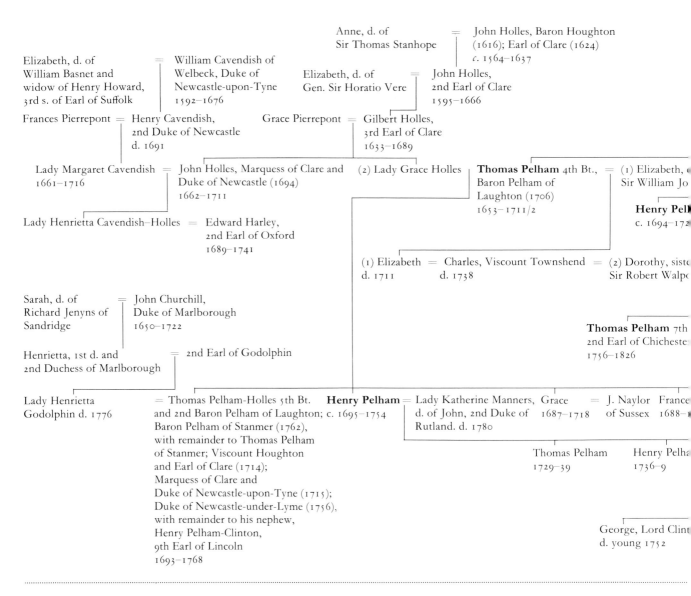

Seven generations of Pelhams, showing the connection with the Holles family from whom Thomas Pelham inherited much of his wealth.

they were able to indulge their tastes on a wider scale by playing the role of public patron as well as private. George Vertue recorded in his *Notebooks* that Henry Pelham was William Kent's 'great patron'; indeed he was.

Politics and architecture in the second quarter of the eighteenth century were dominated by a wealthy aristocracy. This was the age of the great houses of parade, palaces like Wanstead, Houghton and Holkham, and of the ascendency of the Whig families for whom they were built. These grand houses and parks were reflections not only of the aesthetic tastes of their owners, but of their political power. Their uniqueness to their age is demonstrated by the fact that many had been demolished or had fallen into decay before the century was out. Their appearance suggested solid wealth, yet the cost of building, remodelling, repairing and running them was often the cause of financial

embarrassment to their owners. Houghton, Sir Robert Walpole's great house in Norfolk, which more than any other symbolised the Whig ideal of the good life, was practically derelict by the time his son Horace inherited it in 1791. The immense cost of Houghton, and of his other houses, had overtaken even Sir Robert's income. After Walpole's fall in 1742, the Earldom of Orford was an empty honour; and Horace wrote of his father in 1745, 'It is certain he is dead very poor; his debts amount to £50,000, his estate is a nominal £8,000 a year much mortgaged'. Houghton, however, survived just long enough to be inherited in 1797 by the Earl of Cholmondeley who secured its restoration. Claremont, the Duke of Newcastle's great house in Surrey, failed to survive the death of its owner in 1768.

In 1714, before he was twenty-one, Thomas Pelham had inherited the Dukedom of Newcastle, estates in eleven counties and an annual income of £27,000. Yet

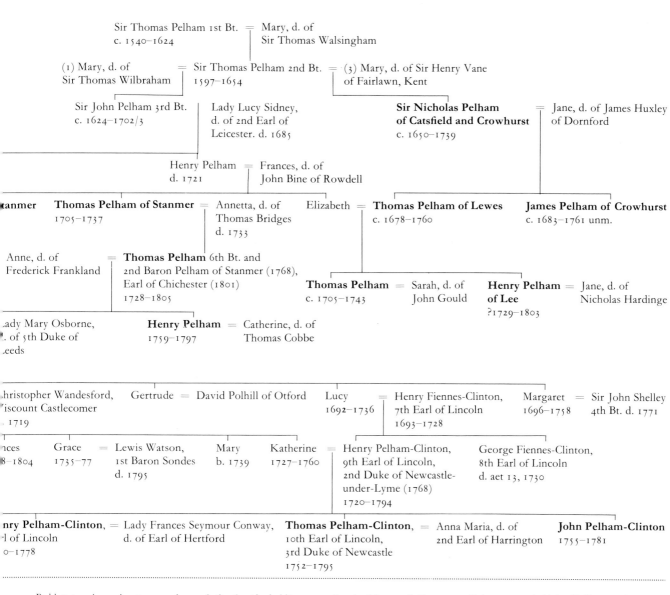

Bold type above denotes members of the family holding seats in the House of Commons. Below: seats held by Pelhams 1691–1794.

LEWES	1697–1702	Thomas Pelham (later Baron Pelham)		1741–1761	James Pelham of Crowhurst
	1702–1705	Sir Nicholas Pelham of Catsfield			
	1705–1741	Thomas Pelham of Lewes	SEAFORD	1717–1722	Hon. Henry Pelham
	1722–1725	Henry Pelham of Stanmer	NEWARK	1722–1741	James Pelham of Crowhurst
	1726–1727	Sir Nicholas Pelham of Catsfield	RYE	1749–1754	Thomas Pelham jun. of Stanmer (later Earl of Chichester)
	1727–1737	Thomas Pelham of Stanmer			
	1741–1743	Thomas Pelham jun. of Lewes	BRAMBER	1751–1754	Henry Pelham of Lee
	1780–1796	Hon. Henry Pelham of Stanmer	TIVERTON	1754–1758	Henry Pelham of Lee
			ALDBOROUGH	1772–1774	Henry Pelham-Clinton, Earl of Lincoln
SUSSEX	1702–1706	Sir Thomas Pelham Bt. (later Baron Pelham)	NOTTINGHAM-SHIRE	1774–1778	Henry Pelham-Clinton, Earl of Lincoln
	1722–1754	Hon. Henry Pelham			
	1754–1768	Thomas Pelham jun. of Stanmer (later Earl of Chichester)	WESTMINSTER	1774–1780	Lord Thomas Pelham-Clinton (later 3rd Duke of Newcastle)
HASTINGS	1715–1722	Henry Pelham of Stanmer	EAST RETFORD	1778–1781	Lord John Pelham-Clinton
	1728–1741	Thomas Pelham jun. of Lewes		1781–1794	Thomas Pelham-Clinton, Earl of Lincoln (later 3rd Duke of Newcastle)

despite the emoluments of the great offices he held for fifty years, he died leaving an estate worth only £9,000. His spending was compulsive, but it was, at least in his own eyes, directed to the service of his King and country, and to maintaining the position which he believed was essential to the success of his political ambitions.

Henry and Thomas Pelham and their five sisters were the children, by a second marriage, of Sir Thomas Pelham, a wealthy Sussex landowner. Sir Thomas was a Whig, who represented his party in the Commons from 1678 until 1706 when he was created Baron Pelham of Laughton. His second wife was Lady Grace Holles, the daughter of Gilbert, 3rd Earl of Clare and sister of the 4th Earl, who had married Lady Margaret Cavendish, the daughter and heiress of Henry, Duke of Newcastle. When Lady Margaret inherited her father's estates, they were found to be encumbered with debts. Her husband agreed to assume responsibility for discharging these, and in return obtained his wife's rights over the property she inherited. Later he was created Duke of Newcastle in his own right. His only child, a daughter Henrietta, was heir to the great Holles estates, and would have inherited them as well as those of her Cavendish grandfather, had not her father decided to alter his will.

The Duke of Newcastle's decision had a profound effect on his nephews Thomas and Henry Pelham, for when he died in 1711, the bulk of these estates passed to the Duke's eldest nephew Thomas, then a young man of seventeen, and still a student at Clare Hall, Cambridge. On 23 February 1713, Lord Pelham died at his family home, Halland Place in Sussex, and the young Thomas succeeded to his father's Barony and to his Sussex estates. The English system of primogeniture, which meant that Thomas, as the elder son, inherited virtually everything, caused Henry, his younger brother, to be financially dependent on him for much of his life; but Thomas, who despite his great wealth was dogged by an almost paranoid feeling of insecurity and fell constantly into debt, relied greatly on the advice and reassurance of his more level-headed brother. Their characters differed enormously, as did their political style and architectural tastes.

This background of wealth and family connections eminently qualified the two brothers for successful participation in political life, and both quickly showed an aptitude for the way in which it was conducted in the first part of the eighteenth century. 1715 was the year of the first general election of George I's reign and the first opportunity for Thomas to indulge his genius for electoral management. The influence of the Ministry in elections was a great factor in controlling the com-

2 Nottingham Castle, the Holles seat on the Duke's northern estates. 3 Newcastle House, Lincoln's Inn Fields – his London house.

position of the House of Commons – not only by virtue of the personal wealth and family connections of its members, but also because of the extensive political patronage at the disposal of the more important members. Places in the Dockyards, the Customs and Excise, or the Office of Works, were often used to secure amenable voters; and in the disposal of ecclesiastical patronage, account was almost invariably taken of the recipient's political views. To secure the goodwill of electoral magnates in counties or boroughs, there were sinecures or grants from the Civil List and the Secret Service Fund to be disposed of. Such ways of influencing voters were most effectively used to secure government majorities when they were in the hands of one man. Newcastle became that man. He had the initial advantages of great personal wealth, which he spent lavishly in the Whig interest. He had the control of seven boroughs, and a decisive voice in the choice of candidates for at least four counties. He also took an intense delight in organisation, and concerned himself with the minutest details of electioneering, wherever he or his colleagues could exercise pressure.

Although there were national funds and sinecures on which he could draw to support his schemes of patronage, maintaining his interest in local areas was an expensive business and one which had to be met from his private purse. He would make contributions to local charities and provide special help in times of stress; he would take the lead in celebrating national events like royal birthdays or anniversaries and great victories in war; he would provide appropriate cups or plates for races and other local contests; he would entertain the local nobility and gentry, as well as using his influence at Court and in Parliament for local causes and the advancement of local persons. A grandee whose duties were such needed to live in a style which expressed his capability of performing them.

Newcastle was fortunate in inheriting four major houses. In Sussex there was Halland Place, an old Elizabethan manor house. Inherited from his father, this was the true Pelham seat and his childhood home. In the same county, there was Bishopstone, his favourite hunting lodge. From his uncle he inherited Newcastle House in London, which became the administrative centre of his great empire; and from the same source came his northern seat, Nottingham Castle, a great house of the seventeenth century.

The grand style in which he used these houses was set early in his life when, in 1714, he celebrated his coming of age at Halland Place. The great affair was reported in the *London Newsletter* a few days later:

On Wednesday last came of age Lord Pelham and at his seat in

1 Claremont, the Duke of Newcastle's seat in Surrey, designed by Sir John Vanbrugh around an existing house built by Vanbrugh for himself.

Sussex he made a noble entertainment, where were dressed seven oxen, fifteen sheep, six calves, eight bucks, and so proportionable of fowls etc. There were eighty stands of sweetmeats on the first table, ... forty-nine hogsheads of strong beer, seven hogsheads of claret, besides champagne, burgundy etc. The aforesaid feast cost two thousand pounds.

In addition to the enormous cost of such entertainments and of maintaining households which could provide them, Newcastle had to cope with the high cost of building and repair, and of running large stables. By 1715 work was being carried out to improve and mod-ernise all four inherited houses. For this, the young man turned to an old friend and fellow member of the famous Kit-Cat Club, Sir John Vanbrugh, who had acted as architect to Pelham's uncle. The Kit-Cat Club had evolved during the later years of William III's reign, with the particular aim of working to ensure the Protestant succession of the House of Hanover after the death of William and Anne. By 1700, it included most of the prominent and ennobled Whigs of the day. Vanbrugh's employment as architect by many of its

The Great Room rises behind the right hand wing. 2, 3 Elevation and Plan of Chargate, Vanbrugh's original house. 4 Sir John Vanbrugh.

members puts him firmly in the Whig camp. As well as being Newcastle's architect, Vanbrugh acted as intermediary between the young Duke and Sarah, Duchess of Marlborough, whose granddaughter Henrietta Godolphin became his Duchess on 2 April 1717.

Vanbrugh was given general supervision of the remodelling of Newcastle House as early as the spring of 1715 when the work of fitting new windows and adding new wainscot started. By 1717 he told the Duke that the house was nearly finished and would soon be

ready for him. In 1718, Newcastle requested that Vanbrugh should survey Nottingham Castle to see if it would be adequate for his needs – he had not yet been to see it himself. Vanbrugh found it in better condition than he expected and wrote congratulating 'your Grace upon his being master of this Noble Dwelling'. Newcastle decided to see for himself and made a trip there that winter, after which money was spent refurbishing the house. It was however never much used.

The repair and remodelling of the Duke's houses

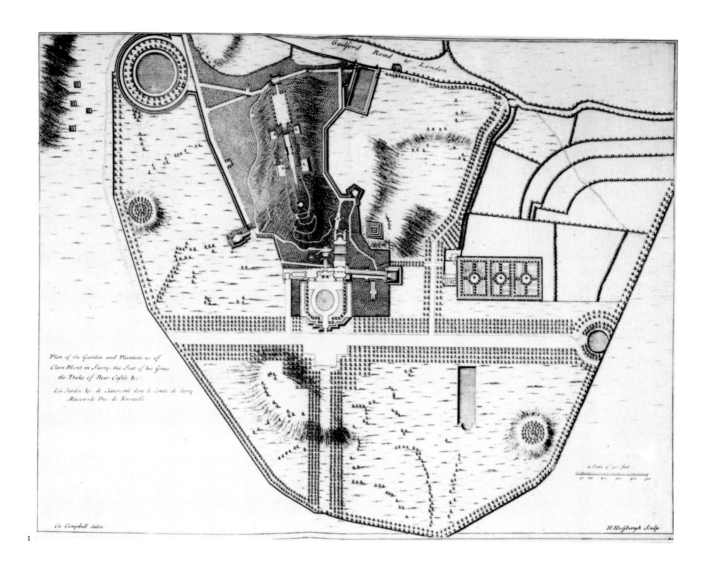

The gardens at Claremont as designed by Charles Bridgeman. Woods and winding paths are contained within a geometrical layout.

was by no means a once-and-for-all affair. Continued expenditure throughout his life often led him into debt. In 1737 his brother Henry wrote him an admonishing but affectionate letter in which he comments,

> . . . purchases and repairs at Lewes, I know Dear Brother that that has been a great expense to you, but what ruins you, is that at the same time near five thousand pounds laid out at Newcastle House, continued expenses from additions at Claremont, hounds and other vast ones at Bishopstone, and now new buildings and alterations going on there.

Claremont was the only house which he did not inherit, and it was built to fulfill a significant gap in his inheritance. What the young man lacked, and felt he had to have, was a seat conveniently located near London and the Court, where he might entertain and find recreation. As early as October 1714 he had bought from his friend Vanbrugh, the castellated house at Esher, called Chargate, which Vanbrugh had built in 1709–10 for his own occupation. By 1716 Newcastle managed to secure the copyhold of the surrounding estate, and the name was changed to Claremont. Vanbrugh's little house was strategically located, but it was certainly not large enough for the needs of a grandee with the pretensions of the young Duke. Work started

2 The Bowling Green and Vanbrugh's Belvedere in 1733–4. 3 Bridgeman's circular basin with the grass Amphitheatre and a temple beyond.

immediately to alter and extend the existing house by adding two large wings on either side to give a frontage of some three hundred feet. The view of *c.* 1750 attributed to J. F. Rigaud shows the arrangement.

At the centre of this composition is Vanbrugh's own Chargate, its crenellations replaced by a straight parapet and a pedimented centre, approached by flights of steps. On either side stretch the two arcaded wings, stepping forward slightly to create a shallow forecourt and to emphasise the central block. The predominantly horizontal composition is then given a series of vertical accents: the corner towers to the wings, the paired

chimney stacks, and the two clock towers behind. In 1719–20 Vanbrugh added a Great Room at the back of the right-hand wing. This was about one hundred feet long, two storeys high, and bigger than any other single room he built.

A Great Room was essential to a house of any pretension during the first half of the eighteenth century. It was the setting of those essentially new forms of entertainment, the assembly, the ball and the rout. Of these the most important was the assembly, 'a stated and general meeting of polite persons of both sexes, for the sake of conversation, gallantry, news and play', as a

1 *The Duke of Newcastle (right) with his brother-in-law, the 7th Earl of Lincoln, by Kneller. In the background is the Claremont Belvedere.*

definition of 1751 put it. An assembly would take place in the evening, and guests might expect to dance, play cards, drink tea, eat supper, or on great occasions, to do all of these things.

After dining with the Duke of Chandos, in September 1720, Vanbrugh wrote to Newcastle, 'He talked to me of your Grace's New Room at Claremont . . . I have, however, done all I can to prevent his coming till tis quite done that it may Stair in his face, and knock him down at Once'. Alas the appearance of that great interior may never be known for it was demolished apparently without record. Records of Newcastle's hospitality however do exist, and clearly it was prodigious. He entertained George I in 1717, without the benefit of his Great Room, and George II in 1749 with it. On the latter occasion the entertainment included music, bell-ringing and gunners for the royal salutes. In 1755 his Steward of the Household, John Greening, recorded, 'My Lord Duke had a Grand Company at Dinner here

on Monday, there were fifty-two Noblemen, the most I ever saw here at one Dinner and His Grace was pleased to say he never saw a Dinner better served and everything as well as possible'.

Country house recreation was not confined to the house alone. As much care, and in some cases more, was lavished on the gardens and the landscape which surrounded the house. Newcastle took a great interest in his gardens; and work started at Claremont soon after the alterations and extensions to the house were under way. By 1727 the garden at Claremont was described as 'the noblest of any in Europe . . . a Magnificent Taste and Way of Thinking'. The style was set by Vanbrugh's Belvedere which sat on that 'Mount' behind the house from which Claremont derived its name. This picturesque pavilion, containing one high room above another, survives still to dominate the landscape. That it was used for entertaining, as well as for ornament, is certain, for it was originally

2, 3 Stanmer in Sussex, designed by Nicholas Dubois, seat of a junior branch of the Pelhams. 4 Thomas Pelham of Stanmer (1705–37).

glazed and panelled, and contained among other things 'a closet for Mr Macklin and the Butler' and a 'hazard table'.

Around this little building Charles Bridgeman created a landscape garden in the new 'natural' style. In his essay *On Modern Gardening*, Horace Walpole wrote that Bridgeman 'disdained to make every division tally to its opposite, and though he still adhered much to straight walks with high clipped hedges, they were only his great lines; the rest he diversified by wilderness, and with loose groves of oak'. To Bridgeman, Walpole also credited the invention of the ha-ha which provided an uninterrupted visual link with the surrounding landscape, whilst preventing the animals grazing there from entering the grounds. All these ingredients appear in the plan of Claremont given in Colen Campbell's *Vitruvius Britannicus* (1722): the pleasure garden protected by the ha-ha, the straight terraced walk dropping down from the belvedere to the bowling green and, outside the rigid geometry of the terraces, a wooded wilderness laced with winding paths. Subsequent to Campbell's engraving a huge grassed amphitheatre was created above the circular lake, a feature unique to Claremont.

Newcastle's position as co-ordinator and dispenser of Whig patronage ensured that the Pelham family as a whole were heavily involved in politics during his lifetime. In 1717 Newcastle's brother, Henry, was returned for Seaford, one of Newcastle's pocket boroughs; and in 1722 he became member for Sussex, which seat he held until his death in 1754. Henry Pelham's rise in politics, which brought him to the Treasury, eventually as First Lord and Chancellor of the Exchequer for eleven years, was largely the result of his own abilities. Cousins and uncles, whose votes in the Whig interest were their most significant contribution or who acted as Henry and Thomas's agents, owed

1 Lucy, Countess of Lincoln. 2 Gateway at Oatlands by Inigo Jones. 3, 4 Unexecuted designs for a villa at Oatlands by Lord Burlington.

their positions almost entirely to the influence of the two brothers.

In the first half of the eighteenth century there were three main branches of the Pelham family in Sussex, all descending from Sir Thomas Pelham Bt of Laughton. Thomas and Henry represented their generation in the senior line, Thomas becoming the 5th Baronet on his father's death, as well as succeeding to his Barony. Their first cousins, Thomas and Henry Pelham of Stanmer, represented the next senior branch and were the sons of Lord Pelham's younger brother, Henry Pelham of Stanmer. Representing the junior branch were Thomas and James Pelham, the sons of Lord Pelham's uncle Sir Nicholas Pelham of Catsfield. The three sets of brothers all held Whig seats in Sussex and

so, when they came of age, did the sons of the two junior brothers.

The two Lewes seats were important ones, and Newcastle saw to it that there were always Pelhams represented there. Traditionally, one seat was held by the Pelhams of Catsfield and Crowhurst. Sir Nicholas Pelham held the seat from 1702 to 1705 and then was succeeded by Sir Thomas Pelham of Lewes who held it for a further twenty-six years, encouraged no doubt by a place of £500 a year (later raised to £1,000) at the Board of Trade, secured for him by his cousin, the Duke.

Possibly to strengthen the Whig interest there, he gave his first cousin, Henry Pelham of Stanmer, the other Lewes seat in 1722. When Henry died in 1725, still in his early thirties, Newcastle was forced to bring

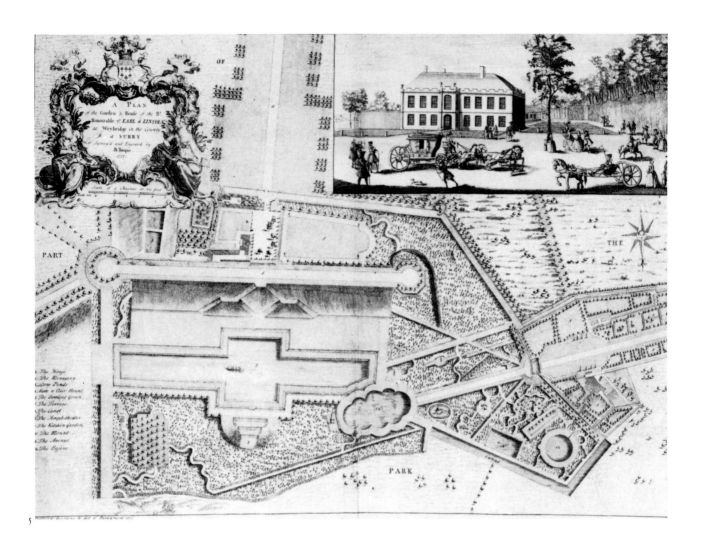

5 *Rocque's plan of 1737 showing the gardens at Oatlands. Burlington's villa may have been designed to stand on the main north to south axis.*

back his great uncle Sir Nicholas, long since retired and then seventy-five years old, to hold the seat until it could be filled by Henry's brother, Thomas of Stanmer, from 1727 to 1737. Maintaining the right sort of men in so many seats must have been a very taxing occupation; but it was one that Newcastle relished, although he complained a good deal about it. During his fifty years in politics, he saw eleven different members of the Pelham family represent the Whig interest in eight different seats. Six of these were in Sussex.

Newark, at the centre of Newcastle's Nottinghamshire estates, was the seat James Pelham of Crowhurst, held from 1722 to 1741. James was a second cousin to Newcastle and the son of Sir Nicholas Pelham. His career shows more clearly than that of any other mem-

ber of the family how ministerial patronage could be used to secure support in Parliament. James Pelham started life as a soldier, seeing active service in the War of the Spanish Succession. But as a friend of the Walpoles, and second cousin of the great Pelhams, he soon exchanged his military career for a political one. In 1710 he had written to Walpole's brother, 'I am convinced you intend to keep your promise of making me a great man'. In the Hastings elections of 1715 and 1722 he acted as agent to the Duke of Newcastle, who appointed him his secretary and in 1722 returned him for Newark. On the formation of the Prince of Wales's household in 1728, Pelham was appointed secretary to the Prince. He resigned the post in 1737 when he voted with the Administration, and against his master, on the Prince's allowance. In 1741 he was transferred to Hastings, with a view to relieving him of the expense of the Newark elections. Discontented with his financial position, he complained to Newcastle, reminding him of the loss which he had suffered by Newcastle's buying South Sea stock for him, and of £2,000 which he had lent the Duke. In the course of the next ten years he was made Deputy Cofferer of the Household under Newcastle's nephew Lord Lincoln, given a sinecure in the Customs of about £700 (held for him by his nephew, John Pelham), and granted a second secret service pension of £500 a year. Still discontented, he wrote to Newcastle again in 1750,

> The King is so gracious as to allow me five hundred a year . . . but as I have nothing to show for it 'tis most likely any alteration in the Ministry would put it out of my power to ask a favour of this sort. What I propose is a pension upon Ireland of six hundred for 21 years, the exchange etc. would bring it lower than what I receive . . . I mentioned this to Mr Pelham who approves of my trying it at this time; both my offices are less than anybody has for near thirty years constant expensive attendance, the cofferer to be sure is a very precarious tenure.

However, on meeting with a refusal from Newcastle, he declared himself 'entirely satisfied.' Needless to say, he voted with the Government in every recorded division.

Throughout these years, James Pelham looked after Newcastle's electoral interests in Sussex, particularly in Hastings, Seaford and Rye. He was also on occasion used as a whip for Newcastle's private party in the House. In 1751, when Pitt was in hot water for speaking and voting with the Opposition on the Navy estimates, Newcastle sent a letter to 'dear Jemmy' desiring that, in view of the 'able and affectionate manner' in which Pitt had defended him against attacks in recent debates, 'neither you, nor any of my friends would give in to any clamour . . . that may be made against him from any of the party on account of his differing as to the number of seamen.' Pelham was instructed to show this letter to seven of the members owing their election to Newcastle, and presumably the others were dealt with by Newcastle himself. In about 1754 James Pelham's health began to decline. He did not stand in 1761, and died in December that year, unmarried and still in possession of his pension and sinecure.

Just as the Pelhams were active as leaders in politics, so did they make a considerable mark as patrons of architecture and landscape design. In 1722 the Stanmer Pelhams started to rebuild their seat in Sussex. Since their cousin Newcastle started work at Claremont, there had been several significant developments on the architectural scene: Leoni's edition of Palladio had been published and Colen Campbell had prepared the way for a Palladian revival in England by the publication of the first two volumes of *Vitruvius Britannicus* and by building houses according to Palladian rules. The Stanmer Pelhams went to Nicholas Dubois, who was not only an architect but had translated Palladio for Leoni's edition of the *Four Books*. Thus Dubois was obviously imbued with different principles of architectural design to those of Vanbrugh, but was well known to the Duke's architect, for in 1719 he had been appointed Master Mason at the Board of Works, of which Vanbrugh was Comptroller from 1702 to his death in 1726. Stanmer, although not an outstanding building, displays the more restrained elements of Palladian design, implying its relationship to Classical design by its proportions, rather than by the use of applied orders. The best room in the house is the dining room with its screen of Corinthian columns at one end, although the style of decoration suggests it was completed rather later than the carcass of the house.

A more positive attempt at Palladian design was made by the Duke's sister Lucy and her husband the Earl of Lincoln. Lord Lincoln had inherited from the Earl of Torrington the estate of Oatlands at Weybridge, very near to that of his future brother-in-law at Claremont. Lord and Lady Lincoln were laying out the grounds at Oatlands by 1725; and it seems likely that the Palladian building, for which designs by Lord Burlington have survived, must have been projected at about this time – certainly before the Earl's premature death in 1728, when he was succeeded by his eldest son, then aged eleven. Burlington's little villa seems never to have been built; and the Earl's death is perhaps the most likely explanation.

The surviving drawings indicate a square single-storey building, raised on a basement and covered by a simple pyramidal roof. The elevation contains direct quotations from Palladio: the rusticated centrepiece from the Villa Pisano at Bagnola, and the flanking window-cases, seemingly clamped to the walls by blocks as at the Palazzo Thiene. The whole composition is reminiscent of the entrance front of the Villa Emo at Castelfranco. But the use of the curiously rusticated order may have been inspired by a source much closer to home – a surviving gateway at Oatlands designed by Inigo Jones, for Queen Anne of Denmark in 1617, when the place was still a royal palace.

The plan of the building is as idiosyncratic as its

COLOUR: *The House of Commons in Session in 1710 by Peter Tillemans. It shows the old Commons Chamber, which was burnt down in 1834.*

elevation, and leads one to question whether it was designed as a residence in itself or, like Burlington's own villa at Chiswick, as an adjunct to an existing house. At the centre of the building is the principal room, apparently with no means of natural lighting unless by a lantern in the roof, which is not shown on the elevation. The room is based on a square with two apsidal extensions beyond screens of columns which serve to define the square. The walls are lined with alternating columns and niches, leaving space for two entrances but no fireplaces. This space must therefore have relied entirely on its architecture for decoration; one can imagine no arrangement of furniture here other than the most casual. The room may therefore have been designed as a *tribuna* for the display of sculpture.

To the period of this design must also belong the form of the gardens shown in Rocque's map of 1737, for it is unlikely that much work was done to them in the years following Lord Lincoln's death in 1728; Lincoln's eldest son died two years after he succeeded, and his second son, who then inherited, was by 1737 still only seventeen. Assuming then that the Rocque plan shows the gardens much as they were ten years earlier, it is tempting to look for a site within them for Burlington's villa. One does not have to look far if one accepts the idea that it might have been built as an adjunct to the existing house, as at Chiswick. The principal north to south axis of the layout runs past the main front of the old house. A new building erected to the west of the house on the space which seems in the plan to be no more than a carriage sweep would both terminate the avenue to the south and command views northwards over the Canal to the Amphitheatre beyond.

In London, houses were built for the Hon. Henry Pelham and for his brother-in-law, the Hon. Richard Arundell. Arundell was the son of Lord Arundell of Trerice and half-brother of the 'architect' Earl of Pembroke. He married a daughter of the 2nd Duke of Rutland, Lady Frances Manners, in 1732, six years after Henry Pelham had married her sister Lady Katherine. Both Pelham and Arundell took leases on the site immediately behind Burlington House which Lord Burlington was developing as a private estate. Their houses, Numbers 32 and 34 Old Burlington Street respectively, were designed by Colen Campbell and formed part of a group whose design was considered *avant garde* for their time. Campbell's continuous astylar façade in stock brick with stone dressings and no articulation of the party walls created an important prototype for the uniform street architecture of the eighteenth century. In his description of the street in 1734, James Ralph clearly recognises this importance.

The first four houses, opposite to the Duke of Queensborough's stable-gate, are, beyond comparison, in the finest taste of any common buildings we can see anywhere: Without the least affectation of ornament, or seeming design of any remarkable elegance, they have all the elegance that can be given to such a design, and need no ornament to make them remarkable. In a word, I would recommend this now as a sample of the most perfect kind for our modern architects to follow; and if none of our squares had a worse set of edifices in them than these, we should never regret the want of better.

Three storeys high, with dormers in the roof, the entire front was thirteen windows wide, four belonging to Number 31, the largest house. The plans were arranged in two mirrored pairs and internally the accommodation was similarly planned: a back room and a front room, divided by a transverse wall from the front staircase hall which was two storeys high, the service stair, and a second small back room. Each house-plot extended westward to Cork Street, all but Number 34 (which was on the corner) having long gardens terminated by a wall against which was built a privy. At the back of Number 34 a basement extended below the greater part of the garden and included a large, groin-vaulted kitchen. At the Cork Street end of the site stood a garden house, fronted by a portico and containing a central room with a coved ceiling, flanked by a smaller room on each side to house a privy and a cold bath.

Although leased by deeds dated between September 1719 and March 1725/6, the houses were constructed between 1718 and 1723. Number 34 was the first to be built, Colen Campbell receiving from Arundell the second of his payments as architect in August 1718. Payments to tradesmen continued until 1723, three years after Arundell took up residence. The southern pair were started slightly later. In the summer of 1718 it had looked as if the poet Alexander Pope would take the site of Number 32 for a house to be built under Campbell's supervision; but by February the following year he had abandoned the idea and Campbell himself took on the lease. Although Campbell referred to the house in his will of 16 January 1721/2 as being 'lately erected and built and now almost compleatly finished by me,' he never took up residence there, and in the same year it was occupied by Henry Pelham.

A drawing by Campbell of a design so similar to that executed at Number 30 Old Burlington Street and which is inscribed 'for the Hon: Henry Pelham Esq: begun in 1720 in Burlington Gardens but never finished

Whitehall looking towards Charing Cross, with Inigo Jones's Banqueting Hall on the right, c. 1746. Detail from a painting by Canaletto.

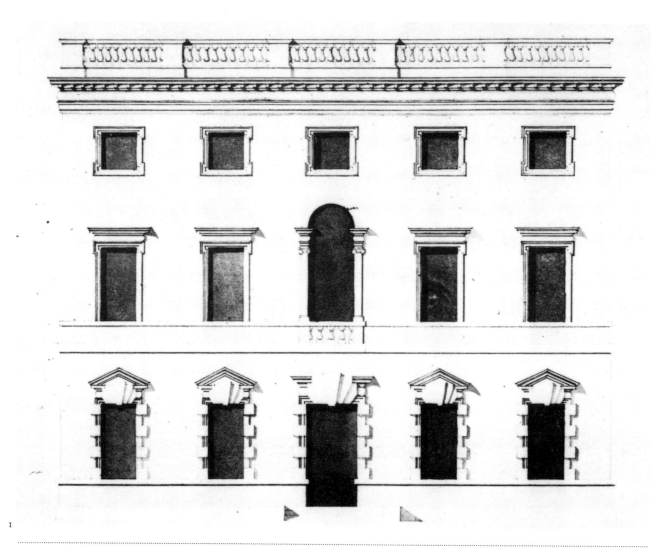

1 *Drawing by Colen Campbell inscribed, 'for the Hon: Henry Pelham Esq: begun in 1720 in Burlington Gardens but never finished C:C.'*

C:C.' suggests that Pelham may have originally intended to take the lease of Number 30. Perhaps due to the complications or expense in constructing that house (it remained incomplete until Sir Michael Newton took on the lease in 1725 and spent £1151 6s 9d fitting it up), Pelham decided to take the more modest house at Number 32, which as we know was 'almost compleatly finished' by January 1721/2.

By now Henry Pelham's political career had taken shape, his close association with Walpole, which ultimately led to his succeeding him as Prime Minister in 1743, was firmly established. When Walpole succeeded Sunderland as head of the Treasury in April 1721, Pelham exchanged his court post under his brother (then Lord Chamberlain) for a seat on the Treasury Board. After Sunderland's death in 1722, the Pelham brothers sided with Walpole against Carteret, who was replaced as Secretary of State by Newcastle in 1724, Henry Pelham becoming Secretary at War.

Having shown themselves to be builders, Whigs and Palladians, it would be surprising if the Pelhams had not become acquainted with William Kent. Until 1726, the year he succeeded Thomas Ripley as Master Carpenter at the Board of Works, Kent's talents as a designer were still largely unproven, his output having hitherto been limited mainly to painting. In that year work started on his interiors at Chiswick House and also at Houghton where Horace Walpole says his father, Sir Robert, was 'persuaded to employ him'. Whether Pelham, who until 1724 had been at the Treasury with Walpole and who is known to have been his close associate, had recommended Kent to his master, can be no more than a matter of conjecture, but that the Pelhams were amongst Kent's earliest architectural patrons is clear. According to John Gay, writing in October 1725 to General Dormer at Rousham, Kent had made vast alterations to Newcastle House in Lincoln's Inn Fields in 1725. And it was Henry Pelham's

2 and 3 Kent's ceiling design for Henry Pelham and interior wall composition for Richard Arundell. 4 31 and 32 Old Burlington Street.

brother-in-law, the Hon. Richard Arundell, who helped to secure for Kent the post of Master Carpenter in 1726. Arundell had been appointed Surveyor-General of the Works in that year and, being essentially a political man although generally recognised as a pundit on matters architectural, he badly needed the support of a man like Kent. He tried hard to obtain for Kent the Comptrollership, but Sir Robert Walpole gave this to Thomas Ripley. Arundell then urged Burlington to use his influence to make Kent accept the post of Master Carpenter.

Kent had already worked for Richard Arundell and Henry Pelham, designing interiors for their houses on the Burlington estate. When in 1727 Kent, under the patronage of Lord Burlington, published in two volumes the *Designs of Inigo Jones with some Additional Designs* (by Lord Burlington and himself), several of the designs executed for these men were included. Plate 63 shows three chimney pieces: 'the first is at the Earl of Bur-

lington's, the second is at the Hon. Mr Arundell's and the third at the Hon. Mr Pelham's, Secretary at War'. Plate 66 is of a ceiling 'at the Hon. Mr Pelham's' and Plate 67, an interior wall composition 'at the Hon. Mr Arundell's'. Lord and Lady Lincoln, the Duke and Duchess of Newcastle, the Hon. Henry and Lady Katherine Pelham and the Hon. Richard Arundell are all listed in the front of the publication as subscribers. Sadly none of Kent's work has survived in these houses, for both were considerably altered by successive owners.

If by moving into Number 32 Old Burlington Street, Pelham felt cheated of the little Palladian palace that Campbell had originally designed for him, he found another opportunity to build on that scale and in that manner when, in 1730, he was appointed Paymaster of the Forces. The appointment brought with it an official residence at the Horse Guards. The residence and office which Pelham inherited had been built in the seven-

1 The Paymaster's Office, Whitehall. Begun in 1732 while Henry Pelham was Paymaster of the Forces. 2 Screen wall in Pelham's office.

3 *Maurer's view of Whitehall, c. 1750. The Paymaster's Office is between Horse Guards and the Admiralty. Opposite, the Banqueting Hall.*

teenth century and was by 1730 perhaps dilapidated, and certainly unfashionable. Pelham immediately set about rebuilding it. A royal warrant of 20 October 1732 refers to 'the Work begun by our Order of Rebuilding an Office for the Paymaster General of Our Forces and Stables for our Horse Guards', and approves £1,000 on account. The final accounts to a total of £3,842 10s 11d were passed on 19 June 1733.

Henry Pelham left the Burlington estate at the end of 1732 and leased the house to another brother-in-law, Lord William Manners, who lived there until 1774. Pelham's new home in Whitehall still stands, immediately to the north of the Horse Guards, its sober front of brick and stone owing much to the example of Colen Campbell. This was perhaps not coincidental, for the building had been constructed under the supervision of one John Lane, Surveyor to the Horse Guards. Lane was a joiner by trade and perhaps the same John Lane whose accounts survive for joiner's work at Campbell's Rolls House and at Number 34 Old Burlington Street, and who also acted as Campbell's 'builder' at Compton Place, Eastbourne. Certainly the Whitehall elevation of the Paymaster's Office has something of the feel of both the Rolls House and of Campbell's 'Burlington Gardens' design of 1720.

Inside little survives today of John Lane's building apart from the Paymaster's Office itself on the ground floor. This is a conventional enough room for its date except for the treatment of the wall at one end of the room. Here one can perhaps detect the influence of Kent, for the wall opposite the chimney piece is designed as a screen with circular framed openings above doors on either side of a central arched recess – an arrangement which reminds one of the screen in Kent's dining room at Raynham Hall.

Kent's appointment in 1726 as Master Carpenter had secured for him an influential seat on the Board of Works, later to be reinforced by his appointment in 1735 as Master Mason and Deputy Surveyor, positions which he retained until his death in 1748. Horace Walpole's suggestion that the Duke of Newcastle and Henry Pelham were in part responsible for his appointment is fully consistent with the character of Office of Works elections at this time and the influence which these men held in respect of its composition. During the middle years of the eighteenth century the architectural initiative in England passed largely from the Crown to the aristocracy, who maintained it by their influence over placemen whose election to key appointments was determined more by the exigencies of political patronage than by professional qualifications. The relationship between the Office of Works and the Treasury was critical. All contracts for specific works had to be renewed every March both by the Treasury and by the Board; in matters of substance the Board was to do 'nothing but by the King's and Lords of the Treasury's direction', and all officers except the Clerks

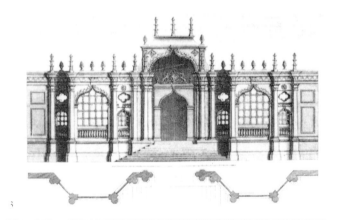

1 *William Kent. His Designs for the Office of Works while Henry Pelham was at the Treasury: 2 The Royal Mews, Charing Cross.*

of the Works were appointed by patents which had to be approved by the Treasury. This meant that, should the Treasury Lords wish to influence the activities of the Board, they were certainly in a very good position to do so. Many of the so-called placemen on the Board had close connections with the Pelhams, and if not actually appointed by them, they usually had reasons to be loyal to them.

Since the death of Wren, the post of Surveyor-General became a virtual political sinecure. When Richard Arundell left it for a more political appointment in 1737, he was succeeded by the able but essen-

tially political Henry Fox. Both Arundell and Fox were appointed by Walpole, but as the Pelhams became more established, and particularly during the period when, one after the other, they held the premiership, an increasing number of officers on the Board owed their places directly to them. When Fox moved on to the Treasury in 1743, it was Henry Pelham whose influence secured the appointment for the Hon. Henry Finch, a silent ministerialist and for thirty-seven years Whig member for Malton. By then the sinecures of Paymaster, Surveyor of the King's Private Roads, Surveyor of the Royal Gardens and Waters, and Ranger and Keeper of

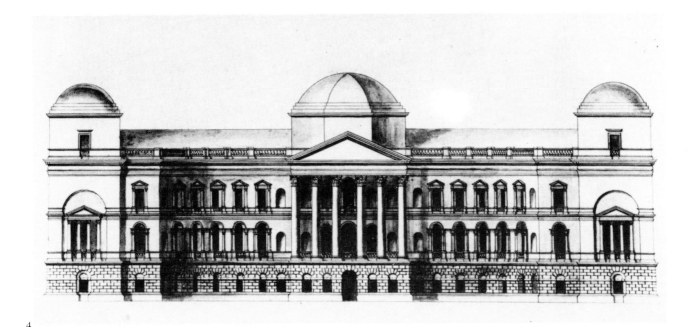

4

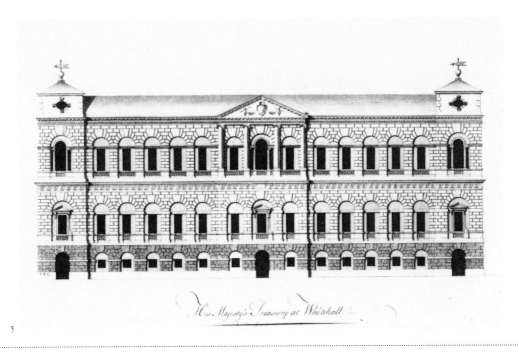

5

3 Screen for the Court of King's Bench in Westminster Hall. 4 The Houses of Parliament, which were never built. 5 The Treasury, Whitehall.

St James's Park, Hyde Park and Green Park, were all in the Pelham gift.

As early as 1726 Newcastle's influence was such that when the Board received from him 'a letter setting forth that it was of the utmost importance to His Majesty's service that John Thompson Esq alderman be chosen Sheriff of London and Middlesex for the remainder of this year, in the room of Sir Jeremiah Murden deceased; and desiring the Board to make use of their credit with the officers and tradesmen employed in this office', the Board obediently 'ordered that a messenger go immediately to the several persons concerned in this office, and not only to insist upon their giving their vote to the said John Thompson Esq. but to use their utmost credit with all others having votes in the election of Sheriff, in whom they may have any interest, to engage them to exert themselves in favour of the said Alderman Thompson.'

But the Pelhams' interest in the Office of Works was certainly not purely political. Both patronised its architects and craftsmen for their private building projects, thus demonstrating a confidence in their abilities outside the sphere of political manipulation. Henry Pelham showed himself to be extremely interested in

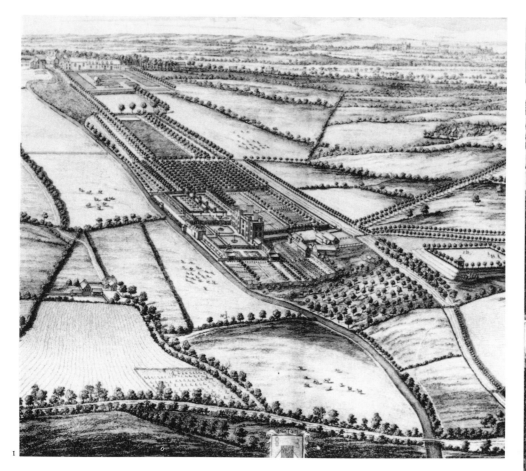

1 Esher Place, Surrey, as it was in the time of Sir Thomas Cotton. It was substantially in this form when Henry Pelham purchased the estate.

public building as well as private. Indeed, despite the apparent scope for corruption within its structure, the Office of Works managed to fulfil its functions in a competent enough manner right up to the day in 1782 when the superstructure of placemen was swept away. During the period between 1718 and 1782 almost every English architect of importance held a post in the Office of Works; and for many years it was as much the stronghold of Palladianism as it had formerly been of Wren's empirical Baroque.

Kent's work, which was so influential in setting what became almost a house-style in the Office, was carried out during the period when the Pelhams were at their most influential. The Royal Mews, alterations at the Royal Palaces and Westminster Hall, and the rebuilding of the Treasury and the Horse Guards all belong to this period. Henry Pelham, in his position at the Treasury, must have been closely involved in the plans for rebuilding that office and, as one of the Commissioners for the building of the new Houses of Parliament, he must have been disappointed when, just as plans had been agreed in 1739, the outbreak of war

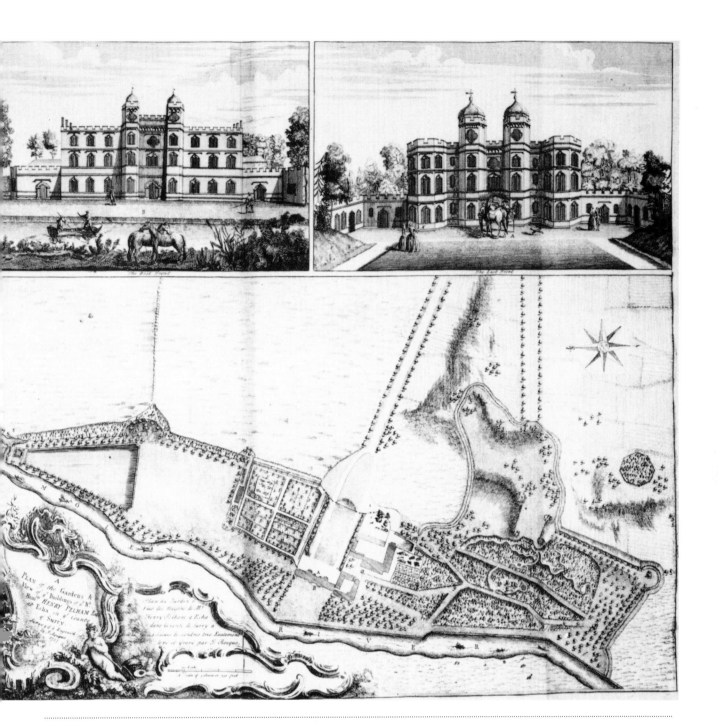

2 *Rocque's plan and views of Esher, published in 1737. They show the buildings and landscape created by William Kent for Henry Pelham.*

with Spain, which lead to the costly War of the Austrian Succession, put paid to Kent's great scheme. The new Parliament buildings were never built, but after the Treaty of Aix-la-Chapelle in 1748 Pelham managed to push through the rebuilding of the Horse Guards on the basis of designs made by Kent.

Henry Pelham's marriage in October 1726 may have given him both the incentive and the opportunity to build in the country, for he received some £10,000 as a marriage portion from the Duke of Rutland and at the same time his brother made over to him certain of the Pelham lands in Sussex. In 1729, he purchased a small estate at Esher close to his brother's Claremont, and here William Kent designed for him a country villa set in a landscape garden. Esher and the country houses of Henry Pelham's brother, the Duke of Newcastle, could hardly have been more different, and were as expressive of their different characters as of their differing means. Esher was conceived as a villa; Claremont was essentially a house of parade. Esher aimed to impress not so much by its size as by the taste of its owner. It was designed not as a seat, but as a retreat from the city and

1 Luke Sullivan's view of Esher Place in 1759. 2, 3 and 4 William Kent's drawings for the entrance porch, a Belvedere and the Fishing Temple.

public life. James Thomson in his quartet of poems, *The Seasons*, wrote of:

. . . . Esher's groves,
Where in the sweetest solitude embraced,
By the soft windings of the silent Mole,
From courts and senates Pelham finds repose.

The concept was Palladian, but the style of its execution was something altogether different.

When Pelham bought his estate, he found there the ruinous Tudor gatehouse of a long lost palace of the Bishops of Winchester. It had been built in the late 1470s by Bishop Waynflete as the entrance to the courtyard of an older palace. It passed to the Crown after the death of Wolsey, to whom it had been lent by Bishop

5 *Laughton Place, Sussex, in the 18th century. 6 The surviving Tudor tower. The Gothick work was done for the Pelhams and may be by Kent.*

Fox. By 1700 the palace had gone, but the gatehouse survived to become the core of a private residence for Sir Thomas Cotton, who for his greater convenience added three-storey wings on either side. It was substantially in this form that Pelham found it in 1729.

Taking his cue from Waynflete's tower at the centre, Kent rebuilt the two wings in Tudor Gothic style, chosen no doubt for its picturesque association with the original, rather than in a spirit of careful stylistic revival. He had no compunction about replacing the original windows in the tower itself with his own unscholarly brand of Gothic or about refitting the interior. Horace Walpole, whose Gothic flights at Strawberry Hill twenty years later showed a far greater

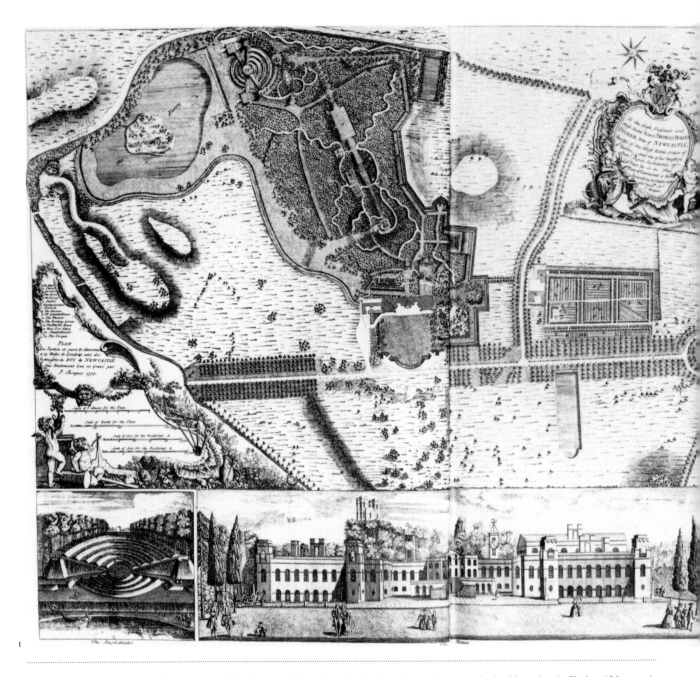

1 *Rocque's plan and views of Claremont, published in 1738. They show Kent's alterations and new garden buildings for the Duke of Newcastle.*

preoccupation for archaeological accuracy, thought little of Kent's forays into this style.

> As Kent's genius was not universal, he has succeeded ill in Gothic. The King's Bench at Westminster and Mr Pelham's house at Esher, are proofs of how little he conceived either the principles or graces of that architecture.

Walpole might equally have cited another piece of Kentian Gothic and one which like Esher was the result of Pelham patronage. At about this time the old Tudor tower at Laughton, which was all that survived of the original Pelham seat in Sussex, was given a curious Gothic 'skirt', thus converting it into a small country house. The detail of the alterations, as Mr John Harris has pointed out, is most reminiscent of Kent's work at Esher. It therefore seems likely, in view of the Pelham connection, that the alterations were designed by him.

If Walpole was critical of Kent's attempts at Gothic, he was full of praise for his gardens. Walpole's belief in Kent's genius for landscape has already been alluded to, but of Esher he wrote to George Montague in 1748, 'Kent is Kentissime there.' In the design of landscape, Walpole recognised Kent's painter's eye as invaluable, and at Esher he suggested the existing prospects of Sir Thomas Cotton's landscape aided his

2, 3 *Kent's own drawings for naturalising a terrace below the Belvedere and modifying another to improve the view from the Great Room.*

genius. 'They marked out the points where his art was necessary or not, but left his judgement in possession of all its glory.' Kent designed several garden buildings for Esher; some are illustrated with Rocque's plan of 1737. Other designs, in Kent's own hand, survive for the Belvedere and a Fishing Temple.

The buildings were contrived not only to complement the landscape in static picturesque compositions, but as incidents on a walk of discovery and as settings for informal entertainment. Walpole's account of the day 'Miss Pelham gave the French an entertainment at Esher,' describes this perfectly.

The day was delightful, the scene transporting, the trees, lawns, concaves, all in the perfection in which the ghost of Kent would joy to see them. At twelve we made the tour of the farm in eight chaises and calashes, horsemen and footmen, setting out like a picture by Wouverman. My lot fell in the lap of Mrs. Anne Pitt, which I could have excused, as she was not at all in the style of the day, romantic, but political. We had a magnificent dinner, cloaked in the modesty of earthenware; French horns and hautboys on the lawn. We walked to the belvedere on the summit of the hill, where a threatened storm only served the beauty of the landscape, a rainbow on a dark cloud falling precisely behind the tower of a neighbouring church, between another tower, and the building at Claremont. Monsieur de Nivernois, who had been absorbed all day and lagging behind, translating my verses, was delivered of his version, and of some more lines, which he wrote on Miss Pelham in the belvedere, while we drank

Rocque's view of 1754 showing Bridgeman's circular basin at Claremont after it had been naturalised by Kent. The island temple survives.

tea and coffee. From thence we passed into the wood, and the ladies formed a circle on chairs before the mouth of the cave, which was overhung to a vast height with woodbines, lilacs and laburnums, and dignified by those shapely cypresses. On the descent of the hills were placed the French Horns; the abigails, servants and neighbours wandering below the river – in short, it was Parnassus as Watteau would have painted it. Here we had a rural syllabub, and part of the company returned to town; but were replaced by Giardini and Onofrio, who with Nivernois on the violin and Lord Pembroke on the bass, accompanied Miss Pelham, Lady Rockingham and the Duchess of Grafton who sang. This little concert lasted till past ten; then there were minuets, and as we had seven couples left, it concluded with a country dance – I blush again, for I danced, but was kept in countenance by Nivernois, who had one wrinkle more than I have. A quarter after twelve they sat down to supper, and I came home by a charming moonlight.

The 1730s were years of great activity for Kent in the field of landscape design. He was working now at Stowe, Rousham and Euston, as well as advising Pelham's brother at Claremont, and his nephew at Oatlands. At Claremont, his efforts were devoted to softening the hard edges of the Bridgeman layout, and to adding a number of garden buildings.

Rocque's map of Claremont dated 1738 shows how Kent had modified Bridgeman's landscape by opening up a vista from the south towards the Belvedere and then setting in it a temple, and by naturalising the North Terrace to improve the view 'Fronting Ye Great Room.' Kent's own drawings of these improvements

survive. His other great contribution was to enlarge Bridgeman's basin at the west end of the garden, transforming it into a serpentine lake containing an island complete with temple-pavilion. Kent's management of water was, according to Walpole, his greatest triumph.

Of all the beauties that he added to the face of this beautiful country, none surpassed his management of water . . . The gentle stream was taught to serpentine seemingly at its pleasure . . . Its borders were smoothed, but preserved their waving irregularity. A few trees scattered here and there on its edges sprinkled the tame bank that accompanied its meanders . . .

Having worked at Claremont and Esher, it was virtually inevitable that Kent should work on the third of that great Pelham triumvirate of Surrey gardens, Oatlands. Here his work commenced much later. By now its owner was Henry Pelham's nephew, the 9th Earl of Lincoln. After 1744 Lincoln became Pelham's son-in-law too, having married his daughter Katherine. After losing his father at an early age, Lincoln had been taken under the wing of his uncle. Since leaving Oxford, he had travelled in Italy and France in the company of his tutor Joseph Spence and his old school friend Horace Walpole. On his return he lodged with his uncle at the Paymaster's residence and was made Lord of the Bedchamber to the King. In 1743 Lincoln was in Norfolk with his uncle, visiting Houghton, Raynham

The 9th Earl of Lincoln with his wife, Katherine, on the terrace at Oatlands, by Devis. The canal is shown here as a winding river.

and Euston, all houses or gardens at which William Kent had worked. It is therefore hardly surprising to find, in July 1745, Kent writing to Lady Lincoln about a proposed visit to Oatlands, or for that matter Joseph Spence referring to 'Mr Kent's pretty building on the old terrace.'

From the time of his marriage until he sold Oatlands in 1788, Lincoln was active in altering and improving the landscape there. He took little part in public or political life and had few worries either about a career or the future of his family. During the lives of his two uncles, he was provided with a number of lucrative sinecures and after their deaths he expected to inherit the Dukedom of one and the estates of both. From 1745 to 1753 he and his wife used 10 Downing Street as their London house, Katherine's father, then Prime Minister, preferring to live in his own new house at 22 Arlington Street.

An account of the building of Henry Pelham's house in Arlington Street must wait until the next chapter, for since the story of that house is the chief subject of this book, it is appropriate that it be retold in more detail than space here can allow. Suffice to say in the present context that Pelham's architect was Kent and that building commenced in 1740 and continued until Pelham's death in 1754, six years after the death of his

architect. The first section of the house however was sufficiently habitable for Pelham to take up residence there in 1743, the year in which he became Prime Minister.

Pelham's twelve years as George II's first minister are little remembered, for he was not a great orator, nor were his achievements particularly notable. They demonstrated more than anything his gift for political conciliation in achieving a 'broad-bottom' administration, and his shrewd financial sense in reducing the National Debt. His ministry, for practical purposes, consisted of himself, his brother and Lord Hardwicke. As George II remarked in 1750, 'they are the only Ministers; the others are for show'. In this triumvirate, Pelham confined himself as far as possible to domestic matters, leaving foreign affairs to Newcastle, with Hardwicke acting as recipient of one brother's complaints about the other.

Although head of the Treasury and chief minister in the House of Commons, Pelham lacked initially that indispensable attribute of an eighteenth-century Prime Minister, influence with the King. This belonged to Lord Carteret who gained it by giving in to the King's views on foreign affairs, at the cost of his own popularity in the Commons.

In doing so, Carteret underestimated the power of

the Commons and the timing of Pelham. In 1742 the Commons had forced the King to give up Walpole; in 1744 they forced him to give up Carteret. When in 1746 Pelham with most of his colleagues resigned as a protest against their opponent's continued influence with the King, they had to be recalled after a two-day interregnum had shown that a Bath – Granville ministry (Carteret had been created Earl Granville) could not raise sufficient support to govern.

Having greatly enhanced the security of his position by the removal of Granville, Pelham set about winning over the brains of the opposition, including those of William Pitt, whose support he procured with a lucrative sinecure. A snap general election in 1747, which gave him a comfortable majority, consolidated his position. To include in office both Pitt and Henry Fox, and not merely to secure their nominal services but to use their debating talents as well, was an achievement no other minister could parallel. A 'broad-bottom' had been achieved.

Pelham's new majority and the termination of the War of the Austrian Succession by the Peace of Aix-la-Chapelle in 1748, cleared the way to what Pelham described as 'my one selfish ambition'. He wrote to his brother,

You know, I have had very little comfort in the great scene of business, I have long been engaged in. I have no court ambition, and very little interested views; but I was in hopes, by a peace being soon made, and by a proper economy in the administration of the government, afterwards, to have been the author of such a plan, as might, in time to come, have relieved this nation from the vast load of debt, it now labours under; and even in my own time, had the satisfaction of demonstrating to the knowing part of the world, that the thing was not impossible. Here, I own, lay my ambition.

His ambition was to lower the rates of interest on government debts and strictly reduce government expenditure. Walpole had made an attempt at the former, but had failed, fearing to lose support in the City. Pelham however had a broader base of support, and had incurred the influential support of Sir John Barnard who had been spokesman in 1737 for the City opposition to Walpole. In 1749 Pelham was successful in introducing a scheme for reducing the interest on the National Debt from four to three per cent. This made it possible to float large-scale loans and raise the taxes which financed the Seven Years War.

The death of the Prince of Wales in 1751 further improved Pelham's position by depriving the opposition of its rallying point. Pelham had by now, despite earlier conflicts on a foreign policy which had involved large payments to foreign princes, made his peace with George II. When in 1751 he expressed a wish to retire with the post of Auditor of the Exchequer (a life sinecure worth £8,000 a year), the King told him, instead of retiring, to hold it in the name of his nephew and son-in-law Lord Lincoln. George II even came to compare him favourably to Walpole, who, he told Newcastle in 1752, 'managed the money matters very ill; he did not indeed give money abroad, but he gave it away liberally at home,' adding, 'he was a great man, he understood the country, but that with regard to money matters, your brother does that, understands that much better.'

Pelham died unexpectedly at his house in Arlington Street on the eve of the general election in March 1754. He was the first Prime Minister who 'had the honour of dying a commoner'. To his contemporaries, his chief virtue was that he set an example of integrity in public life. Horace Walpole, who was no friend of the Pelhams, said 'he lived without abusing his power, and died poor,' and George II, who had gone to such lengths to keep Carteret instead of Pelham, lamented, 'Now I shall have no more peace'. He was not mistaken.

During the period of his premiership, Pelham must have had little time for building. But, in addition to the continuing work to his own house, he found in 1745–6 an opportunity to pay homage in a very practical way to the prophet of English Palladianism, Inigo Jones. In that year Pelham's wife, Lady Katherine, succeeded Sir John Jennings as Ranger of Greenwich Park, an office for which the Queen's House, designed by Jones for Anne of Denmark, was the official residence. Despite a few occasions when the monarch exercised his right to use the building for his own purposes, the house had been the residence of the Ranger since 1690. More recently its use by the Royal Hospital, as a residence for the Governor, had been made possible by making the Governor, Ranger of the Park as well. Responsibility for the building's upkeep had reverted to the Office of Works; and in 1730 the post of Clerk of Works at Greenwich was revived. Although in this year it had been found necessary to spend £440 on repairs to the roof, when Lady Katherine became Ranger in 1745, work to the cost of £4,500 was put in hand under the supervision of James Paine. At such a cost, the 'repairs' carried out must have constituted a major restoration of the building. The figure spent represents about a fifth of the total expenditure of the Office of Works that year, and almost a thousand pounds more than the cost

COLOUR: *The Rt. Hon. Henry Pelham (c. 1754), George II's first minister for twelve years from 1743 to 1754. Painting by William Hoare.*

The Right Hon.ble Henry Pe
Chancellor of the Exchequer

William Hoare: 1 Thomas Pelham-Holles, 1st Duke of Newcastle. 2 Henry Pelham-Clinton, his nephew, who succeeded as 2nd Duke in 1768.

of rebuilding the Paymaster's residence at the Horse Guards in 1733.

Pelham's last act of public architectural patronage was to initiate the rebuilding of the Horse Guards at Whitehall. Although moves to erect a new building were first mooted in 1745 when designs were drawn up by William Kent, it was not until after peace was declared, that the Treasury felt they could seriously consider going ahead with the project. In the summer of 1749 the Board of Works was called upon 'to lay before their Lordships a Plan for rebuilding the Horse Guards, together with an estimate'. Henry Fox, now Secretary at War, attended a Board Meeting on 11 July, 'looked over the plans and elevations in this office intended for Building the Horse Guards', and asked for a plan to be made of the old building 'as it now is that the same may be laid with new Designs before Mr. Pelham'. On 9 August 1749 the Board 'considered and made several alterations to the Plan intended for the New Horse Guards'; and on 5 September they sent a set of drawings to the Treasury with an explanatory letter. The building which they envisaged was much more than a mere guard house; it was virtually a new War Office. The plan provided not only for the accommodation of the Horse and Foot Guards, but also for the Secretary at War, the Judge Advocate-General, and the Commissioners of Chelsea Hospital, together with a chapel and a room for holding courts martial. As a former Secretary at War, Pelham must have been particularly interested in the scheme.

The project was put under the supervision of the Board of Works, and instructions given to proceed forthwith. John Vardy and William Robinson were appointed joint Clerks of Works; and craftsmen were selected who were known to the Board or were Patent Artisans. Many were known personally to Henry Pelham, for among the lists of those working at the Horse Guards were a number who had worked at Pelham's

COLOUR: *The Horse Guards at Whitehall by Canaletto, showing construction of the clock-tower in 1753 three years after building started.*

1 The Old University Library, Cambridge. It was designed by Stephen Wright in 1754 for the 1st Duke, who was Chancellor of the University.

house in Arlington Street. One such, Joseph Pickford, a mason, had been added to the list at Pelham's specific request, and built the north wing. John Lane, the Surveyor to the old Horse Guards and who built the Paymaster's residence, was employed as a joiner.

The central building was the first to be erected. Its foundations were laid in the summer of 1750 and the clock-turret was built in 1753. The north wing was finished about the same time, but the south wing, containing the Foot Guards' quarters, was not begun until 1754. The building as a whole was completed in 1759. Thus Pelham lived to see at least part of the work finished, and with it the almost complete transformation of the area in which he had spent his working life.

The story of the Pelhams' patronage does not end with the death of William Kent, nor indeed with that of Henry Pelham. During the building of 22 Arlington Street, William Kent was assisted by a clerk who did the 'measuring'; his name was Stephen Wright. When Kent

Garden buildings constructed at Oatlands for the 2nd Duke of Newcastle: 2 The Temple of Venus. 3 The Grotto. 4 The Temple of Vesta.

died in 1748, Wright took over supervision of the whole project. The Pelhams found in this young man a natural successor to Kent. Though not as inventive as his master, he proved himself well able to follow in the tradition which had been set for him. Naturally enough, he was essentially a Palladian architect, although his work at Milton Manor, near Oxford, shows that, like Kent, he could also make Gothic designs if called upon to do so.

Wright joined the Office of Works in 1746 as Clerk of Works at Hampton Court; and in 1754 he became Clerk of Works at Richmond New Park Lodge. With the backing of the Duke of Newcastle, he became Master Mason and Deputy Surveyor in 1758, but never obtained the Comptrollership, despite importuning his patron on the two occasions when events made his appointment look almost possible. Perhaps Newcastle felt that promotion to this important post would mean that Wright would have less time to execute the private commissions for which he was using him.

In 1754, when Newcastle was Chancellor of Cambridge University, he gave £500 towards the building of a new front for the University Library. The design which he insisted be adopted was Wright's. The building still stands, probably Wright's finest work and one which rivals his master's greatest achievements.

As at Arlington Street, so at the Duke's estate at Claremont and his nephew's at Oatlands, Wright continued where Kent left off. To both, he added garden buildings in the style of his master. For Lord Lincoln at Oatlands, he built a virtual replica of Kent's Temple of Venus at Stowe, as well as a circular Temple of Vesta, based on the Roman one at Tivoli. Since he continued to supervise work at Oatlands until as late as 1776, he may also have been responsible for the Grotto, built in the 1760s and later transformed into a shimmering Aladdin's cave by the Lane brothers of Tisbury. Much planting was done at this time and tulip trees, acacia, cedar, magnolia, maple, walnut and juniper were introduced – a step forward in botanical terms from Kent, whose limited palette of beech, larch and cypress was criticised by contemporaries. Close by the house there was a melon ground and peach-forcing house.

People came from far and wide to see the gardens at Oatlands; and as reports went back with the visitors, so its fame spread. Thomas Pococke attributed such fame to its terrace; Joseph Farrington admired its view – west to St Anne's Hill and east to Old Walton Bridge, under the central arch of which the eye was deceived in to thinking the lake actually flowed.

Not far away was Hampton Court Palace. William Hickey described in July 1768 a great regatta on the Thames between Oatlands and the Palace, and the lavish hospitality his party were offered by the Earl of Lincoln.

The Earl of Lincoln, who has a beautiful house at Weybridge, near Walton Bridge, having with him a large party of nobility, male and female, upon a visit, adopted various modes of amusing them, amongst others he planned what was termed a Regatta, to which all the gentlemen of the neighbourhood who kept boats were invited. The whole were to assemble at the foot of his Lordship's terrace, from thence in procession (the order of moving being previously arranged) drop gently down with the stream to Hampton Court, in the garden of which an elegant collation was prepared in tents put up for the occasion. After remaining there till towards sunset, they were to pull up again to his seat, where a magnificent dinner awaited them, with fireworks and superb illuminations, the night to conclude with a Ball. This Entertainment we determined to partake of, as far as with propriety and civility we could; and having heard and seen the costly preparations the noble host had made for the reception of his party, we agreed at least not to disgrace the cavalcade we intended to accompany. We accordingly had our cutter entirely new dressed and fitted up. She was painted of a bright azure blue, with gold mouldings and ornaments, the oars and every article finished in the same way, richly embellished with aquatic devices. The awning was of the same colour, in silk, as were the dresses of the eight rowers, the jackets and trousers being trimmed with an uncommonly neat spangle and foil lace, and made easy, so that we could row perfectly well in them. We wore black round hats with very broad gold bands and small bright blue cockades in front. The ensign was of richest silks; under the awning we had capital French horns and clarinets, the performers being dressed exactly like the rowers.

We sent the cutter, covered with matting, by West Country barge to Walton, where we assembled in the morning of the day of the entertainment, and having equipped ourselves at the inn close to the bridge, we started from thence to attend the Regatta. The novelty, as well as the splendour of our appearance, drew every eye upon us, and we undoubtedly made a very showy and brilliant figure, far surpassing any one of the boats in the procession. We pulled what is called the Man of War's stroke. The rapid manner in which we moved in all directions and our masterly manoeuvres, surprized, and seemed highly to gratify the ladies of the party, so much so that nothing but our boat was attended to. Thus we accompanied the noble party to Hampton Court, at times rowing ahead, and then again dropping astern to the Fleet. Upon bringing to, Lord Lincoln sent a servant to our helmsman to enquire who we were, and having ascertained that we were gentlemen, he very politely came in person to our boat, returned his own and his party's thanks for the great addition we had made to their entertainment, and requested our company, to partake as well of their cold collation as of the dinner in the evening. This we civilly declined, but our band continued playing alternately with their own while they remained at Hampton Court, his Lordship sending us an abundant supply of refreshments, with ices and iced wines of all sorts. The repast being over, we attended that procession back to Weybridge, our band playing martial tunes whilst the company were landing. Being all on shore, we arose, and took leave with three cheers, which were most cordially returned by the gentlemen and ladies waving their handkerchiefs, and Lord Lincoln again very politely thanking us for our company.

Within four months of the occasion described by Hickey, Lord Lincoln's uncle, the great Duke of Newcastle, died childless at the age of 75. He had been head of the powerful Pelham clan for fifty-five years and had held office continuously, with the exception of a few months in 1756–7, for forty-five. The last eight of these were as Prime Minister, in succession to his brother Henry. His cousin Thomas Pelham of Stanmer, who was in constant attendance during the last years of his life, succeeded to the Sussex estates, as well as to the Pelham Barony. His Duchess had £3,000 as her jointure. His nephew, Lord Lincoln, succeeded to the remainder, as well as inheriting the Dukedom of Newcastle.

The new Duke had little need either of Newcastle House or Claremont. Both were quickly sold off, the latter to Lord Clive who already had a mortgage of £25,000 on the property. The Duke, who was not interested in politics and whose wife had died in 1760, seems now to have spent an increasing amount of time away from London on his estates in the North of England. In the year of his uncle's death, he started to build a new seat for himself at Clumber in Nottinghamshire. His architect was Stephen Wright, who also designed several less important buildings for the Duke in the North, including a bridge across the Trent at Newark (1775). When in 1775 the Duke's son, the Earl of Lincoln, moved into his grandfather's old house in Arlington Street, it was Wright again who supervised the repairs and alterations.

Although Newcastle lived until 1794, Wright's death in 1780 seems to mark the end of the great era of Pelham patronage. The remaining years of the Duke's life were devoted to the pleasures of the country and of sport. In his memoirs, his old school-fellow and former friend, Horace Walpole, wrote of him, that his 'exceeding pride kept him secluded from the world, and rarely did he appear either at Court or in Parliament'. In 1788 he sold his estate at Oatlands to the Duke of York. Francis Wheatley's painting of the same year, 'The Return from Shooting', which shows the Duke with his dogs and his keepers in the park at Clumber, seems to symbolise his final withdrawal from London and the stage on which his two uncles had played such prominent parts for half a century.

It is indicative of the peculiarity of the age in which the Pelhams lived, that there survives very little of the houses and gardens on which they lavished so much time and money. It is no whim on the part of the writer that this chapter has been illustrated mainly by paintings and engravings; there is little left to be photographed. The Duke of Newcastle's house at Claremont survived only for the lifetime of its builder. Lord Clive demolished the house as soon as he bought it, and employed 'Capability' Brown to build him something more fashionable. Neither Henry Pelham nor his brother had sons to succeed them, and their nephew, to whom what was left of their estates passed, preferred to build a new house rather than live in those which he inherited. Of the three great Surrey gardens created by the Pelhams, only those at Claremont survive, and have

recently been restored by the National Trust. Henry Pelham's Gothic villa at Esher lasted for the lifetime of his daughter Frances, but when she died unmarried in 1805, it was sold and its wings were demolished. Waynflete's Tower still stands somewhat forlornly at the centre of a suburban housing estate. Only fragments of Kent's plasterwork survive inside – fan vaulting above a lost staircase, a giant scallop shell in a window embrasure, ribbed vaulting in the hall. Outside no longer, as Alexander Pope once wrote of Esher, do 'Kent and Nature vie for Pelham's Love'. Oatlands too has suffered from its proximity to London. The famous views are now obscured by encroaching development, and its many garden buildings have been reduced to little more than something to trip over on a Sunday walk. Nottingham Castle was gutted by fire during Reform Bill riots in 1831, and virtually rebuilt as a municipal museum in 1875–8. Only fragments of Halland Place and the Tudor tower at Laughton remain standing.

Two Pelham seats survived intact into the twentieth century. Clumber remained the principal seat of the Dukes of Newcastle until 1938 when it was demolished. Stanmer, the seat of the Sussex Pelhams, still stands, although it is no longer a home of the Pelhams, the 9th Earl of Chichester having sold the house and a large part of the estate to Sussex Corporation in 1947.

A change of use to offices has saved the two last London houses of the Pelham brothers, although Newcastle House was much altered by Sir Edwin Lutyens in 1930. Number 22 Arlington Street, now called William Kent House, has recently been restored by its present owners. The story of this house is told in the remaining pages of this book.

The Return from Shooting, painted by Francis Wheatley in 1788. It shows the 2nd Duke of Newcastle with his keepers and dogs at Clumber.

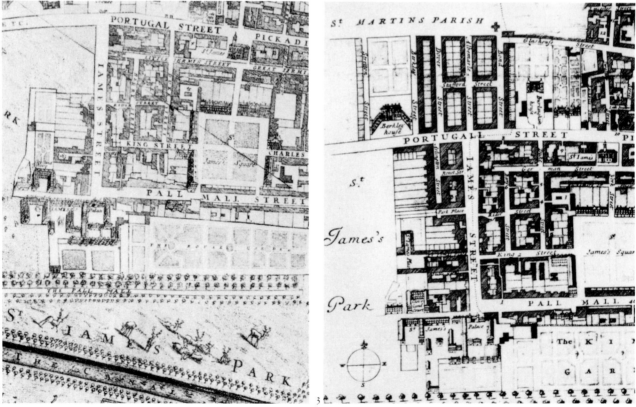

1 St James's and Westminster, 1714–22. 2, 3 Maps of 1682 and 1689 show the Park before and after development by Lord Arlington.

NICHOLAS THOMPSON

22 ARLINGTON STREET
IN THE 18TH CENTURY

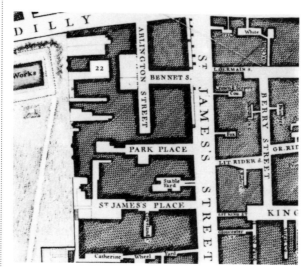

Detail from Rocque's map of 1746.

In 1740, Henry Pelham purchased from his old enemy William Pulteney a house at 22 Arlington Street, London. Pelham, at the time still Paymaster General, had been living in his official residence at the Horse Guards. The move may partly have been prompted by the early death, in November 1739, of both his sons, for after that Horace Walpole says their mother would 'never go to Esher, or any house where she had seen them'. Indeed, according to Walpole, they moved immediately from Whitehall, and by 1741 were living at a house in Spring Gardens, Charing Cross.

By 1740 Arlington Street had become very fashionable, as well as being 'absolutely the ministerial street'. Pelham's new neighbours were Lord Tyrconnel to the north and Lady Codrington to the south. Further down the street were the Earl of Cholmondeley, the Duchess of Norfolk and Lord Carteret – another of Pelham's political enemies. Sir Robert Walpole had lived in the house now occupied by Lady Codrington from 1716 until he became England's first Prime Minister in 1732, at which point he moved to 10 Downing Street. After his resignation he returned to the street, buying Number 5 across the road. His son, Horace Walpole, was born in the street, at his father's first house there.

Proximity to the seat of government and to the Court, which had moved officially from Whitehall to St James's in 1698, was at the root of the area's popularity; and the deep sites on the west side of the street with their frontages to Green Park made this part of Arlington Street especially attractive. The *New Review of London* described it in 1728 as 'one of the most beautiful situations in Europe, for health, convenience and beauty; the front of the street is in the midst of the hurry

Sutton Nicholls's view of St James's, Square, c. 1727, showing St Albans' 'stately uniform piles', built at the end of the 17th century.

and splendour of the town; and the back is in the quiet simplicity of the country'.

Like most of the Parish of St James's to the east, Arlington Street had been laid out during the last quarter of the seventeenth century. In 1682 Charles II granted six acres at the north-eastern corner of St James's Park to Henry Bennet, Earl of Arlington, the man perhaps best remembered as the first 'A' of the notorious CABAL ministry of 1667. In 1686, a Royal Licence to erect buildings on the site was granted by James II. Brome's map of the parish of St James's, dated 1689, shows how the six acres were developed in two streets bearing the Earl's family names and titles. Terraces of houses were laid out with their fronts along the line of the streets, and on the west side of Arlington Street, with long gardens stretching back to the Park.

St James's was developed in much the same way, following the creation of the Parish in 1685, a year after its founder Henry Jermyn, Earl of St Albans, had died. The street pattern of the area south of Piccadilly has,

save for the later creation of Lower Regent Street and Waterloo Place where William Kent's gardens to Carlton House once stood, remained little altered to the present day.

Kip's engraving of the area, dated 1714–22, shows the uniformity of the houses, in particular those in Lord St Albans' great piazza, St James's Square. Kip might have exaggerated this, but a reference to St Albans' 'Stately uniform piles' at a time when the Square was just coming into being, suggests that some overall regularity was certainly achieved.

Very little of the first generation of domestic building remains visible in the area today; the only seventeenth-century building of any consequence remaining is the Church of St James. Indeed on most of the sites, the structure which exists there today is likely to be the third or fourth building. Extensive rebuilding took place in the eighteenth century, and by the time Henry Pelham came to the area, the process had already begun. The original construction was not always the

James Bowles's view of the Square, c. 1752, showing some of the houses rebuilt. The Duke of Norfolk's new house can be seen on the right.

best. The houses had been built in the fever of speculation, and many soon became dilapidated. On the other
hand changing architectural taste, bringing a desire for
a more sophisticated plan and a more modish appearance, was doubtless an even stronger motive to rebuild.
An interest in architecture as an art, rather than merely
as a means of securing a roof over one's head, absorbed
many in the fashionable world of the time. It is significant that, when in 1715 Leoni published the first volume
of his edition of Palladio, interest was sufficiently general for seventeen of the twenty-one known residents of
St James's Square to have become subscribers.

The first substantial rebuilding in the Square did not
start until 1726, when Number 4 was rebuilt behind a
restrained Palladian façade of brick and stone. The
formula, which owes much to Campbell's prototype on
the Burlington estate, did not significantly disrupt the
feeling of homogeneity. It set the style for further
rebuildings by other Palladians, such as Flitcroft and
Brettingham, and was still in use more than twenty

years after for fronting what amounted to a virtual
palace on the east side for the Duke of Norfolk. A
comparison of Sutton Nicholls's view of the Square in
1727 with that made by Bowles in 1752 shows that,
despite the alterations, the Square retained a considerable measure of uniformity. Some relished this outward
plainness. Sir John Fielding described the Square as
follows:

St James's Square is beautiful and spacious . . . Although the
Appearance of the Square hath an Air of Grandeur, yet that by no
means resulteth from the Pomp and Greatness of the structures
about it; but rather from a prevailing Regularity throughout, joined
to the Neatness of the Pavement. The Basin in the Middle contri-
butes not a little in producing the Effect. The Houses are built more
for the Convenience of their opulent and noble Possessors, than for
causing Surprise in the Beholders.

Exterior modesty however, concealed an interior splendour. Behind those regular fronts, money and imagination were lavished to proclaim the taste and the wealth
of their owners.

By the second decade of the eighteenth century, the

1 The gardens at Carlton House as laid out by William Kent for Frederick, Prince of Wales. They later made way for Carlton House Terrace.

great popularity of the assembly room and pleasure garden, those public meeting places of polite society, were causing ambitious hostesses to try to emulate them in private. At first they hired public rooms for large parties, but soon they were arranging their own houses to provide, first, a Great Room that could accommodate a large assembly, and then later, a whole series of rooms through which guests might wander and where card-tables, supper, and music might be set up at the same time. In country houses of the early part of the century, apartments tended to be strung out in a straight line. In London houses the greater restriction of space, and the need to use all of it to maximum effect, led to the attractive and convenient arrangement of providing a top-lit central staircase surrounded by a circle, or half-circle (depending on the width of the house), of interconnecting rooms.

The house which Henry Pelham bought in Arlington Street formed part of the original seventeenth-century development. To a follower of architectural taste like Pelham, it must have seemed quite out of fashion; and by 1740, it may well have become dilapi-

dated. In any case Pelham determined immediately to pull it down, and redevelop the site. Fortunately he was not obliged to maintain the building line along the street, as the occupiers of houses in St James's Square undoubtedly were. This factor, combined with the considerable length of the site and the fact that one end of it gave directly on to the park, led to an unusual plan for the new house. In his design Pelham's architect, William Kent, combined certain conventions of the terrace house with those of the larger mansions set behind forecourts along the north side of Piccadilly. He placed the house not against the street, but against the Park, creating two full-height canted bays which gave views across it from all the back rooms. The house was approached from the street in a ceremonial fashion, that also provided privacy and security for the occupants.

Set back from the street, behind a paved forecourt protected by iron railings with gates, was a low three-bay building of one storey on a basement. In the centre a pair of panelled doors gave admittance to a square hall where footmen would wait on visitors. Credentials established, the visitor would be escorted along a

2, 3 *Devonshire House and Burlington House, private palaces set back from Piccadilly behind enclosed forecourts.* 4 *4 St James's Square.*

vaulted arcade, open to a courtyard on the south side. This second courtyard lay between the front-building and the main house. Only did the visitor then reach the house proper. A second internal sequence of spaces ultimately brought him up a grand top-lit staircase to the Great Room which ran the full width of the house on the first floor, overlooking the inner courtyard. The plan of the main house was twice as deep as it was wide and consisted of two ranges of accommodation, one in front and one behind the top-lit staircase. Inside the house, therefore, the quite conventional arrangement provided a set of three good rooms on each floor.

Externally all parts of the building were soberly dressed in the restrained Palladian idiom; and in this it was typical of many town houses being built at the time. The form and proportions of the principal front were based on a concept inherited from Italian Renaissance architects, who in turn had drawn it from the Ancients' rules for proportioning the Classical order of a temple front. This was combined with a decision, which suited the social requirements both of Renaissance Italy and of Georgian England, to make the

first floor of the house the most important. The combination of the functional and the aesthetic worked very well, for it allowed the principal floor and the 'chamber' floor above it, to occupy the highest portion of the Classical order, that of the columns and their capitals. The ground floor with its lower rooms was expressed as a plinth (or the basement of the temple). At the top of the house, the implied order would be terminated by a cornice, or full entablature, above which the dormer windows to the garrets would be set back into the roof, scarcely visible from the ground floor. The principle can be seen very clearly by comparing the two main fronts of Colen Campbell's Marble Hill at Twickenham. On the one side the centrepiece has a full Ionic temple front complete with pediment; on the other side none – but the proportions of the undecorated elevation nonetheless derive from the decorated one.

This was the basis for proportioning the street elevation of a London house in the eighteenth century. By 1740, it was familiar both to Kent and Pelham, whose official residence in Whitehall had been rebuilt

1 A Town House from Andrea Palladio's Quattro Libri, *published in 1570. 2, 3 Colen Campbell's Marble Hill House, Twickenham.*

on just these lines in 1732–5. Kent applied it at 44 Berkeley Square and at 22 Arlington Street. Of the two houses, Arlington Street is the more idiosyncratic, for the approach to the house through an arcade open to a courtyard militated against a central point of entry; it demanded instead access at one side. The disruption to symmetry which this involved was to a certain extent reduced by the use of arched openings at the ground storey level for both the house and the arcade, thereby carrying the rhythm of the fenestration across the point of disruption where the arcade joined the house. This arrangement, which Kent seems first to have used at Arlington Street, appears again at the Horse Guards, a few years later.

The actual process of constructing Henry Pelham's house is minutely recorded in the surviving Building Accounts for the years 1740 to 1754, now in the British Architectural Library at the Royal Institute of British Architects. The old house was pulled down in 1740, and most of the materials were sold off during the following year. Meanwhile work had started at the Park end of the site on the construction of the Main House. By November 1741, this was slated and, by October 1742, glazed. The Arcade and the Front-

Building, with the forecourt paved and the front gates in place, were complete by December 1742. With the house watertight, the plasterers and the wood-carvers moved in to complete their work in time for Henry Pelham to move into the new house, albeit still unpainted, by May of the following year. On the 25th of that month, Horace Walpole wrote to Sir Horace Mann from his own home across the Street,

I have been looking at the fathers in God that have been flocking over the way this morning to Mr Pelham, who is just come to his new house. This is absolutely the ministerial street: Carteret has a house here too, and Lord Bath seems to have lost his chance by quitting this street.

Pelham therefore moved in just before taking up his appointment as First Lord of the Treasury, which came, after much delay, by special messenger from the King at Worms on the evening of 23 August.

The principal rooms of Henry Pelham's house lay on the ground and first floors. On the ground floor a narrow vestibule (often referred to as the Passage Room) led from the Arcade to the Staircase; to the left of it was the Dining Parlour. The space immediately behind these two was taken up by the Staircase Hall and a Waiting-Room at the foot of the stairs. Beyond that,

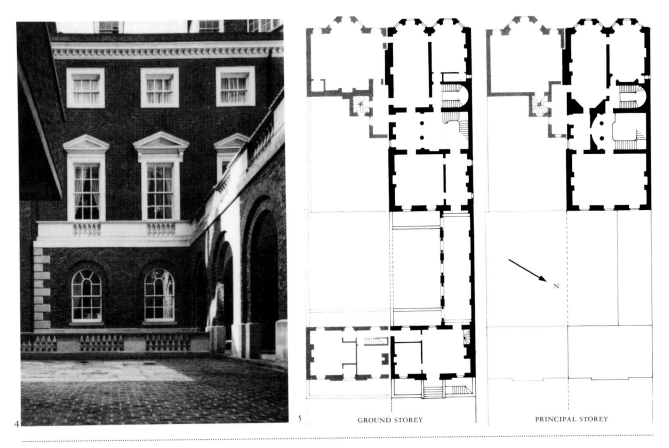

GROUND STOREY   PRINCIPAL STOREY

22 Arlington Street: 4 Elevation of the main house in 1981. 5 Plans showing its two-stage development by William Kent in the mid-18th century.

and overlooking the Park, was the Long Room; and next to it was Pelham's Library, slightly shorter in length to allow for a secondary stair behind the main one. On the first floor the Great Room occupied the full width of the front of the house; and on the park side of the stair were the main Bedchamber and Dressing Room in much the same arrangement as the rooms below. Behind a screen of columns at the top of the stairs was the Vestibule which probably served as an ante-room or closet to the Dressing Room and the Great Room. Further bedrooms were provided on the chamber floor above. The domestic offices and servants rooms were restricted to the basement and to the garret floor in the roof.

The Building Accounts show that the principal rooms were elaborately fitted up. On the first floor the Great Room, Bed Chamber and Dressing Room were all given enriched ceiling frames, Corinthian entablatures and enriched friezes; on the ground floor the Library had an 'Ionic entablature and frame, enriched frieze – sofeat with flowers &c', the Long Room an 'enriched entablature and enriched Ceiling frame with flowers and enriched frieze', and the Dining Parlour an 'Ionic cornice and Ceiling frame, with Circle enriched

in D°, with flowers &c', Chimney-pieces were mainly of 'veind' or statuary marble, the pair in the Great Room costing as much as £123 5s 5d each. Over the chimney-pieces there were frames carved in wood. For Lady Katherine's Dressing Room, William Barlow carved 'ornamental Circular frames in festoons, foliage flowers and Ribands', and in Pelham's Dressing Room there were '4 festoons of Husks' carved by James Richards. Carving was otherwise mainly limited to doors and door cases, dados and picture frames. The Staircase Hall must have appeared much as it does today, having 'a circular skielight with reveald Beams, losenges, Frett and flowers', a 'screen at the head' and 'screen at the foot' of the great stair, and its handrail decorated with 'foliage work'. On the walls, the plasterer provided an 'enriched frieze, enrichments with festoons shells and foliages, flowers, Dentill cornice, long trusses.' No mention, however, is made of a gallery at second floor level. The present gallery is a copy of one existing before the 2nd World War, and which may have been a later insertion.

When Horace Walpole observed the bishops flocking across the street to Pelham's new house, they were undoubtedly going to attend his levée. Great men (and

William Barlow Carver is Creditor To A Bill
of Carving ending Xtmas 1748 —

Dressing Room ground Story To 179 run of 5 Leaved grass
at 2, 25..9 of 9 leaved Do & bead & space at 10. 12 run of 5
leaved grass & bead & space at 6, 67..8 large egg & tongue at 8 } 6 12 2¾

Long room ground Story To 18..5 run of 7 leaved grass. 3 leaved Do & husk & space to Architrave at 9, 2..8 run of raheing
leaves & tongues to door frieze at 3..2. 5 ft run of egg & tongue
at 6 6..2..7 leaved grass —   1 14 0¾

Repairing Cappitalls in the Staircase &c Carver 3 days ² at 3..6   12 3

Ladys dressing room A Large Chimney frame carv'd   4 6 —
                                                    _____
                                                         20 ..4 ..6

James Richards Carver Credᵗ To A Bill July y 9, 1749
To 4 festoons of husks in Dressing room ground Story }   6 ..a ..o

William Barlow Carver is Creditor To A Bill
dated y 24 of September 1750
To 38..4 run of golass to 3 picture frames in the
dressing room Ground Story —   at 10 p ft }   1 ..12 ..4
                                                    _____
                                                       239 ..16 .. 6

1 Detail from page 78 of the 18th century Building Accounts, describing carved work executed by William Barlow and James Richards.

the King) held a levée every morning. It started while the giver of the levée was being powdered and curled in his bedchamber or dressing room. A select few might be invited to talk to him there, but most would have to wait patiently outside until he appeared in the ante-room. Levées were particularly used to present petitions or to ask for favours and positions. For the Pelhams such business was, as we have seen, a highly important element in the maintenance of their political power. That they were 'fathers of God' who Walpole saw hurrying to the house, was not surprising, for the Pelhams' promotion of bishops for their staunch Whig principles was notorious. When the Duke of Newcastle resigned the premiership in 1762, Walpole wrote that 'there were not three bishops on the bench who did not owe their mitres to him.'

Pelham's levées at Arlington Street would most likely have taken place in the two ground-floor rooms overlooking the Park, the larger of the two performing the role of ante-room to the smaller Library, or Dressing Room (as it is later referred to), where more private business would have been discussed. In using a library for this purpose, Pelham may have been consciously following Sir Robert Walpole's example at Houghton, where Kent had designed a small library which was used in this way. The relationship of Pelham's library to the back stair was important, for it not only permitted him to descend from his bedchamber above without passing through the crowd awaiting him in the ante-room, but it also provided an opportunity for those he particularly wished to speak with, to by-pass the main curcuit and come directly to the inner sanctum. The custom of conducting serious business like this had been set by Charles II, whose inner circle of advisers would meet in the King's closet or cabinet (a small private room beyond the state bedroom). The King's cabinet council was the ancestor of the Prime Minister's Cabinet of today.

Lady Katherine's levées would have been held upstairs in her dressing-room. They would have been much more intimate and less official occasions, and conducted in mixed company. No doubt they would have played cards, for Lady Katherine was fond of gambling. Her daughter Frances took after her; according to Walpole she managed to dissipate a fortune of £70,000 in this way.

2 Laroon's 'The Nobleman's Levée' (detail) shows the sort of activity that would have taken place on the ground floor of Henry Pelham's house.

That the house worked satisfactorily as the residence of the King's chief minister is borne out by Pelham's decision to live there throughout his term of office. Number 10 Downing Street, which his master, Sir Robert Walpole, had had annexed to the appointment in perpetuity, he offered to his son-in-law and daughter, the Earl and Countess of Lincoln. But whatever the advantages of the site, and the arrangement of rooms, the Arlington Street house was not very big. This is something Pelham must have felt, for in 1743 he took advantage of Lady Codrington's departure from the site immediately to the south to start extending his house. Whether or not this had always been the intention is not clear. Certainly the design of the first house, and the manner in which it was extended, hardly suggest forward planning. However, it does appear from the Deeds Register that Pelham bought both plots from William Pulteney at the same time; the combined sites had always been referred to as Number 22, and the writer has found no record of a sale to Henry Pelham after that date. The continued occupation of the southern plot by Lady Codrington could be explained by a tenancy agreement, but the manner in which Pelham developed the two sites is less comprehensible.

Following Lady Codrington's removal to 18 Arlington Street, demolition of the house on her part of the site was put in hand immediately. New building work proceeded rather slowly. The first task was to make the enlarged site secure, and to present a unified front to the street by extending the existing front-building to the south. This was done quite simply by building a replica alongside the original, complete with a blank door to balance the existing front door. Work started in 1744, and was complete by 1747. In 1745 the arcade court was extended to cover the full width of the two sites, with paving laid over underground vaults.

The extension of the house itself did not start until all this was finished. Its purpose was to provide a Great Room on the ground floor en suite with the existing rooms which overlooked the Park. In fact the addition included very little more than this. The ground floor was entirely taken up by the Great Room (it is referred to as this throughout the Building Accounts), a small closet, a circular newel stair and a passage linking the room and the stair to the space at the foot of the main staircase. A richly decorated and deeply coved ceiling which gave the Great Room a floor to ceiling height much in excess of the other rooms on the ground floor meant there was no room for accommodation above it at first floor level; and craftsmen's accounts refer only to work at basement, ground and chamber storeys. Reference by the joiner and carpenter to some work to a 'messanine' must therefore refer to what little space remained between the Great Room and the chamber floor. The carcass of the new addition was started in the summer of 1747, and by Christmas it had been slated. Finishes were executed the following year, and painting and gilding were complete by 1750.

When first complete the room must have caused quite a sensation. It is mentioned twice by Horace Walpole, who in one instance cites its magnificence as one of three examples to illustrate that in Architecture, Kent's taste 'was deservedly admired'. The other two examples were Lady Isabella Finch's staircase at 44 Berkeley Square and the Temple of Venus at Stowe. Walpole's confirmation that Kent was the designer of the Great Room is helpful, for Kent's death in April 1748, meant that the decoration of the room was not executed during his lifetime. The last bill to be paid 'dr. William Kent Esq.' was to Richard Hughes on 16th December 1747, for slating the 'New Building'. Payment to Kent for his own services are not referred to in the Building Accounts, although some are recorded against Pelham's account at Hoare's Bank – three in the 1730s which must relate to other work, and one on 16 February 1748 in the sum of £298 5s, which may relate to his work at 22 Arlington Street.

Kent had been assisted throughout the period of building by Stephen Wright, who is first mentioned in 1741, when he was treated to breakfast and dinner when he measured the first floor. During Kent's lifetime 'measuring' work seems to have been Wright's main function, but after 1748 he appears to have taken over the role of supervising architect. In November 1751, he was paid directly for 'making drawings for the several parts and finishings of the Great Room. Dº. to the Screen at the foot of the Great Staircase. Dº. to the Steps from the Park into the dressing room, and together with measuring, abstracting and writing out the Severall Artificers Accounts of the whole additional Building and attendance on the severall works'. The basic concept of the Great Room however must surely have been Kent's; and indeed Walpole confirms this in another reference, when he mentions the 'fine room and ceiling designed by Kent, as the rest of the house was'.

Its design reminds one immediately of the Saloon at 44 Berkeley Square, which pre-dates it by a few years. In both, the bed of the ceiling, a honeycomb of polygonal coffers divided by richly moulded and gilded ribs, seems to derive from Italian ceilings of the High Renaissance, like those of the Villa Madama in Rome and the Doge's Palace in Venice. At Arlington Street the inverted brackets which divide the deep cove into a series of bays are elements used by Kent at Burlington House and at Worcester Lodge, Badminton. But what gives both ceilings their most Kentian flavour are the paintings 'en grisaille' depicting the Loves of the Gods and which decorate the many small coffers. One might assume them to be the work of Kent himself, if the Accounts did not suggest that by the time of Kent's death the room may not even have been plastered. The plasterer's work was not measured until the end of 1748, and measurement of painting and gilding did not take place until the end of 1750.

Although it looks convincing enough, it is difficult to say with any certainty just how much of the present plasterwork is original. From the Building Accounts it would appear that, in outline at least, the ceiling must have followed the same format as it does today. In detail there appears to have survived until the beginning of the present century more of the plasterwork described in Robert Dawson's account than now exists; 'Corinthian Cornice and Architrave, . . . Frieze in foliage, Basketts of fruit etc., Festoons on Cove with husks, berrys and Flowers, . . . women's heads' are all elements which can be seen in Edwardian photographs of the room. William Barlow's account for carving includes the embellishment of door and window surrounds, and elaborate shutters with 'semi-Octagonal' pannells with foliage shells etc . . . Soffit Panells with Dish Festoons Foliage etc . . . long pannells on Shutters with vases foliages and festoons flowers etc.' These may be the ancestors of the rather simpler octagon panels on the shutters today. For the centre of the east wall Joseph Pickford carved a great chimney-piece in statuary marble with a frieze of 'festoons of fruit and Flowers etc.' John Marsden, the joiner, made the dados, and the upper walls were battened for hangings.

Apart from describing in detail the work involved in building Pelham's house, the surviving Building Accounts are interesting for the information they provide on the tradesmen and supervisers employed. Many of their names can be traced to other projects where Kent was architect, and several were involved with projects for the Office of Works.

The following tradesmen and craftsmen were em-

22 Arlington Street: The Great Room rehung with crimson damask as in 1754. It was the principal element in the second phase of building.

ployed at 22 Arlington Street between 1740 and 1754. The value of work for which they were responsible is shown alongside each trade.

RALPH CRUTCHER, bricklayer   £3,426 3s 4d

JOSEPH PICKFORD, mason   2,689 14 10

JOHN MARSDEN, JOHN RICHARDSON,
joiner/carpenters   5,306 8 9

RICHARD HUGHES, JAMES RUSSELL,
slaters   109 15 11

JOHN DEVALL, plumber   1,209 17 10

RICHARD MINNS, RICHARD COBBETT,
glaziers   276 0 9

JOSEPH PATTISON, ALEXANDER WITTON,
CHRISTOPHER MARTIN, BENJAMIN HOLMES,
smiths   1,462 7 7$\frac{3}{4}$

EDWARD MIST, ANDREW JACKSON,
JOHN WILKINS, paviors   222 16 6

ROBERT DAWSON, plasterer   1,222 3 2

JAMES RICHARDS, WILLIAM BARLOW
GEORGE MURRAY, carvers   364 0 6

JOHN JONES, THOMAS ABBOT,
painters   294 4 9

JAMES NEALE, gilder   88 9 0

THOMAS EVANS, gold beater   115 14 0

STEPHEN WRIGHT, measurer   87 12 0

The total cost of building during the period for which records survive was £17,306 1s 8¾d. This includes additional payments under the heading of Contingencies (£372 3s 9d) and also payments to the book-keeper (£60 9s).

These craftsmen must have formed a tightly-knit team. Most of them were used to working together and some, like the Mists and the Devalls, were connected by marriage. William Barlow was an executor of Kent's will, which had been witnessed by John Marsden. Joseph Pickford, John Devall, Benjamin Holmes, Robert Dawson and William Barlow were all working at the same time for Lady Isabella Finch at 44 Berkeley Square. Marsden, Pickford and Neale worked at Holkham. Hughes and Devall collaborated on repairs to the roof of Westminster Hall in 1748; and when in 1750 the King and Pelham had approved Kent's designs for the rebuilding of the Horse Guards, Crutcher, Devall, Minns, Richardson and Richards were all appointed members of the team which was to carry out the work. Joseph Pickford was subsequently added to the list at Pelham's specific request, and built the north wing.

Several of the craftsmen held official posts in the Office of Works. John Devall was Sergeant-Plumber from 1742 to 1769. Richard Minns was Master Glazier from 1745 to 1761, when he was succeeded by his colleague Richard Cobbett. In the previous year George Murray succeeded his master, James Richards, as Master Sculptor and Carver in Wood. Richards was perhaps the most distinguished of the craftsmen to work at Pelham's house. He had been Master Sculptor since 1721, when he succeeded Grinling Gibbons in that post, and had collaborated with Kent during his early years as an architect, over the Great Drawing Room at Kensington Palace. For Kent again, he worked on Queen Caroline's Library, St James's Palace, at the Treasury and on the Royal Barge. He was also associated with Colen Campbell at Marble Hill, The Rolls House, Compton Place and Burlington House.

The familial network within the Office of Works was not only limited to the craftsmen. Richards' daughter, Elizabeth, married the architect Isaac Ware. Although his name does not appear in the Accounts, Ware himself may have been involved in the building of Pelham's house. John Harris, Curator of the RIBA Drawings Collection, has attributed to Ware, on stylistic grounds, a drawing belonging to Columbia University which appears to be of the west front of 22 Arlington Street, before the extension to the south was made. A number of Office of Works architects were engaged in superintending progress at Arlington Street, and Isaac Ware, who was Clerk Itinerant and Draftsman (1728–66) and Secretary to the Board (1736–66), may well have produced some drawings for Kent. He certainly did this for a number of Kent's other projects, such as the Courts of Justice, 10 Downing Street, the Royal Mews, and the Horse Guards. In addition to Kent, Stephen Wright, Thomas Ripley and William Robinson are recorded as certifying payments to craftsmen for work at Arlington Street. Wright who had initially acted as measurer and had long been Kent's assistant, was a natural successor when his master died. After 1748 he appears also to have acted as Pelham's agent: Pelham's account at Hoare's Bank records twenty-three payments made to Wright between May 1751 and August 1756 amounting to £4,733 8s (the last two were authorised by Pelham's executors).

Several tradesmen's bills were 'examined' by Ripley and Robinson – their names usually appear jointly. Neither man was a particularly distinguished architect in his own right, but both had associations with

22 Arlington Street: The first floor Saloon redecorated, as originally, in white and gold. It was the Great Room of Pelham's first house.

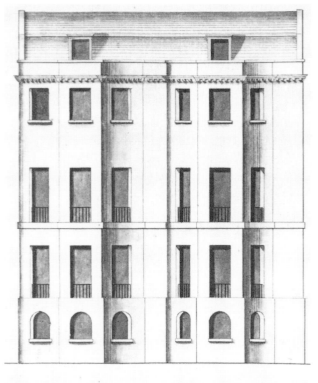

West Front . next the Park

2

1 Drawing inscribed 'West Front next the Park', attributed to Isaac Ware. 2 Projecting bays overlooking the Park at 22 Arlington Street.

Kent, and both were officials of the Board of Works. Ripley, who was Walpole's protégé and executant architect at Houghton, was Comptroller from 1726 and became Clerk of Works at Greenwich Hospital in 1746. Robinson, who had served under Ripley at Greenwich, and later supervised the building of the Horse Guards with John Vardy, ultimately succeeded Ware as Secretary to the Board in 1766.

Henry Pelham had only a short time in which to enjoy his completed house. On the eve of the General Election of 1754, he caught a chill from walking in the Park and died suddenly on 6 March.

In the same month an Inventory was made of the contents of the house. It survives today in the Greater London Record Office. In it are identified by name all the rooms in the house, the furnishings which they contained and also their value. The total contents of the house were put at £1,969 17s 6d. Of this, £865 11s represents the value of the contents of the 'Great Room, closet and passage', the most expensively furnished part of the house. The contents of the 'Blue Drawing Room and closet' adjoining the Great Room were valued at £291 8s. Next in value came a bed chamber, which contained all the linen (£131 3s), and fourthly the Dining Parlour (£125 16s 6d). The Inventory is repro-

duced in full as an Appendix to this book, but it is perhaps worth making a number of points here about the general character of the furnishings in the principal rooms.

Much is made of the hangings and coverings in each room. Curtains were generally of the sort that drew-up in festoons, and the choice of fabric related to the importance of the room. The new Great Room had crimson damask curtains and wall hangings to match. The Blue Drawing Room (Long Room in the Accounts) also had matching curtains and hangings; but these were of mixed damask, a rather cheaper material which contained linen as well as silk. In the Bed Chamber, curtains and bed hangings were in matching blue moreen, and in Henry Pelham's Dressing Room, the curtains were of green lutestring lined with tammy.

Many of the items of furniture were protected by covers. Seat furniture had cases in linen or check; the glass chandelier in the Great Room was hung 'with silk lines and tassels with a linen case'; and a large Persian carpet in the same room was protected by a baize cover. More generally, Turkey carpets were the normal form of floor covering.

The style and design of individual pieces of furniture is difficult to assess from the Inventory, but one might expect the twelve 'mahogany carved and gilt chairs upholstered in damask and three windows stools to match' in the Great Room to have been specially made, and to have been Kentian in appearance – similarly the painted, plain and carved terms in the passage and at the 'foot of the great staircase'. Several tables with marble tops and carved frames (sometimes painted, sometimes gilt) can be traced to the Building Accounts. Pickford was responsible for the tops, Marsden for the frames, Abbot for the painting, and Neale perhaps for the gilding. The Dining Parlour contained two such pieces, used no doubt as side tables, for, characteristically at that period, the dining table appears to have been kept (when not in use) outside in the passage.

Pictures there were in the house, but not in great quantity. In the Great Room hung two whole length portraits of King George II and Queen Caroline, two large historical pictures (attributed in the margin of the Inventory to 'Vandick' and 'Castilione'), and an unidentified picture over the fireplace. The Royal portraits may have been the 'whole lengths' by Kent which Walpole had seen at Esher and cited as evidence that Kent's 'portraits bore little resemblance to the persons that sat for them, . . . the colouring was worse, more raw and undertermined than that of the most errant journeymen to the profession'!

A 'coloured print of Mr Pelham', a 'fruit picture by Mich Ang⁰' and two pictures by Canaletto, which are also listed in the Inventory, probably hung in the adjacent passage. All five paintings in the Blue Drawing Room were landscapes; and in the Dining Parlour, they were mainly portraits – the Duke and Duchess of Newcastle, the Duke of Richmond on horseback and Sir Robert Walpole. Two of the doors in this room had oval pictures above them and the other, a bust of Lord Pembroke. There also hung here 'a large picture of the School of Athens' which was presumably the one left to Pelham by William Kent in his will and described as 'the School of Athens after Raphael'. Kent left to Lady Katherine a 'head of Edward the Sixth', but the Inventory does not reveal whether or not it was in the house at the time.

It is interesting to read in the Inventory of the furnishings of the original Great Room on the first floor. By 1754 it had been completely eclipsed by the new room below, and was furnished rather poorly as a bedroom, with a '4-post iron bedstead with blue serge throw-over furnishings' and no window curtains. Individual pieces of furniture were in unfashionable woods such as walnut or oak. The total value of the contents was just £32 16s 6d.

In his will, Pelham left to his wife what 'plate, pictures, books, furniture and household goods' she might think she needed for her own use. The house itself was left to the Hon. Richard Arundell and John Roberts Esq. for and during the term of ninety-nine years, with the proviso that Pelham's son-in-law and daughter, the Earl and Countess of Lincoln, should live in it if they wished at a rent of £300 per year, but otherwise allowing them to 'let the same for the most money or best rent that can be got'.

Richard Arundell and John Roberts had both been closely associated with Pelham during his lifetime. Arundell, Pelham's brother-in-law was also, according to Walpole, a 'bosom friend'.

John Roberts was Pelham's private secretary and was responsible, among other things, for dispensing the large sums of Secret Service money required to maintain the Whig interest in the Commons. Wraxall, in his memoirs, said that Roberts paid each ministerial member between £500 and £800 per annum, and that the names of the recipients were entered in a book seen only by the Prime Minister and the King. Roberts had always been close to Pelham: he owned property in Esher and had a room at 22 Arlington Street. His services were rewarded by a series of sinecures. Apart from a shared interest in Pelham's house, he was also granted, on the Prime Minister's death, a pension on the Irish Establishment. He died in 1772.

Neither Roberts nor Arundell lived at Arlington Street after Henry Pelham's death; and nor did Pelham's daughter and son-in-law. In 1755 Lady Katherine moved to Berkeley Square, and the house was let, first to Earl Gower until 1768, and after him to the Duke of Grafton until 1775. Pelham's daughter

The Hon. Henry Pelham with his secretary, John Roberts, at Esher.

Granville Leveson Gower, Earl Gower (1721–1803), by Reynolds.

Katherine died in 1760. Her husband, who became 2nd Duke of Newcastle on his uncle's death in 1768, chose to spend most of his time in the North. But their son Henry, Earl of Lincoln, newly married in 1775, decided to make his grandfather's house his home, and lived there until his early death in 1778.

1755–1768

GRANVILLE LEVESEN GOWER

SECOND EARL GOWER

Granville Leveson Gower had been Lord of the Admiralty under Pelham from 1749 to 1751. He took the house at 22 Arlington Street on succeeding his father as 2nd Earl Gower in December 1754. His years there saw his rise both as a politician and a courtier, culminating in his appointment as Lord President of the Council in 1767, and his creation as Marquis of Stafford the following year.

The writer has found no evidence or record of alterations to the house during Lord Gower's tenure. This is perhaps not surprising for during his occupation, he began, with the help of his architect Sir William Chambers, to build in Whitehall one of the most import-

ant London town-houses of the period. Gower House was started in 1765 and, although finishing touches were still being added as late as 1774, it must have been habitable enough for Lord Gower to have moved there from Arlington Street by the end of 1768.

Although Lord Gower seems understandably not to have made any alterations to Pelham's house, his neighbours in the street were busy rebuilding and altering their houses. By the end of the period of his occupation, the street had taken on the outward appearance which it was to retain well into the twentieth century. Sir William Chambers acted as architect for two of Gower's neighbours. In 1772–3 he made alterations to Number 19, a house already altered by Robert Adam in 1763–6 for Sir Lawrence Dundas Bt.; and at Number 21 he built a new house for Lord Weymouth in 1769, which still stands. Sir Lawrence's house had belonged to Lord Carteret in Pelham's time and had been rebuilt for him along the same lines as Pelham's – that is to say using the long site to create an internal courtyard. As at Number 22, the main and front buildings were connected by an arcade open to the courtyard. The arrangement particularly suited Pelham and Carteret as politicians for it meant that the London mob could be kept at bay, and relative peace and security enjoyed in the main house. In November 1742, Horace Walpole, writing to Sir Horace Mann from Number 5, refers to an incident when the good sense of this arrangement must have been made very apparent.

I laughed at myself prodigiously t'other day for a piece of absence; I was writing on the King's birthday, and being disturbed with the mob in the street, I rang for the porter, and with an air of grandeur as if I was still at Downing Street, cried, 'Pray send away those marrowbones and cleavers!' The poor fellow with the most mortified air in the world replied, 'Sir, they are not at our door, but over the way at Lord Carteret's'. 'Oh', said I, 'then let them alone, maybe he does not dislike the noise!'

In the 1750s Henrietta Louisa, Countess of Pomfret, rebuilt the house at Number 18, following much the same plan as Lord Carteret next door. But here Sanderson Miller, who was responsible for its design, clothed the house in Gothic dress. It became known as Pomfret Castle. Inside too the rooms were Gothic in style, with vaulted ceilings and perpendicular tracery on the walls, executed in stucco.

Sadly the Countess did not live long to enjoy her pretty new house, for she died in 1761 on her way to Bath. Shortly after, Lady Sophia Carteret moved into the house, so conveniently placed next door to her father. Lady Sophia also lived there only a short time, for in 1765 she married William Petty, 2nd Earl of Shelbourne, who bought the still-unfinished mansion in Berkeley Square, designed by Robert Adam for Lord

19 Arlington Street: 1 Sir Lawrence Dundas with his grandson, by Zoffany. 2 Corridor linking the front building to the main house.

18 Arlington Street: Sanderson Miller's house for Lady Pomfret.

Bute. It later became known as Lansdowne House. After Lady Sophia had left Number 18, the house was occupied for less than a year by Lord Louis Farmer, and then from 1766–87 by William Hamilton, who was Chancellor of the Irish Parliament for most of this period. Hamilton is perhaps best remembered by his nick-name 'Single-Speech Hamilton', which he gained for the famous (and only) speech he made in the heated Commons debate in 1755 against Newcastle's system of subsidies for retaining England's allies against France.

Number 17 had been occupied by a single family for longer than any other house in the street. By 1710 it belonged to the Marquess of Dorchester, who was created 1st Duke of Kingston in 1715, and was the father of the famous, and literary, Lady Mary Wortley Montagu. The house remained in the family until 1770, when the 2nd Duke sold it to the Duke of Hamilton, although it was let for a short period from 1729–33 to Lord Monson, whose son, the first Lord Sondes, later married Henry Pelham's daughter Grace in 1752. Its long association with one family since the beginning of the eighteenth century may explain the somewhat old-fashioned appearance of this house in Buckler's view of 1831, with its sash boxes fitted flush with the brickwork, an arrangement forbidden by Law in new houses after 1709. Indeed Number 17 was probably the only

original Arlington Street house to have survived into the nineteenth century, albeit with more Palladian additions at the back facing the Park.

1769–75
AUGUSTUS HENRY FITZROY
THIRD DUKE OF GRAFTON

By the time the Duke of Grafton came to Number 22, the west side of Arlington Street exhibited a remarkable variety of building forms and styles. Grafton was then still Prime Minister, and in the same year married for the second time. His public and private lives had been somewhat in turmoil, for he had begun to neglect his business, and had outraged the already lax morality of his day by behaving as though, to use the words of Horace Walpole, 'the world should be postponed to a whore and a horse race.' The 'whore' in question was Mrs Anne Horton, described as 'the Duke of Grafton's Mrs Horton, the Duke of Dorset's Mrs Horton, everybody's Mrs Horton'. She was the daughter of a tailor in Bond Street, and travelled to Jamaica with Mr Horton, a West India merchant. Later she fled from him to England and in April 1768 appeared with the Prime Minister at the Opera in London. This liaison was more than his own marriage could stand and, after twelve years of married life, his Duchess eloped with the Earl of Upper Ossory, whom she married on 26 March 1769, just three days after the Act dissolving her first marriage had become law. In May, Grafton married Elizabeth Wrottesley, daughter of the Dean of Windsor; and Mrs Horton later married Viscount Maynard, in 1776.

After unsuccessfully urging Lord North of the desirability of a reconciliation with the American Colonists, Grafton resigned as Lord Privy Seal, nearly six years after giving up the Premiership to him in 1770.

Throughout his life, his pack of hounds at Wakefield Lodge in Northamptonshire, the official residence of the Ranger of Whittlebury Forest, and the races at Newmarket, occupied much of his time. He established the Wakefield Lawn Races, which continued until 1788 and were 'attended by the elite of the sporting world'. It was to this that he retired from politics in 1775.

The Duke must have felt quite at home in Henry Pelham's house, for both his childhood homes, Wakefield Lodge and Euston Hall, bore the impress of William Kent's genius. Grafton's father, the 2nd Duke, had employed Kent to lay out the park at Euston in the late 1730s and, in 1746, to build a Banqueting House there. The 2nd Duke, like his grandson, had a passion for fox-hunting; and William Kent designed for him the hunting-lodge at Whittlebury Forest. Furthermore,

1 Augustus Henry Fitzroy, 3rd Duke of Grafton (1735–1811) by Pompeo Batoni. 2 Henry Pelham-Clinton (1750–78) and his brothers, by Hoare.

Euston had been the home of the 3rd Duke's great-great-grandfather, the Earl of Arlington, to whom Charles II had granted the corner of St James's Park on which his London house now stood.

1775–80
HENRY PELHAM-CLINTON,
EARL OF LINCOLN

The 2nd Duke of Newcastle had four sons, three of whom predeceased him. Henry was the second son and, after his eldest brother George had died young in 1752, was known by the courtesy title Earl of Lincoln. In 1772, at the age of 22, he was returned by his father for Aldborough, and in 1774 was elected unopposed for the County of Nottinghamshire. A year later he married Lady Frances Seymour Conway, daughter of the Earl of Hertford. A London house was by now a virtual necessity. His grandfather's house in Arlington Street being available to him, he was quick to set about its repair and modernisation. His father's protégé Stephen Wright, who of course knew the house well, supervised the work.

Building Accounts for the years 1775–8 survive in the Newcastle Collection of manuscripts at the University of Nottingham. Reading through them, one gets the impression that the house had become dilapidated – windows and floors had to be replaced, glazing and plastering renewed, and slating repaired. But the house must also have seemed old fashioned to the young Lord Lincoln, and its Palladian interiors somewhat heavy in the neo-Classical age of Adam.

In addition to repairs, a number of improvements were made on the ground and first floors. These seem to have been directed at lightening the effect of the existing decorations. In several rooms the frieze and architrave of the entablatures were removed, leaving only the cornice. This was done in the two first-floor rooms overlooking the Park. The rooms were then repainted and the walls hung with paper. The carver, Richard Lawrence, embellished the Library on the ground floor with 'three bunches of ribbands, one drop of floroons, and one single floroon' as well as repairing 'several other pieces that was broke to the festoons'. Minor modifications were made by him to the old Great Room on the first floor and the Long Room on the ground floor. Lawrence substantially altered the Dining Room, which by then had both a new floor and new windows. Here he carved a niche built to take a new sideboard made by him in Adamesque style.

Apart from endless repairs and renewals of locks, hinges, grates, gates and railings, William Palmer, the blacksmith, installed an extensive system of bells throughout the house in 1775. The larger rooms were fitted with two or three separate 'pulls', connected by cranks and wires running through the house, which rang bells outside the Servants' Hall in the basement. The installation was something of an innovation, and reflected a growing concern for both privacy and informality amongst the owners of large houses. It meant that the constant attendance of servants in the main part of the house was no longer necessary; they could be summoned from remoter parts by the ringing of a bell. The 1st Duke of Newcastle had referred to his servants as his 'family'; his great-nephew's attitude to his household was, perhaps, less paternal.

The team of craftsmen assembled to carry out the repairs and improvements was similar in character to the one that had built the house for Henry Pelham, and they worked, predictably enough, under the direction of Stephen Wright. The majority were also employed by the Office of Works; and the reappearance of the name of Devall is an indication that the craftsmen dynasties of earlier years still flourished. Accounts submitted by the following craftsmen survive for work carried out between 1775 and 1778.

	£	s	d
JOHN GROVES, bricklayer	306	2	5
JOHN GILLIAM, mason	138	11	11
JOHN RUSSELL, WILLIAM KELSEY AND JOHN WEST, carpenters and joiners	483	9	6
ROBERT GRIFFITHS, slater	15	18	0
JEREMIAH DEVALL AND CO., JEREMIAH DEVALL AND GEORGE HOLROYD, plumbers	96	5	2
JAMES LOTON, glazier	122	3	4
WILLIAM PALMER, smith	203	16	0
WILLIAM PILTON, wyre worker	9	9	4
ALEXANDER BRODIE, patent stove maker	197	19	0
J. PHILLIPS, WILLIAM MEREDITH, paviors	82	3	11
THOMAS CLARK AND CO., plasterers	146	19	1
RICHARD LAWRENCE, carver	26	4	0
R. & ELIZABETH WRIGHT, EDWARD BETTS, painters	143	7	4

The total expenditure recorded, which includes £19 15s 6d paid to Wright as Surveyor and £18 to Lord Tyrconnel for two years ground rent for the Stables in Bruton Mews, is £2,090 4s 6d.

Devall, Kelsey and West had been involved in the rebuilding of the King's Bench Prison (1770–3) and Groves, Gilliam, Kelsey and West were part of the team which rebuilt the Fleet Prison in 1780–1. When the Office of Excise was rebuilt in 1768–70 under the direction of William Robinson, Devall, Lawrence, Kelsey and West were all employed. Groves, Russell, Gil-

liam, Palmer, Devall, Holroyd, Clark and Lawrence all worked under Sir William Chambers at Somerset House between 1776 and 1795. Lawrence, who must have been rather older than the rest, had worked with Henry Pelham's carver, James Richards, at the Queen's Library, St James's Palace. In 1760 he succeeded Richards as Surveyor and Repairer of Carved Work at Windsor. He had worked before under Stephen Wright at the Manor House, Milton (1764–73).

Thomas Clark, who was one of the most successful plasterers of the later eighteenth century, had also worked with Wright – at the Old University Library, Cambridge in 1758. In addition to his employment by the Office of Works (he held the post of Master Plasterer from 1752 until his death in 1782), he worked at Holkham Hall, Norfolk (1745–60), Milton House, Northamptonshire (1750), Norfolk House, St James's Square (1755), Ashburton Place, Sussex (1760) and at Sir Richard Lyttleton's house in Burlington Street, London (1765). Number 22 Arlington Street was one of his last commissions.

Lord Lincoln may never have seen the work complete, for he died in France in October 1778. After his death, outstanding accounts for work to the house were settled by his father, the Duke of Newcastle. Lincoln's only son died within the year, and his widow must shortly have moved out with their small daughter Katherine, who survived. Lincoln's younger brother, Thomas, eventually succeeded to the Dukedom of Newcastle on his father's death in 1794.

1780–87

CHARLES MANNERS

FOURTH DUKE OF RUTLAND

The last two decades of the eighteenth century saw two more men with Pelham connections living at Number 22 Arlington Street; and one of them must have been responsible for the addition of a new dining room alongside the old one. The addition appears clearly on Horwood's map of 1792–9, but there is no mention of it in the Accounts for Lord Lincoln's alterations. Of the two men who followed Lincoln, Charles Manners, 4th Duke of Rutland, and Sir Sampson Gideon, 1st Baron Eardley, the first would appear to be the less likely. The Duke of Rutland was Lady Katherine Pelham's great nephew. He had the house from 1780 to 1787. On succeeding his father as 4th Duke in May 1779 at the age of twenty-five, he gave up his Cambridge University seat, for which he had been returned unopposed in 1774 while still under age, to the younger William Pitt. His main interests lay, of course, in Leicestershire where

1 Charles Manners, 4th Duke of Rutland (1754–87) by Reynolds. 2 Sir Sampson Gideon (1745–1824) and his tutor, Signor Basti, by Batoni.

he had inherited his father's estates at Belvoir; but in February 1783 he was appointed Lord Steward of the Household and given a seat in the Earl of Shelbourne's cabinet. His time in London was short, for when Pitt succeeded Shelbourne as Prime Minister later that year at the age of twenty-five, he induced Rutland to accept the post of Lord Lieutenant of Ireland. Rutland was the first of three occupants of 22 Arlington Street to hold this post.

His time in Ireland was shortlived, for he died in Dublin in the summer of 1787 following a great tour of the country during which he was entertained at the seats of the Irish aristocracy. Wraxall's description of a typical day during the tour would suggest that his fatal 'fever' might have been brought on by complete exhaustion!

During the course of the tour, he invariably began the day by eating at breakfast six or seven turkey's eggs as an accompaniment to tea and coffee. He then rode forty and sometimes fifty miles, dined at six or seven o'clock, after which he drank freely, and concluded by sitting up to a late hour, always supping before he retired to rest.

When he was in Dublin the entertainments of the viceregal court were of the utmost magnificence; and the Duke and Duchess 'were the handsomest couple in Ireland'. At first Pitt had been anxious to reform the

Irish Parliament, but Rutland had felt this was 'difficult and dangerous to the last degree'. He appears quickly to have made up his mind in favour of a legislative union; and in a letter to Pitt written in 1784 he said, 'Were I to indulge a distant speculation, I should say that without union Ireland will not be connected with Great Britain in twenty years longer.'

1787–98

SAMPSON GIDEON

FIRST BARON EARDLEY

It must have been with a certain feeling of smugness that Sir Sampson Gideon moved into the Duke of Rutland's house in Arlington Street in 1787, for Gideon had clashed with him on a number of occasions and been obliged to defer. Now, by his early death, Rutland had made way for Gideon.

Sir Sampson Gideon's father, also Sampson Gideon, had been one of Pelham's chief advisers. He was born in London in 1699, the son of a Portuguese Jew, who had settled in England. He began business there at the age of twenty, with a capital of £15,000; and he rapidly amassed a fortune, investing it mainly in landed estates, which at his death in 1762 were valued at £580,000. He became 'the great oracle and leader of Jonathan's

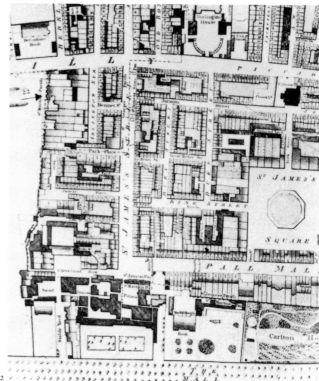

1 Sampson Gideon after becoming Baron Eardley in 1789, by J. Jackson. 2 Horwood's map of 1792–9, showing an addition to the front of

Coffee House in Exchange Alley' (afterwards the Stock Exchange in Threadneedle Street) and was almost wholly relied on by the Government for raising loans. It was he who, in 1749, advised Henry Pelham, and carried through the consolidation of the National Debt and the reduction of interest payable. Although closely connected with the Government, he took no part in supporting the measure introduced by the Pelhams in 1750 to naturalise Jews, despite the fact that his religion prevented the fulfillment of his great ambition to be created a baronet. He did however bring his children up as Christians, having married a Protestant wife; and, out of respect for the father, George II made the son a baronet, when still a boy of thirteen. Thus when Gideon senior died in 1762, his son, aged seventeen, was a baronet with a fortune of half a million pounds.

Throughout his life he spent this fortune extravagantly, and indeed upset a great number of people this way, particularly when he did so to further his political ambitions. Although he did not enter business like his father, he was a heavy subscriber to Government loans. He embarked on a political career early in life, but it was not until 1770 that he obtained a seat. In that year a vacancy occurred in the County representation of Cambridgeshire, where Gideon's father, shortly before his death, had purchased Lord Lincoln's estates. When neither the Yorkes nor the Manners, the two great county families, produced a candidate, Gideon offered

himself, and was nominated with Lord Hardwicke's support in opposition to Thomas Brand. After an expensive canvass, Brand agreed to withdraw, receiving £1,000 compensation from Gideon, whose expenses were said to have been 'not less than £5,000'. Gideon retained the seat without contest until the election of 1780, when the Duke of Rutland's brother and Lord Hardwicke's nephew, both recently come of age, were introduced as candidates.

Gideon's property in the County was not equal to theirs, nor had he made a very favourable impression in the County while its representative. Hardwicke's nephew Philip Yorke wrote in April 1780,

It is rather remarkable to see how violently the common freeholders are prejudiced against Sir Sampson Gideon. I went to pay my compliments to a room full of them . . . and they all declared they would choose their countrymen for their Members, and not a Jew. Besides, said one, he is so great a fool, so weak a man, he is always asleep and never did any business in his life.

and in May,

I wish Sir Sampson would give up, it would save an enormous deal of money, and his will be thrown away as he stands no chance whatever of succeeding, and will in all probability meet an unpleasant reception at the nomination meeting.

Gideon did not give up, and angered by rumours of a union between his opponents, 'made rather an imprudent declaration . . . to the printer of the Cambridge paper, that he had a hundred thousand pounds ready to spend upon this election'. His extravagant campaign

22 *Arlington Street since the publication of Rocque's map of 1746 (p. 103).* 3 *Dayes's view of the houses backing onto Green Park in 1797.*

continued until polling started; and he only withdrew when, at the end of the first day's poll, it was clear that he was far behind the other two candidates.

Although badly hurt by the Cambridgeshire experience, Gideon was quick to find another seat, and was returned unopposed for Midhurst in November of the same year. He retained the seat for three years and then, at the General Election of 1784, stood for Coventry, which seat he won and held until 1796. During his political career he faithfully adhered to Pitt and, when in July 1786 Pitt suggested to the Irish Administration that 'two or three' Englishmen should be included in the next creation of Irish peers, Gideon's name was mentioned. The Duke of Rutland, in his capacity as Lord Lieutenant, firmly objected. It was therefore not until 1789, after Rutland had died, that Gideon got his peerage – and then not until he had changed his name from Gideon to Eardley, though as Thomas Orde, Chief Secretary for Ireland, had remarked, he 'has made it but a half measure, for the cloven foot is sadly exposed by the preservation of Sampson'.

By this time he had been living for two years in the house of his old adversary, now vanquished – the house built by the Prime Minister whose administration had relied so much on his father's talents, but who had refused to honour him because of his race. Could it then have been in a gesture of triumph, as a symbol of his come-uppance, that he built a great new dining room alongside the old one, looking out through tall windows across the courtyard? And did he hang in it some of his father's remarkable collection of paintings, many of which had been bought from Sir Robert Walpole, who had once lived in a house on the site where the new room now stood?

Horwood's map confirms that the room had been added before Gideon left the house. Surviving battens on the walls behind the present decoration delineate a shallow barrel-vault to the room, a form characteristic of the last years of the eighteenth century. Robert Adam and Henry Holland used it in the houses which they designed; and examples survive very close to Arlington Street: Adam's first floor drawing room at 20 St James's Square (*c.* 1774) and Holland's Subscription Room at Brook's Club (*c.* 1778). These are early examples; but the form continued to be used as late as the nineties by James Wyatt and John Carr of York. The new dining room at Arlington Street, which must have looked very like Carr's great drawing room at Farnley Hall (1786–90), has now been restored to conform to the evidence found of its earlier shape.

Lord Eardley left the house in 1798. He lived until 1824, and died somewhat ironically on Christmas Day. In the 1770s he had rebuilt his father's house, Belvedere, near Erith, Kent, and may well have spent his last years there.

John Jeffreys Pratt, 1st Marquess of Camden (1759–1840), by Sir Thomas Lawrence. He lived at 22 Arlington Street from 1798 to 1837.

5

NICHOLAS THOMPSON

22 ARLINGTON STREET
IN THE 19TH &
20TH CENTURIES

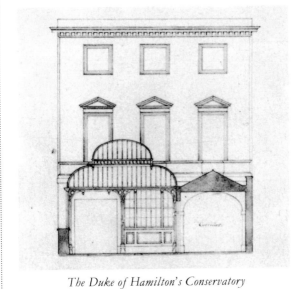

The Duke of Hamilton's Conservatory

The changes to the house during the second half of the eighteenth century were slight when compared to those which were to follow during the next century and a half. These reflect more than anything else changes in society, and in its attitudes to domestic and social life during those years. The period however starts firmly in the eighteenth century tradition, with Lord Camden's occupation of the house.

1798–1837
JOHN JEFFREYS PRATT, 2ND EARL
AND 1ST MARQUESS OF CAMDEN

It was shortly after he succeeded to a cousin's estates in Sussex and Kent in 1797, and almost four years after he succeeded to his father's title in 1794, that Lord Camden came to live at Number 22 Arlington Street. He remained in occupation until 1837, just three years before his death. Although his tenure was largely during the nineteenth century, he was essentially an eighteenth-century figure. The pattern of his early life would have been familiar to his contemporaries. Within a year of leaving Cambridge, he was put up at Bath during the General Election of 1780 by his father, who had been Recorder of the City since 1759, and was returned without opposition. In the same year, as a reward for his father's services, he was appointed one of the tellers of the Exchequer, and held that office until his death. The post was extremely lucrative, so much so that an attempt was made in 1812 to limit the emoluments accruing to it; these had increased from £2,500 per annum in 1782 to £23,000 in 1808. Remarkably, from that moment Camden relinquished all further income arising from it. By the time of his death it would have amounted to upwards of a quarter of a million pounds. For his patriotic conduct he received the formal thanks of Parliament.

His early life was, according to his father, typical of a young man about town.

They go to bed about three in the morning, rise at eleven, breakfast, ride to the park, till it is time to dress – then dinner, and the evening of course dedicated to amusement . . . They talk a little politics at their Clubs . . . but with respect to the real state of the Country they neither know nor care about it.

Although holding minor ministerial appointments almost continuously, he made no political impact until his appointment as Lord Lieutenant of Ireland in 1795. In holding that office, he shared with the English Cabinet responsibility for the policy of repressing the Catholics which ended in the rebellion of 1798. He was hated by the Irish, who saw him as a figurehead of English repression, and blamed by the English for his dilatoriness in attacking the rebels. When the rebellion broke out in May, Camden panicked. He sent his wife and family back to England for safety and entreated the English Government to send out a military man, Lord Cornwallis, to succeed him. By the time Cornwallis arrived in Dublin, the rebellion was practically at an end. Camden returned to England, and moved into 22 Arlington Street the same year.

Despite his failure to control the rebellion, Lord Camden was not without his admirers. He was strongly in favour of the Union of Great Britain and Ireland; and there were those who imagined that he would have been a better person to carry it into effect than Cornwallis. The Bill was eventually passed by Pitt's Administration in 1780. It enacted that there should be one Parliament for the United Kingdom, that four bishops, twenty-eight temporal peers and one hundred commoners should sit for Ireland in that Parliament, and that free trade should be established between the two countries. Camden continued to be consulted on Irish matters throughout the remainder of his life; and there was some talk in the early years of re-appointing him as Lord Lieutenant. However, for all this, his opinions appear not to have carried great weight. In 1805 he succeeded Lord Sidmouth as President of the Council and, in September 1812, was created Marquess of Camden and Earl of Brecknock.

How much of his time he spent at Arlington Street is really not known. He seldom took any prominent part in the debates of the House of Lords. He continued where his father left off in developing the Camden Town Estate in North London, and carried out alter-

ations to his country houses in Sussex and Kent. The Wilderness, near Sevenoaks, in Kent was Lord Camden's principal seat; and he died there in 1840 at the age of eighty-two.

Something of the state in which Lord Camden left his house in Arlington Street can be gleaned from the *Civil Engineer and Architect's Journal* of 1840 which describes his successor's improvements. Clearly the writer thought Lord Camden's house extremely old fashioned, complaining that 'like too many other mansions in London, (it) had been consigned to the tasteful hands of the upholsterer and whitewasher'; in place of painting on the walls, which was now becoming fashionable, there was but 'dabbed and spotted paper'.

Henry Somerset, 7th Duke of Beaufort (1792–1853) by Cosway.

1838–53

HENRY SOMERSET,

7TH DUKE OF BEAUFORT

The man who effected the transformation of this old-fashioned interior into what must have been one of the most lavish schemes of its time was Henry Somerset, 7th Duke of Beaufort. He had succeeded to his father's dukedom in 1835 and, with it, the great house at Badminton in Gloucestershire. The family's original

William Kent's arcade as decorated by Eduardo Latilla in 1840 for the Duke of Beaufort. This scheme survived until the First World War.

London house had been in Chelsea, but was sold in 1829 to Sir Hans Sloane who demolished it.

The 7th Duke was evidently a man of some refinement, for a contemporary remarked of him that 'it was impossible to have the slightest communication with his Grace, without being struck by his inherent courtliness, which was enhanced by a fine port, a commanding figure, and a countenance whose features were cast in a truly noble mould'. He had, in his early twenties, while still Marquess of Worcester, been aide-de-camp to the Duke of Wellington in the Peninsular and, in 1814, married the great Duke's niece, Georgiana Fitzroy.

Georgiana died after a few years; and by the time the Duke moved to Arlington Street, he had married again – this time to his former wife's half-sister, Emily Culling-Smith. The match gave rise to endless gossip, for it was said to be within the prohibited degrees of affinity, and so voidable by sentence of the Ecclesiastical Court. But no such sentence was passed, and the Marriage Act of 1835, whilst specifically forbidding all such marriages in the future, legalised those that had taken place in the past.

Henry Somerset is perhaps remembered more as a sportsman (he figured as one of the great hunting men of his time in the pages of *Nimrod*) than as a patron of the arts. He was, however, interested in both music and drama and, whereas he did little to alter the house at Badminton, he set about the transformation of 22 Arlington Street as soon as he had taken it over. The Duke was in the vanguard of taste in looking to the Continent both for inspiration and for craftsmen; and in deciding he would prefer to have his walls painted, not papered. At first it was proposed to employ German artists, who he had been told would do it better and more cheaply than Englishmen, but 'while negotiations were going on, Mr Latilla was mentioned to the Duke as having been engaged in similar works, and having been directed to send in designs, was immediately employed'.

Eduardo Latilla had gained a reputation for perfecting a new system of fresco decoration, but had never had the opportunity to display his talents to the full. He had, according to the *Civil Engineer and Architect's Journal*, worked as a boy for the architect John Nash, who had brought home from Italy a collection of designs for the loggia of the Vatican and some Italian artists, whom he later employed to paint part of his own house in Raphaelesque style. Latilla, apparently, was responsible for finishing the work after the Italians had left; and from then on he devoted his life to fresco painting. In 1842, he published a book entitled *A Treatise on Fresco, Encaustic and Tempora Painting*. Fresco technique involves painting in water-colour a plaster surface before it has time to dry. In the 1830s, it was becoming an important facet of the then fashionable interest in polychromy. Fresco painting became popular throughout the next decade, and gained impetus from the various competitions held in association with the new Houses of Parliament.

At 22 Arlington Street, Latilla worked in association with the architect Owen Jones. Jones had travelled extensively in the 1830s, and developed an eclectic decorative vocabulary which formed the basis of his highly influential book, *A Grammar of Ornament*, published in 1856. Jones insisted most emphatically on the use of colour in decoration, declaring that 'form without colour is a body without a soul'. The results of the association of these two men at 22 Arlington Street must have been startling to say the least. Even Latilla, writing several years after the work had been completed, felt obliged to remark that he had applied colour 'to an extent that in description might alarm, though as a whole, it had received the approbation of many of the first artists and men of taste.' None of these interiors have survived; and the only visual record of their appearance is an early photograph of the 'arcade' as Latilla must have left it, 'in biagio or chiaroscuro with trophies and medallions, something in the Roman style'.

The Staircase beyond, like the Arcade, was 'decorated with representations of medallions and architectural ornaments'. Three other rooms on the ground floor were redecorated at the same time: the Dining Room, added alongside the original front at the end of the eighteenth century, the Great Room overlooking the Park, and a small oval room added as a link between the two. The Journal reserved its greatest praise for the Dining Room whose 'light elegance', it said, 'both by day and by night is equally effective'. Its description of this lost room is worth repeating in full, for it must have been remarkable by any standard.

This apartment may be about thirty feet by twenty, and sixteen feet high, having on one of the long sides three windows, the opposite side an entrance door, another and a chimney at one end of the room, and at the other end folding doors leading out of it. Six large panels are thus left, which are painted with two series of subjects, one representing the seasons, and the other Hebe and Ariadne. As a banquetting room the decorations of course are of a Baccanalian character, and without departing from the character of the antique, are not repulsive to modern taste. The whole style is a similarly happy adaptation of ancient principles, and without being restricted to any one school, has a unity of character which establishes it as a style in itself. The design of the panels is much in the Pompeian taste, but carried out in accordance with the advance of modern art; the pilasters and arabesques have, perhaps, more of the character of Girolamo Romanino, or his model, the baths of Titus, and the tone of colouring shows a nearer approach to the Herculanean than the Pompeian. The ground of the room is of a lavender colour and upon this a brightness and harmony of effect is produced without spottiness or rawness.

The two panels at each end of the room are devoted to the seasons, the first of which, Spring, is represented by a female figure clothed in white gauze, and floating in true antique style in ambient air. Beneath her is a landscape representing Greek scenery, and under the panel is a mask of a young head in a festoon of spring flowers, daffodils, crocuses, snow-drops etc.

The next on the same side is Summer, also personated by a young female, crowned with a wreath of roses, and holding a garland in her hand, and floating over scenery representing Egyptian subjects. The festoon underneath is of roses and other summer flowers, and contains a mask of Bacchus.

At the opposite end of the room, the figure next the door, that of an older female, is the emblem of Autumn; she is crowned with poppies, and presides over an autumnal landscape. A mask of a warrior reposes on a festoon of grapes, wheat-ears, and other harvest productions. Part of the drapery of this is, perhaps, a little heavy.

The remaining panel of this series is devoted to Winter, a subject treated in a beautiful and effective method. In a deep blue winter sky floats a young female closely draped, with part of her robe brought round her head as a hood. Above her head is seen the constellation of the Pleiades, and to her breasts she clasps a cinerary urn, the emblem of the closing year. Underneath is a representation of iceclad mountains, forming an appropriate finish to this admirable scene, the character of which is indeed well maintained. A mask of a bearded old man is placed on the festoon beneath, which is twined of the holly and mistletoe and other emblems of Christmas.

The other and smaller series of subjects is on the side opposite the windows. One panel is appropriated to Hebe, who, with her golden vase and cup, and usual attributes, flies over a morning scene. The other panel represents Ariadne with the thyrsus, the scene under being a sacrifice to Bacchus. Under each of these panels is a festoon of flowers with a mask of a female head.

There is nothing much to remark in the smaller doors, they have over them each a small panel, containing a vase and flowers. The ornaments of the folding doors consisting of bluish ribbands and of medallions, have much of the character of the baths of Titus, and over the door is an arabesque on a yellow ground. The treatment of

1 J. Buckler's 1831 view of Arlington Street looking north. No 22 is set back and not visible. 2 J. Whittock's view of 1848 from the Park.

these doors is very skilful, the details made to tell well. The chimney and fire-place is of black marble with ormolu ornaments, and over it is a large glass. This chimney was very difficult to bring in, but the treatment has been most successful. Over the glass is a deep chocolate ground panel, with boys carrying grapes, accompanying an infant Bacchus riding on a goat. The several compartments of the room are divided by arabesques consisting of a red staff or thyrsus, with grapes and Bacchanalian emblems. The coving round the room has four corners of a peculiar deep brown used by the ancients, which Mr Latilla names Etruscan brown. Between these are arabesques on a cream-coloured ground, consisting of boys playing with panthers. The ceiling is of a low cream colour, having in the centre a patera, formed of light festoons and flowers. From this depends a lamp ornamented with vine leaves of ormolu, and grapes of ground glass. The carpet is of a plain pattern, and light in appearance; it is of blue and yellow on a maroon ground, with a white border. The furniture is of the simplest description, a mahogany table and red morocco chairs. These latter accessories are not the selection of the artist, but it does great credit to the high-minded nobleman who employed him, that he has not, as is too often the case, allowed the furniture to injure the rest of the works. The lamp might have been more in the antique, but it is not offensive. An Elizabethan stove, intended to have been placed in the room, has been removed.

The 'oval saloon leading from the banquetting room to the drawing room' was less admired. 'It has a white ground with festoons of gold ribband, but we cannot say we like the design of these last'. The oval room referred to was in fact not the same one that now connects the two great rooms. It was sited, not on axis, as now, but up against the south boundary of the site giving access to the corners of the two rooms.

The Drawing Room was of quite different character, and demonstrates the highly eclectic approach to decoration at that period. Whereas the banquetting room was essentially Classical in inspiration, the Drawing Room was more mediaeval. 'The design is in a style somewhat of the time of Henry the Fourth', the Journal reports, 'and is of a most gorgeous character, nearly all gold and silver'. The panels however depicted the story of Mary Queen of Scots; and the Journal attributes the design of the room to Owen Jones. It is tantalising that it says no more than this. Had elements of the present ceiling, and the now-lost frieze which appears in Edwardian photographs, not corresponded with entries in the original Building Accounts, one might have believed that nothing of the eighteenth century survived this metamorphosis. But if the appearance of the Duke of Beaufort's drawing room was of the time of Henry IV (i.e. 1399–1413), it may well have had a flat ceiling of beams and joists suspended below the original coved one. This arrangement would certainly have avoided the expense of stripping out the old ceiling, and may well be how it survived.

Extensive though these changes were, they marked

just the beginning of a whole series of transformations by those who, in turn, occupied the house after the Duke's death in 1853.

William Douglas Hamilton, 11th Duke of Hamilton (1811–1863)

1854–70
WILLIAM AND WILLIAM DOUGLAS HAMILTON,
11TH AND 12TH DUKES OF HAMILTON

According to an account of the house published in 1908, the 11th Duke of Hamilton paid £60,000 for Beaufort House, which then became known as Hamilton House. The actual figure is perhaps less interesting than the fact that the house was being sold at all, for this is the first mention of a sale which the writer has found. Certainly during the second half of the eighteenth century, it would appear that the house was being let on a series of short leases by the beneficiaries of Henry Pelham's will, or by their heirs. At what point the freehold of the house passed to the occupier is not clear, but certainly the change in tenure would be one of the reasons why so much more was done to the house during the nineteenth century.

Despite the fact that the Duke of Hamilton spent much of his life abroad, he carried out a number of

The Duke of Beaufort with his second wife, Emily, on a gondola in Venice, by Schiavoni. She was the Duke's first wife's half-sister.

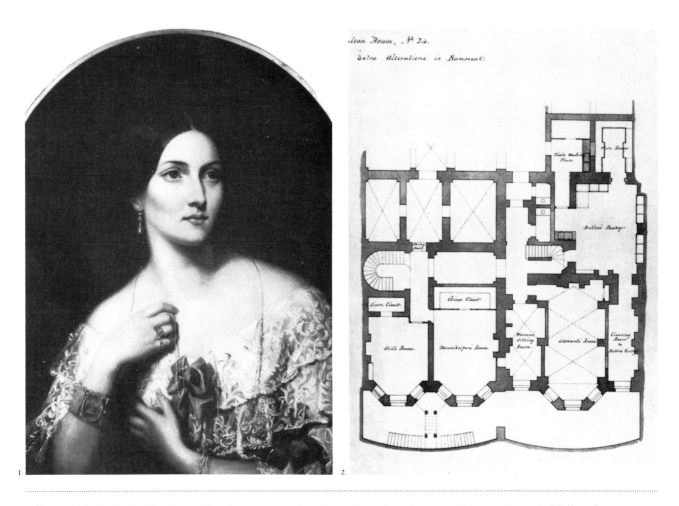

1 *Princess Marie Amélie, Duchess of Hamilton. 2,3,4,5 Alterations to Hamilton House, 22 Arlington Street, by William Burn, 1854–6.*

alterations to his houses in England and Scotland. In 1843, at the age of twenty-two, he had married the Princess Marie Amélie, daughter of the Grand Duke of Baden and a cousin of the Emperor Napoleon III. After his marriage, the Duke lived chiefly in Paris and Baden, taking very little interest in British politics. He inherited his father's London house in Portman Square; but within a year of the old Duke's death, he had decided to buy another. His choice of architect to alter the new house was William Burn, a Scotsman whose practice, by 1830, was larger than that of any other Scottish architect, and who, by 1840, had already designed or altered over ninety country houses, thirty churches, and twenty-five public buildings. Until 1844 he worked from his office in Edinburgh, but then moved to London to take advantage of the numerous commissions he was then receiving from English clients. By the time he was commissioned by the Duke of Hamilton in 1854, he was sixty-five years old. During the following three or four years he worked for the Duke, not only in London, but at the Duke's two Scottish seats, Hamilton Palace and Brodick Castle. Burn showed himself

capable of designing in almost any style, from Greek Revival to Scottish Baronial; but what commended him most to his clients was his attention to planning and, above all, the need to safeguard an owner's privacy from both servants and guests.

Great importance was attached to a well-organised and efficient plan in mid-nineteenth century country house design. This was vital in households that had become increasingly compartmentalised. Individual rooms were reserved for specific functions, and the arrangement of furniture within them became more permanent. Domestic servants were given highly defined tasks and observed a strict hierarchy within their own ranks. In a country house, an entire wing might be devoted to domestic offices and the accommodation of indoor servants. In a town house the basement might be extended, perhaps under the garden, to provide the same kind of accommodation.

Burn's drawings for the alteration of Hamilton House survive in the collection of the Royal Institute of British Architects, and show how, at basement level, the entire site was taken up by domestic offices and

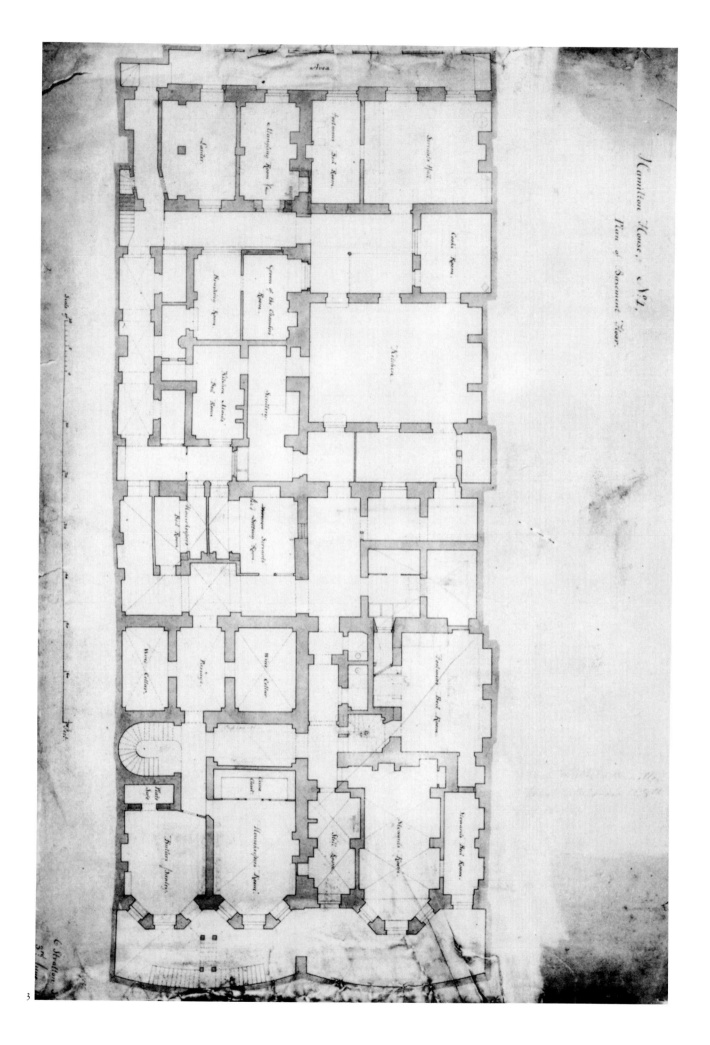

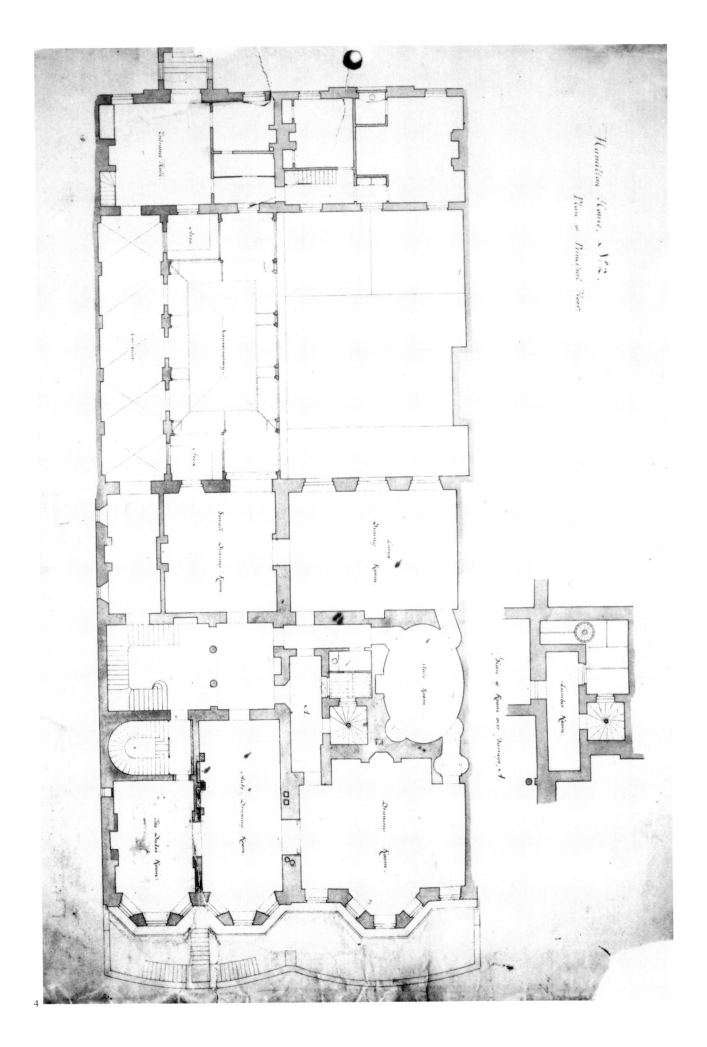

4

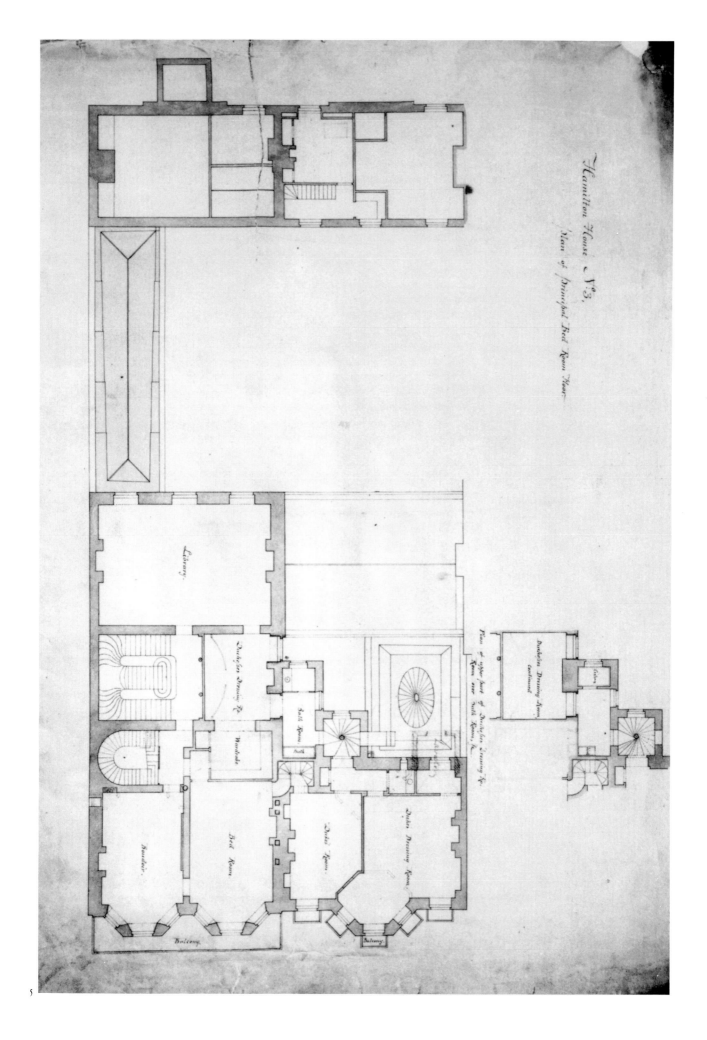

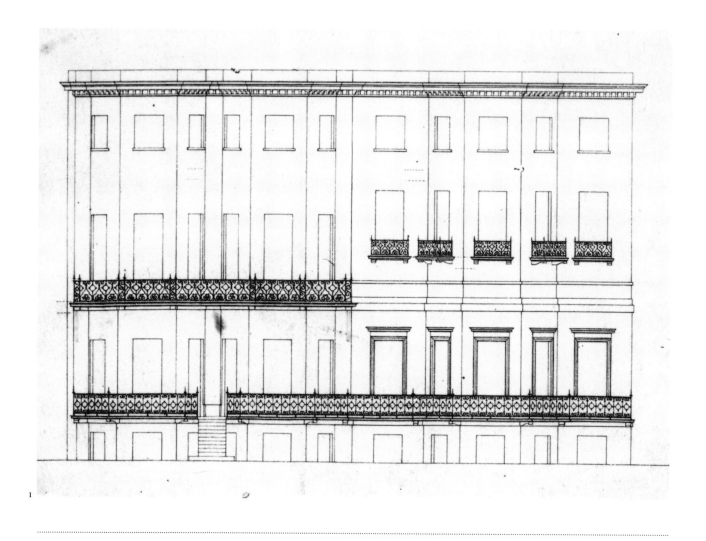

Proposals for Hamilton House by William Burn: 1 Park front. The first floor windows in the right half were raised to light new bedrooms on

servants rooms. There exist two schemes; and for each, rooms are labelled according to the uses to which they were to be put, or the servants who would occupy them. The principles underlying the schemes anticipate the writings of Robert Kerr, whose book *The Gentleman's House*, published in 1864, was devoted to 'the exposition of those details of arrangements which make up the plan of a Gentleman's House'.

The Duke's London household was clearly a grand one, for the drawings show he had a steward as well as a butler. In most households, labour was divided under three heads – the butler, the housekeeper and the cook. The butler was chief of the male attendants on the family, and was responsible for the groom of the chambers and the footmen who worked with him. Particular to his office was the service of wine and the storage of plate, and he was probably his master's personal attendant. The housekeeper was in command of the housemaids, and perhaps a still-room maid. She was responsible for the cleaning of the house, for looking after the

china and linen, and for storing and preparing tea, coffee, preserves, cakes and biscuits in the still-room. The kitchen, and preparation of all other food, was presided over by the cook, who was responsible for the kitchen and scullery maids. In the Duke of Hamilton's household, butler, housekeeper and cook were relieved of the business of provisioning their departments by a steward, who was the chief officer of all, and responsible for ordering and receiving everything supplied to the house by tradesmen. A London house would be maintained by a skeleton staff, supplemented when he was there by servants who had travelled ahead from wherever he was last in residence.

Burn's plans of Hamilton House express vividly the way in which a great London household must have worked. Pride of place is given to rooms for three of its chief officers. In Burn's first scheme, steward, butler and housekeeper are all given rooms on the west side of the house, with bay windows looking across the narrow garden to the Park beyond. In both schemes, the

the mezzanine above the Great Room. *2 Conservatory (above) and Porte-cochère. 3 The 12th Duke of Hamilton (1845–95) by Winterhalter.*

Steward's Room is the biggest and thus suitable, as was the custom in a large household, for use as a dining hall for the upper servants – the valet, butler, head cook, housekeeper, head lady's maid and head nurse, and any 'stranger's servants' of equal rank brought by house guests. Lower servants would eat in the Servants' Hall, which Burn locates at the front of the house and close to the kitchen.

In both schemes, the Housekeeper's Room is in the same place and contains a capacious china closet. The room allocated to the butler in the first scheme, however, is given over to the still room in the second, presumably on the grounds that it was not big enough, for the 'extra alterations' (the second scheme) provides him with a larger internal room lined with cupboards, and with a plate room for the storage of silver as well as areas for plate-washing and plate-cleaning. Both locations are conveniently placed at the bottom of the service stair, and relate well to the vaulted wine cellars in the centre of the building.

The extra alterations appear only to relate to the western half of the house, so that it is likely that the proposals for the eastern half, shown on the earlier drawings, were implemented. This half of the house contained the Kitchen, the largest room of all at basement level. The Cook's Room leads out of it on one side, the Scullery on another, with a bedroom beyond that for the kitchen maids. Between the Kitchen and the Footman's Bedroom is a series of unidentified rooms; some of these must have served as food stores which – apart from the larder under the front building, with windows back and front to allow a through-draught to keep perishable food cool – are not otherwise shown. Under the area between the front and main building is the Groom of the Chamber's Room and, next to it, the brushing room, normally used for the brushing of clothes, but which in London, where the incidence of mud was perhaps less frequent than in the country, might also have served as a base for cleaning shoes and knives, and for trimming, cleaning and filling oil lamps.

Across an open area from these two rooms is the Mangling Room for household laundry, and between that and the Kitchen, a second and smaller bedroom for a footman, from which it would be possible to hear someone arriving at the front of the house.

Three enclosed staircases link this subterranean and completely utilitarian world with the upper parts of the house where the Duke and his family lived and entertained, and beyond them, with the garret bedrooms where, at the end of their long day, the housemaids took their rest. The three floors used by the family would have been as luxurious and comfortable as the servants quarters were utilitarian – the second floor devoted to family bedrooms and the nurseries, and the first to a private suite for the Duke and Duchess. By using the mezzanine space above the great Drawing Room, and by turning the eighteenth century 'blind' windows on the parkside elevation into real ones, William Burn was able to provide a bedroom and dressing room each for the Duke and Duchess, both with lavatories and, for the Duchess, a bathroom and walk-in 'wardrobe' as well. Leading from the Duchess's bedroom is her boudoir. Across the landing of the main stair is the Duke's library.

Curiously, Burn's drawings show a different form for the main staircase at ground and first floor levels. At the lower level the plan is as it is today, but on the floor above it is shown as an 'imperial' stair – a central flight branching left and right into two return flights which lead up to the landing. The existence today of a Victorian handrail, and the similarity of the imperial form in Burn's drawing to the stair which William Kent had created at 44 Berkeley Square, might suggest that this was how Burn had found it, and that its present form is the result of his alterations. However, during the recent restoration, investigation of the flanking walls showed nothing to indicate that an imperial stair had once existed. Perhaps, therefore, this was a proposal by Burns which was never executed, and the new handrail, no more than a repair.

Within the existing building, Burn's drawings indicate only minor modifications at ground level. But two major additions to the house significantly altered its plan, as well as its appearance from the street. The first of these was particularly characteristic of the period – a large glazed conservatory, which was built over part of the internal courtyard. Just as the tendency in nineteenth-century country house design was to bring the landscape into the rooms by dropping window cills to the ground and creating winter gardens and conservatories leading directly off principal spaces, so in London Burn contrived the same effect. On the Park side of the house, window openings on ground and first floors were enlarged, and sliding sashes were replaced by hinged 'french' windows giving onto iron balconies which overlooked the Park. Within the site, the Small Dining Room opened straight into the new conservatory, of which the elaborate form and domed roofs were made possible by advances in glass and iron technology. Here, even in mid-winter, and in the centre of the city, there was always a lush, exotic, evergreen world, perhaps containing plants which the Duke and Duchess had brought back from their travels.

Burn also made alterations to the entrance front of the house, which had never been very satisfactory. It had been built, one must remember, in two stages, the second being a mirror image of the first; this produced, in effect, two front doors. Even with the later addition of a small porch outside the real one, the elevation must have presented an uncomfortable duality. By building a second matching porch, and then creating between them a giant porte-cochère with Tuscan columns, Burn gave the elevation a strong central focus at a scale fitting to the house which lay beyond.

In 1863, less than ten years after the alterations had been completed, the Duke of Hamilton died, it is said from a fall after supper in the Maison Dorée, Boulevard des Italiens, Paris. The Princess Marie Amélie continued to use the house until the end of the decade, when her son, the 12th Duke, whose dissolute life in Paris was remarked upon by Queen Victoria in several of her letters, sold it to Sir Ivor Guest.

1871–1947
SIR IVOR GUEST
AND THE LORDS WIMBORNE

The Guest family were the last to use 22 Arlington Street as a private residence. They held it for three generations until 1947, when the 2nd Viscount Wimborne sold it to the present owners.

For centuries, the belief that land was safe, was one of the rocks on which the upper classes rested. As Mark Girouard has said, 'it was impossible for land to burn down, or to be stolen, or blow up, or sink at sea. It was irremovably there, and one could rely on it'. It was a symbol of power as well as a source of wealth. Until the nineteenth century, the wealth and population of England lay in the country rather than the towns; landowners rather than merchants were the dominating class, and ran the country so that their interests were the last to suffer. But although the tradition survived through most of the nineteenth century, there developed

22 Arlington Street: The Great Room in 1902, as redecorated for Lord Wimborne. The 18th-century entablature has survived intact.

1 Dowlais Ironworks in the 19th century. 2 Canford Manor, Dorset, by Charles Barry. 3 Sir Ivor Guest Bt., 1st Baron Wimborne (1835–1914).

simultaneously a new tradition, which found its roots in the Industrial Revolution, and which recognised the value of wealth derived from other sources. During the last quarter of the nineteenth century the influx of cheap corn from America led to an unprecedented agricultural depression in England. It severely shook the hitherto unchallenged security of families whose land provided their income and supported their great houses. The mystique of land as the basis of status and wealth was finally exploded, and those families who had money in industry and commerce came into their own.

Sir Ivor Guest came from just such a family. His grandfather, John Guest, had left his native Shropshire in the mid-eighteenth century and settled at Dowlais in Glamorganshire, where he established an extensive Iron Works. Until it was closed in 1930, it was the oldest and largest in Wales. His nephew, John Josiah Guest, set the Works on the map, by increasing its

production some twenty-fold in the forty-five years between 1807 and his death in 1852. Paternalistic, philanthropic and popular amongst the twelve thousand families he had drawn around him, he became the first Member of Parliament for Merthyr Tydfil in 1832, and held the seat for the rest of his life. He was created a Baronet in 1838. In developing the Works, and indeed in every aspect of his later life, he was helped and encouraged by his remarkable second wife, Lady Charlotte Guest.

His first wife had died in 1818, a year after their marriage, and in 1833 he married Lady Charlotte Bertie, only daughter of the 9th Earl of Lindsay. Lady Charlotte, an artistic and highly intelligent woman with dynastic ambitions, was determined to establish her family's position by transforming some of her husband's wealth into a country seat. A modest house built in 1826 at Canford in Dorset was purchased in 1846. Within two years remodelling and enlargement had started under

4 22 *Arlington Street: The Ballroom next to the Conservatory, which George Trollope and Sons added for Lord Wimborne in the 1880s.*

the direction of Sir Charles Barry, whose competition-winning designs for the new Houses of Parliament were then being built at Westminster. Lady Charlotte worked closely with Barry during the building of Canford, going over every detail of its design with him. She was extremely interested in art and architecture, and travelled widely to find paintings and objects with which to furnish the new house.

Canford became the family's principal residence, although it seems from Lady Charlotte's diaries that her husband was not altogether convinced that the expense was really warranted. Largely for the benefit of his health Sir John lived at Canford for the remaining years of his life; but significantly he chose to die at Dowlais, amidst the scenes of his childhood. He left behind him a young widow and ten children, the eldest of whom was fourteen. Three years later, in 1855, Lady Charlotte married her children's tutor, Charles Schreiber. The children were brought up at Canford, and most of them

married into landed families. Thomas, her second son, married the sister of the celebrated Victorian Duke of Westminster; and Ivor, the eldest, married Lady Cornelia Spencer-Churchill, the eldest of the six beautiful and gifted daughters of the 7th Duke of Marlborough.

Ivor Bertie Guest had been born at Dowlais in 1835. He succeeded his father, in 1852, at the age of 17. His early adulthood was spent as an officer in the Dorset Imperial Yeomanry, although he soon became involved in politics as a Liberal – a family tradition which started with his father and continued for a further two generations. He later unsuccessfully contested, as Conservative Candidate, the County of Glamorgan and the Borough of Poole in 1874, and the City of Bristol in 1878 and 1880. In 1903 he reverted to Liberalism in reaction to Joseph Chamberlain's campaign for fiscal reform, and what he considered was an undesirable tendency on the part of the Unionist Party to foster ritualism in the Church. He gained strong and active

The Yellow Drawing Room, c. 1890. An ante-room to the Great Drawing Room, it contained many of the best pictures in the house.

support both in his political and religious beliefs from his wife, whom he had married in 1868. Lady Cornelia was by all accounts a formidable lady of strong views, fervent in her adherence to the Protestant faith and in her advocacy of Liberalism. She was the elder sister of Lord Randolph Churchill, and thus the aunt of Winston Churchill, whom she was at great pains to woo from the Tory Party.

It was just two years after their marriage that Sir Ivor and his wife bought Hamilton House. Like their predecessors in this London house, they were not reticent in adapting the place to their needs and tastes, adding to it a large and magnificent ballroom alongside the Duke of Hamilton's conservatory. This new room could be approached either from the Conservatory or the Large Dining Room, and so made a significant extension to the suite of reception rooms. The room itself was elaborately and opulently decorated, with coupled Ionic pil-

asters supporting a full entablature beneath a deeply coved and enriched ceiling. At one end, a raised 'box' with balustraded balcony provided a point of vantage from which musicians could accompany the dancing.

The room was built by George Trollope and Sons, a family building firm established in 1778, which in 1864 had extended its operations to include high-class decorative work. Their new department operated from a building known as the Pantechnicon (now Sotheby's Belgravia) in West Halkin Street, and offered the very latest in fashionable furnishings. Their show rooms were modestly called 'The Museum of Decorative Art'. Trollopes had worked at Buckingham Palace as paper-hangers in 1830, exhibited furniture at the Great and Paris Exhibitions in the 1850s, and had more recently been completing schemes which Cubitts had started in Belgravia. Their work at 22 Arlington Street followed closely on their building of Her Majesty's Theatre in the

The Great Drawing Room. Henry Pelham's room, embellished with inlaid doors, silk-lined panels and a monster chimneypiece.

Haymarket (1868–9), and exhibited much of the same theatrical exuberance. The firm amalgamated with Colls and Sons in 1903, and operates today as Trollope and Colls.

Trollopes may also have been responsible for the redecoration of many of the existing rooms at Hamilton House, for clearly changes were made. Owen Jones's Henry IV Drawing Room was swept away, and the Great Room restored to something like its eighteenth-century appearance, although much embellished. A grossly designed chimneypiece and carved overmantel mirror, inlaid doors and door cases, and walls divided into panels with enriched frames lined with silk damask were the principal features of the new scheme. Leading from this room, the Yellow Drawing Room as it was now called, contained many of the best paintings in the house. E. Beresford Chancellor, in his book the *Private Palaces of London* (1908), lists two portraits by Reynolds,

a fine 'head' by Hogarth, a Van Dyck, a pair of three-quarter length portraits by Van der Helst, a Zucchero, and three paintings by François Boucher. And, as if the collection was not already catholic enough, the room contained two modern paintings as well – Lord Wimborne's first three children, painted by Hicks in 1877, and Watts' celebrated 'Ariadne'. Beyond the Yellow Drawing Room lay the White Drawing Room, that chamber where in earlier days Henry Pelham had received only his closest colleagues. Its decoration in the 1890s would however have made it quite unrecognisable to him, had he been able to return; the white walls with their gilded boiseries would have been more familiar to Louis XIV's first minister. The practice of frenchifying interiors was extremely fashionable at this time. Kent's rooms at Devonshire House, on the other side of Piccadilly, suffered the same fate; and when in 1892 Lord Wimborne's nephew, the 9th Duke of Marl-

1 *The Library on the first floor. Kent's ceiling survives above the Victorian alterations. The door on the left leads to the top of the stairs.*

borough, succeeded to Blenheim, he imported a team of cabinet-makers from Paris to transform the State Rooms there with details copied from Versailles. When later in 1906, the Ritz Hotel was built next door to Wimborne House, the design was quite frankly Parisian, both inside and out.

Upstairs the transformation was less thorough, and contemporary photographs show Kentian ceilings floating above Victorian panelling and bookcases. Lady Wimborne's Boudoir above the White Drawing Room was relatively simple compared to the rooms below. Across the landing from this room lay the more masculine Library, with its massive chimney piece and overmantel and its heavy desk and bookcases en suite. Chancellor identifies the paintings on the walls in this last room – 'a very fine pair of landscapes by J.F.Van

Bloeman, two curious genre pictures by Longhi, a Jan Both, and a very effective seascape of the Dutch school, as well as a fine view of St Peter's as seen from the Tiber by Pannini.' In 1887 electric light was installed throughout the house.

In a period when elaborate social etiquette formed the barrier which jealously guarded the exclusiveness of those 'in Society', these rooms formed the setting for the day to day ritual of calls, tea parties, and 'at homes', which were the *modus operandi* of that elite. Hospitality at Wimborne House, as it was called after 1880 when Sir Ivor was created Baron Wimborne, was justly famous. Dinners and balls there were lavish indeed and often politically orientated.

The justification given for the wealth and privileges granted to Society in the nineteenth century was that its

2 The White Drawing Room, decorated in the French taste. 3 Lady Wimborne's Boudoir with its surviving Kent ceiling. 4 The Ritz Hotel.

members should lead the nation, not only politically, but morally as well. This is not to say the upper classes at that time were prudish or puritanical (how could they be with the Prince of Wales as their leader?); but they were extremely careful of their public image. A far worse sin than adultery was its advertisement, and a public scandal was thought, literally, to betray the whole social class. In 1876 the Guests found themselves caught up in one of the greatest scandals of the period, the Aylesford affair. While Lord Aylesford was accompanying the Prince of Wales on a grand tour of India, Lady Cornelia's brother, the Marquess of Blandford was having an affair with Aylesford's wife. An extremely serious one it was, for they decided to elope, seek divorce and marry. Their intentions caused consternation everywhere. Lord Randolph Churchill man-

aged to persuade his brother not to proceed with his plans for the time being, but felt that, in the long term, only the Prince could prevent disaster by persuading Aylesford not to seek a divorce. Lord Randolph achieved his aim, but not without resorting to blackmail. He went to Princess Alexandra with letters written to Lady Aylesford by the Prince himself. If Aylesford did sue his wife for divorce, the letters would be produced as evidence in court; and if that happened, he told her, it was the Solicitor General's opinion that the Prince would never sit on the throne of England. It was a bad enough business already. Now it took on even more serious proportions. The Prime Minister, Disraeli, was called in; and Queen Victoria was enraged. In the event, the affair was kept out of the courts, but the result was virtual ostracism from court circles for the

The Green Drawing Room (1), Dining Room (2) and Conservatory (3). COLOUR *The Oval Room, built by the 2nd Lord Wimborne*

whole Churchill family. The Duke of Marlborough agreed to accept the post of Viceroy of Ireland as a way of withdrawing from English social life with some dignity, and Lord Randolph went with him as his private secretary.

The episode caused rifts within the Churchill family itself. Lord Randolph's sister Cornelia and her husband sided with the Prince; and when at the height of the affair, in the summer of 1876, his Royal Highness declined to accept their invitation to a ball at Arlington Street, Sir Ivor went to the Prince's private secretary Francis Knollys, to see if he would change his mind. Lord Randolph himself refused to attend the ball, and was incensed when his brother-in-law accused him of being 'completely wrong all thro'. When Randolph replied that whatever he thought, he hoped he would keep this opinions to himself, Sir Ivor retorted that he should do nothing of the kind. The quarrel between them continued for several years, so that after Randolph's return from Ireland in 1880, he had occasion to

write in angry mood to his wife, Jenny, that 'Cornelia behaved very piggily as she has done before on more than one occasion.'

Lord Randolph's return from Ireland in 1880 had been brought about by Disraeli's defeat at the general election that year. After this he went into opposition against the new Liberal Government under Gladstone. In the same year, Sir Ivor was sworn of the Privy Council and created Baron Wimborne, an event which cannot have pleased his brother-in-law who was still excluded from the smartest circles. The difference in their political beliefs may well have had much to do with the quarrel between Randolph and his sister; both she and her husband were staunch supporters of the Liberal movement.

Although relations between the Guests and Lord Randolph were often bad, the mutual regard which existed between that family and Lord Randolph's son, Winston, appears to have been continuously high. Lady Wimborne's deep interest in her nephew's career lasted from the day in 1902, when she listened from the Ladies' Gallery in the Commons to his maiden speech, until her death in 1929. Winston was by his own nature susceptible to his aunt's attempts to woo him from the Tory Party, for both he and the Wimbornes were advocates of Free Trade. When in 1903 Joseph Chamberlain proposed fiscal reforms whereby duties would be imposed on goods imported from foreign countries, Winston received a letter from his aunt at Wimborne House urging him to leave the party: 'Of one thing I think there is no doubt and that is that Balfour and Chamberlain are one, and that there is no future for Free Traders in the Conservative Party. Why Tarry!'

Aunt's and nephew's views exactly coincided. Within ten days of receiving her letter he was writing to Lord Hugh Cecil, '. . . it is my intention that before Parliament meets my separation from the Tory Party and the Government shall be complete and irrevocable, and during the next session I propose to act consistently with the Liberal Party . . . Free Trade is so essentially Liberal in its sympathies and tendencies that those who fight for it must become Liberals.' On 31 May 1904, the first Parliamentary day after the Whitsun recess, Winston literally crossed the floor of the House to sit on the Liberal benches. He was later followed by his two cousins, Ivor and Freddie Guest, no doubt to the gratification of their mother, Lady Wimborne. In 1906 Ivor Guest was returned as a Liberal for Cardiff Boroughs with an unprecedented majority, and held the seat until 1910, when he was sworn of the Privy

Freddie Guest with Winston Churchill at the Colonial Office in 1921.

Council and accepted a peerage as Baron Ashby St Ledgers. After four unsuccessful attempts to enter Parliament, Freddie Guest, the Wimborne's third son, was returned for East Dorset at the General Election of December 1910, and became Chief Whip to the Liberal members of the Coalition Government. His first political speech in 1905 had been made in support of his cousin Winston, whose private secretary he later became.

Wimborne House at this time became the virtual centre of the Free Trade Party, and Winston Churchill was a constant visitor. Ties between Winston and his cousins were, however, not only political. In 1898 he had chosen Ivor to be proof-reader for his first novel, the story of the Malakand Field Force; and later, when he was writing his father's biography, his uncle put a room at Wimborne House constantly at his disposal to work in. Ivor, Freddie and Winston frequently played polo together.

In 1910 the Wimbornes' second son, Henry, joined his brother in the Commons and in 1918 the youngest, Oscar, was returned for the Loughborough division of Leicestershire. At every turn of their political careers,

Chamber Music at Wimborne House by Sir John Lavery. It depicts one of the Quartet Society concerts held in the Ballroom in the 1930s.

their mother was there to advise and encourage – sometimes, if she felt it necessary, to admonish too. When, in 1913, her nephew Winston, then First Lord of the Admiralty, was in deep water over his estimates for Naval expenditure, his aunt did not hesitate to send him her advice. She wrote accusing him of breaking with the traditions of Liberalism, and of being in danger of becoming purely a 'Navy man' and losing sight of the far greater job of leader of the Liberal Party. In the event Churchill prevailed and the estimates were agreed.

When Churchill left the Admiralty in 1915, and his salary dropped from £4,500 to £2,000, it was his cousin Ivor Wimborne who helped him out by inviting him to stay at Arlington Street, until such time as he could move into his brother's house in Cromwell Road.

Apart from Liberalism, Lady Wimborne's other great cause was the Protestant faith, for which she was dubbed the 'Deborah of Dorset'. She founded an institution called Lady Wimborne's Protestant League, and organised and financed its branches throughout the country. In his biography of his father, Winston Churchill's son, Randolph, describes how in Liverpool she was a little unlucky.

She employed an unknown and impecunious young lawyer, F.E. Smith, as the secretary of the local branch and authorised him to take and furnish an office. One day she let Smith know that she was coming to Liverpool to inspect the premises which he had acquired on her behalf. Smith felt that his office was rather bleak and bare, and not at the time being fully conversant with the religious controversies involved, or with the real objectives his patroness was seeking, went out and for a knockdown price bought twelve somewhat inferior reproductions in colour of the Virgin Mary. These he caused to be hung as gracefully as he could contrive on the walls of the office of the Protestant League. When Lady Wimborne surveyed Smith's handiwork she dismissed him instantly.

Randolph Churchill, described his great aunt as a 'highly intelligent old battle-axe', but Winston certainly had 'a great regard' for her, and wrote sympathetically to her on the death of her husband in February 1914.

Lord Wimborne's death meant that his eldest son Ivor succeeded, not only to his title, but, according to the *Complete Peerage*, to some 83,539 acres in Dorset, Glamorgan, Breconshire, Hampshire and Ross-shire, which yielded an annual income of £46,856. His father had continued to run the Dowlais Iron works until 1899, but in that year the Guests amalgamated with two other families of industrialists whose wealth had been founded, like theirs, in the mid-eighteenth century – the Keens who were nut and bolt-makers in the Midlands and the Nettlefolds who were wood-screw manufacturers. The resulting company took its present name of Guest, Keen and Nettlefolds Ltd in 1901, and has since grown to become one of Britain's largest international engineering groups, with subsidiaries worldwide.

The new Lord Wimborne was forty-one years old, had been married twelve years and had three children. His wife was the beautiful Alice Grosvenor, younger daughter of the 2nd Baron Ebury. Since being elevated to the peerage in his own right in 1910, he had served for two years as Paymaster-General in Asquith's Liberal Government, and was currently Lord-in-Waiting to His Majesty King George V. Winston Churchill had been trying for some time to get his cousin a post at the Admiralty, as Civil Lord in place of George Lambert, but Asquith had not been prepared to dismiss Lambert.

On 4 August 1914 war broke out, and Wimborne was appointed to the staff of Lieutenant-General Sir Bryan Mahon, then commanding a division at the Curragh in Ireland. Wimborne's interest in Irish affairs developed quickly, and led him a year later to accept the Viceroyalty of Ireland. He had the post for virtually the rest of the War; and during this period the Dublin Court became famed for its hospitality. Lady Cynthia Asquith, the Prime Minister's daughter-in-law, visited the Viceregal Lodge on two occasions, first in 1915 and then again during the following year. Her impressions are recorded in the diaries which she kept. Tremendous ceremony was maintained and everything was hugely grand. She becomes quite giggly over the endless curtseying and other Court etiquette. The Wimbornes are referred to as 'Their Majesties', or 'His Ex' and 'Her Ex', and often Lady Wimborne is just 'Queen Alice'. Both played their parts to the full, Lord Wimborne – somewhat theatrical in his insistence on correct procedures, Lady Wimborne – 'heaven born manner, smile and dimple, and most conscientious'. Lady Diana Manners, who listed Lord Wimborne among her older admirers and who, until her marriage to Duff Cooper, was his neighbour in Arlington Street, stayed with them in Dublin. Whilst being impressed by the splendour of their Court, she too was somewhat taken aback by the carefully prescribed etiquette. 'On curtseying after dinner to H.E.', she was told by her hostess, 'we don't use the gavotte or Court curtsey but rather the modern Spanish'.

Although Wimborne was popular, events proved too strong for him; and in 1916 the Easter rebellion broke out. It was Wimborne's idea that the leaders, who were known to the police, should be arrested before trouble began, but the approval of the absent Chief-Secretary, Augustus Birrell, could not be obtained, and nothing was done. On 10 May, Lord Wimborne's resignation was in the London evening papers. Had it not been for a public inquiry, at which his

Ivor Churchill Guest, 1st Viscount Wimborne (1873–1939), by Orpen. He became first President of the National Liberal Party in 1931.

1 The 'Italian Garden' laid out at basement level. 2 The enfilade through the south suite of rooms. 3 Plans of the house made in 1946.

evidence created a favourable impression, this might have been an end to his Viceroyalty. In the event he consented to withdraw his resignation, and continued in the post until 1918. In that year, he was asked by the Government to report on the subject of conscription in Ireland. On his refusal to support this measure, his place was taken by Lord French. Wimborne returned to England, and in June was created a Viscount.

For the immediate future he ceased to take much share in politics and turned his attention to business activities. These years also saw the completion of the alterations which had started at Wimborne House while he was still in Ireland. When faced with moving into his parents' house, Lord Wimborne must have felt very much as Sylvia had done in V.Sackville-West's novel *The Edwardians*; as she looked around the rooms in which Lord Roehampton's sisters lived, 'here were too many chairs, too many hassocks, too many small tables, too much pampas grass in crane-necked vases, too many blinds and curtains looped and festooned about the windows. The whole effect was fusty, musty and dusty. It needed destruction, it needed air . . .' At Wimborne House, this is just what it got. Grand ideas, but simpler detailing were the keynotes of the new regime.

In the main the changes were cosmetic, although several major structural changes significantly altered the way in which the house was used. Burn's great Conservatory at the centre of the building was demolished, and the area turned into an open courtyard once more, this time excavated down to basement level. The progression from one room to another now involved following a strict circuit, for one was no longer able to cut across from one side to another, without going right to the front or the back of the house. This circuit of rooms was then enhanced by the reconstruction of the small oval room, between the Dining Room and the Great Room, just a few yards north of its original position, so that, after moving the fireplaces of these two great rooms and putting double doors in their place, the three rooms could be linked on axis. By also replacing the musicians' gallery in the Ballroom with double-doors and creating a library in the space beyond, it was possible to open up an 'enfilade' through a series of no less than six different spaces, which together stretched for a total of 166 feet. In a London house, this was truly remarkable, particularly when one remembers that this suite was matched by a further six rooms on the north side of the house. The complete circuit therefore consisted of twelve rooms in all, providing a sense of

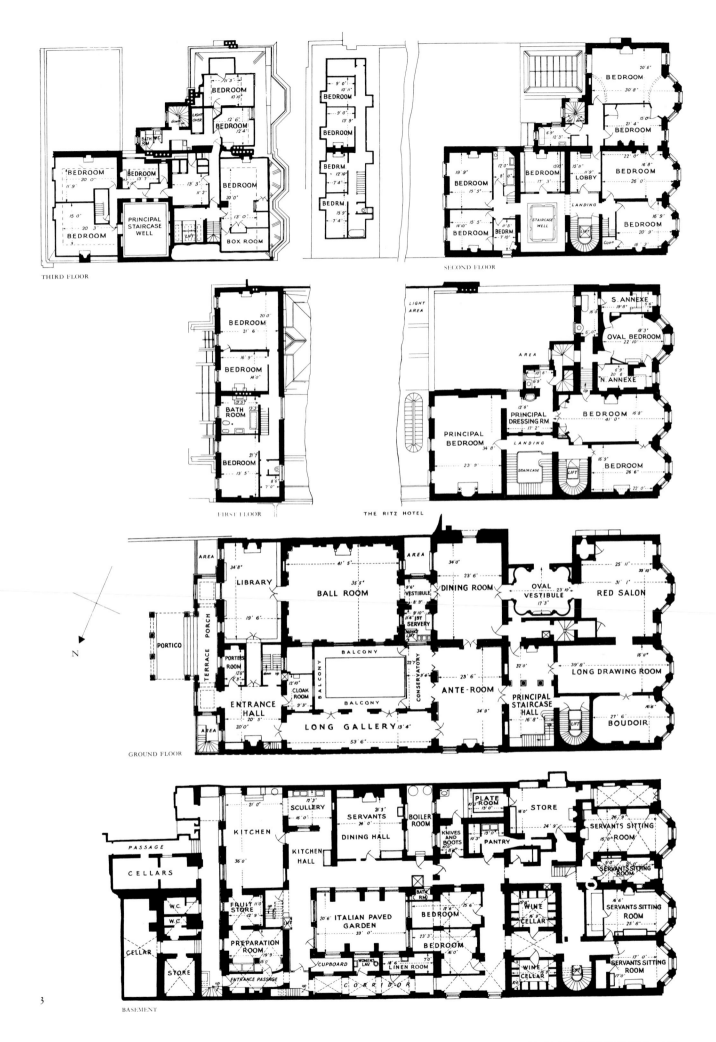

THIRD FLOOR

SECOND FLOOR

FIRST FLOOR

THE RITZ HOTEL

GROUND FLOOR

BASEMENT

3

The house as redecorated for Lord Wimborne c. 1917: 1 The arcade corridor leading to an ante-room decorated with panels 'en grisaille'.

grandeur which could scarcely be imagined to lie behind the modest façade which fronted Arlington Street. In fact the extent of the site equalled that of its neighbour the Ritz Hotel, which lends some credibility to the reply attributed to Lord Wimborne when approached by the proprietor of that hotel, who hoped to annexe the house: 'Wimborne House is not for sale', replied his Lordship. 'How much do you want for the Ritz?' He was looking for space to build a tennis court at the time!

Much of the redecoration at Wimborne House was carried out by Thornton Smith and Co., who were one of the best known firms of London decorators at that time. They were used to working in period styles, and their interiors, like those of their competitors, tended to exhibit the fashion for expensive simplicity which followed the First World War. At Wimborne House, the approach was eclectic. Many of the rooms had little stylistic connection with the architecture of the house,

or indeed with each other. Latilla's frescos in the arcaded corridor were replaced by a similar, but more reserved, scheme of painting. The 'passage room' beyond was thrown together with the Small Dining Room next to it to form an ante-room, decorated with canvasses *en grisaille* set in gilt rococo frames. The Great Drawing Room underwent considerable change, for not only was the fireplace moved, but doors and door-cases were taken out too, and the panelled treatment of the walls removed. In place of all this a simpler scheme was created. A French chimney-piece of the sixteenth century with a tapering hood dominated the room. The walls were hung with crimson damask from cornice to skirting; and early doors and doorcases from the Continent were introduced to complete an effect of romantic mediaevalism. Furniture too was chosen to support the mood: cross-type chairs and heavily carved tables were scattered about, as in the hall of some great château.

3

2 *The Great Drawing Room with an early French chimneypiece.* 3 *Palladian revival on the first floor: Lord Wimborne's Bedroom.*

Where the French influence could be seen in other rooms, it was of a different character – much lighter, and in the style of Louis XVI. The rococo decoration given by the previous generation to the White Drawing Room was now replaced by oak panelling, although not much changed in style. The elegant 'boiseries' which appeared in the Boudoir above, however, represented a more substantial change. Exquisitely carved trophies of drawing and painting implements, flowers and musical instruments, suspended on carved ribbons from the cornice, formed the chief decorative features of this elegant panelled room. It was part of a suite of rooms used by Lady Wimborne, which over-looked the Park. Next to it Kent's little-changed long octagonal room was the Viscountess's dressing room, and beyond, up a small flight of stairs and above the Great Drawing Room, lay her bedroom and bathroom. This part of the house, which had been first used by the Duke of Hamilton, was now completely reorganised to provide an oval bedroom, flanked by narrow closets fitted with shelves and cupboards for Lady Wimborne's extensive wardrobe. All of this survives in its original form, complete with the painted Louis XVI style decoration of the bedroom itself.

This was an extensive suite of rooms for one person, but then Lady Wimborne had three lady's maids, and the clothes she wore were famous. She was apparently outraged once because someone estimated her annual dress expenditure at only £10,000! Both in Dublin, as Vicereine, and in her own house in London, she would cap her every outfit with another. Lady Cynthia Asquith describes her presiding over a banquet in Ireland in an 'exquisite head-dress of ospreys and emeralds'.

The remaining rooms on the first floor of the house comprised Lord Wimborne's own suite of bedroom, dressing room and bathroom. The principal room was William Kent's original Great Room at the front of the house, with its three tall windows looking out over the

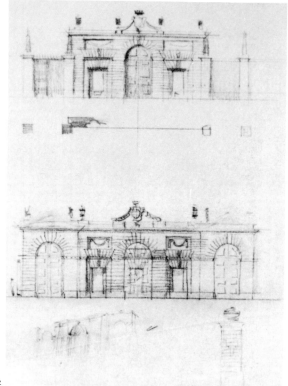

courtyard. This had been the library of Lord Wimborne's parents – a use first given it by the Duke of Hamilton. It now became Lord Wimborne's bedroom. In making the necessary adaptation, he decided to revive its Palladian origins. Kent's frieze and architrave had gone; gone too were the chimney-pieces which existed at either end of the room. If the room were to be made complete again, these would have to be replaced. Lord Wimborne and his decorators, went to another, rather earlier, Palladian house for the necessary detail. Marble Hill at Twickenham, built in the mid-1720s, had come under the care of the London County Council in 1902. In 1917 the Council made a deal with Lord Wimborne whereby, in return for allowing Thornton Smith to take impressions of the ornament in the Saloon there, the Council were allowed to keep the plaster-casts when they had been used. Thornton Smith's account in the sum of £13 10s 0d for the following items survives.

To sending scaffold to Marble Hill Twickenham and plasterer's time and materials, taking impressions of all ornaments in frieze and overmantel etc. to be reproduced.

To supplying and delivering to the London County Council 5 plaster casts of the ornament squeezes at Marble Hill in accordance with the provisions of their letter of permission.

Only one chimney-piece was put back in the room, for Lord Wimborne's bed stood against the chimney breast on the south wall. A grand Palladian doorcase with a pediment and Corinthian columns was added at the centre of the west wall. The Palladian character of the room was thus re-established, a reminder of the house's eighteenth-century origins.

Lord Wimborne's grand style demanded extra rooms for servants as well as for his family and guests, and so two floors were added to the front of the building which overlooked the street. The style of the addition matched that of Kent's original single-storey structure, so that only a change in the type of stone used, and the absence of crown glass in the upper windows,

3 *Ashby St Ledgers: The country house in Northamptonshire created by Lord Wimborne and Lutyens over a period of thirty-five years.*

gave clues to the difference in building dates. Possibly because more use was now given to this part of the house, Lord Wimborne considered erecting a screen wall along the front of the site to enclose the forecourt.

Edwin Lutyens, who had been working for Wimborne on his country house at Ashby St Ledgers, supplied some ideas. Lutyens' rough sketches show alternatives for a Classical frontispiece surmounted by a cartouche and swags, and flanked by gates on either side. One scheme shows the gates enclosed in pedimented surrounds which reflect the twin porches on either side of the portico to the main house. Perhaps it was a good thing that, in the event, nothing so ambitious was carried out – certainly anything as solid as Lutyens had proposed would have made the forecourt a mean and unattractive prelude to the house.

Lord Wimborne's personal involvement in all these changes was considerable, for the alteration and re-decoration of Wimborne House was just one expres-

sion of a lifelong interest in architecture and the arts. His passion for building had started much earlier when, shortly after his marriage in 1902, he purchased the small manor house of Ashby St Ledgers in Northampton-shire. Ashby had been the home of the Catesby family for two hundred years (until their implication in the Gunpowder Plot of 1604), and had then been altered by the Ianson family in the seventeenth century.

In partnership with Edwin Lutyens, who was not only his architect but his great friend, he transformed, over a period of thirty-five years, a modest hunting-box into one of the largest and most romantic country houses to be built in the present century. Right from the start, Guest (as he still was) assumed the role of 'grand seigneur' referring playfully to Lutyens as 'that little architect fellow'. To an unusual extent he deter-mined what should be done, though in fact he greatly respected his friend. Lutyens responded well, finding his client 'nicely outspoken'. The results of their collaboration were irrational and ingenious, and afforded both a great deal of fun.

Alterations began in 1904 with the internal remodelling of the existing house and demolition of some nineteenth-century additions, and was soon followed by the first phase of new additions. In 1909–10 the seventeenth-century east front was 'completed' along the lines of a partially executed scheme of the 1650s. To the north of this was added a mediaeval timber house from Ipswich, which Guest had seen exhibited at the White City and decided to buy. At the same time a new wing was started to the west to include a vast stone hall with open timber roof, and a dining room beyond. In the angle between this and the Ipswich house were built domestic offices with servant's rooms above. The main lines of the gardens were determined by Lutyens in 1904, though they were carried out and modified gradually over the next thirty years. For advice on planting, Lutyens consulted Gertrude Jekyll.

By the early twenties, Lord Wimborne's decision to make Ashby St Ledgers his principal seat and to sell Canford, meant that further additions had to be made to accommodate his widening circle of friends. In 1921, according to Lutyens, a house party, which included the Prince of Wales, had been 'such a terrible squash' that Lord Wimborne decided 'to add lavishly in spite of the hard times'. The outcome was the completion in 1923 of the large north wing which provided more visitor's bedrooms, a mezzanine with twelve servants' rooms, and a new servants' hall with its own pantry on the ground floor. This enlargement in turn necessitated a bigger dining room for parties, which was achieved by extending the existing dining room range westwards. Although the house was substantially complete by now, minor alterations continued right up to Lord Wimborne's death – and indeed after it, for Lutyens designed his patron's memorial in the churchyard adjacent to the house.

The creation of Ashby St Ledgers exemplifies the enthusiasm of the period for romantic houses, for the 'game' of building and restoring, and for entertaining generously and with imagination. It illustrates too the remarkable ambivalence of contemporary figures, who like Lord Wimborne, displayed their wealth conspicuously whilst claiming to sympathise with the plight of the men and women who joined the General Strike in 1926. Indeed, it was Wimborne who helped to accelerate a settlement that year by helping Labour leaders to get in touch with the Government.

In the crisis of 1931, when unemployment had risen to nearly three million and Ramsay MacDonald was forced to form a National Government of all three parties, Wimborne supported the idea, and was elected first President of the National Liberal Party. Wimborne House once again became an important meeting place for the Party, and was the scene of a great Liberal reception on the eve of the State Opening of Parliament each year, just as Londonderry House was for the Conservatives.

Lady Wimborne was extremely interested in music. In 1932 she started a series of private chamber concerts at Wimborne House. Subscription to the 'Quartet Society' entitled its members to enjoy a champagne supper and to listen to music performed in the candlelit ballroom (electric light was not installed in this room until after the War). The first season opened in January with the Brosa String Quartet playing Mozart, Haydn and Beethoven. Later, on 31 March, the bicentenary of the birth of Haydn, the same group played Haydn's D Minor, E Major, and C Major quartets. The concerts continued through the thirties; and programmes were expanded to include works for larger groups of players.

Three years after the start of these concerts, Alice Wimborne met the young composer, William Walton. Despite the considerable difference in their ages (she was at least twenty years his senior), and in the face of jealous indignation from Walton's friends the Sitwells, the two became lovers. After Lord Wimborne's death in 1939, they spent an increasing amount of time in each other's company; and it was during the weeks they spent together at Ravello in Italy that Walton wrote his beautiful Violin Concerto.

In 1937 the Royal Academy exhibited a picture by Sir John Lavery with the title *Chamber Music at Wimborne House*. Although painted with a degree of artist's licence, it conveys the atmosphere of the candlelit ballroom filled with the music of a small orchestra playing before an invited audience. The picture is cleverly composed to include portraits of the key figures – Lady Wimborne on the right and, next to her, Lord Moore (the present Lord Drogheda). On the left, sitting back on the sofa with his legs crossed, is William Walton. Behind him sits Lord Wimborne, making something of a courtesy appearance, for it seems that he never in fact attended these evenings. The harpist is Sidonie Goossens. Close by the orchestra are the Sitwells, and Anthony Asquith who used to introduce each programme with a short talk to qualify the evenings as 'educational' and so avoid payment of Entertainment Tax.

Wimborne House appears, thinly disguised, as the London house of the Marchmains, in Evelyn Waugh's novel *Brideshead Revisited* – 'the big drawing room, . . . the long drawing room, . . . the small drawing room where luncheon parties used to assemble, . . . the gloom

'*I think we might skip the concert tonight, Ivor,*
and find a little lighter entertainment.'

1 Lord Wimborne and his son, the Hon. Ivor Guest, in a Tatler cartoon of 1936 by Tony Wysard. 2 Alice, Lady Wimborne by Cecil Beaton.

. . . of the library, . . . the forecourt, the railings, the quiet cul-de-sac, . . . bays of windows opening into Green Park . . . the light streaming in from the west in the afternoon, . . . the garden door, into the park' from which Charles and Cordelia 'walked in the twilight to the Ritz Grill'. For the purposes of his story, Waugh chose to have Marchmain House pulled down in 1928 to make way for flats. Wimborne House escaped this fate; but four of its neighbours (Numbers 17–20) were demolished in 1936 to make way for a new block called Arlington House.

Just as the ball given for Lady Julia Flyte's first season in 1923 was for Marchmain House 'the last ball of its kind given there, the last of a splendid series', so the music of the Quartet Society played the swan-song of Wimborne House as a private palace. The thirties saw the house probably at its grandest; but, as a private house, they saw it at its end. In June 1939 Lord Wimborne died. In less than three months, England declared war on Germany, and everything changed. Lord Wimborne's son, the 2nd Viscount, never occupied the house fully. Like many great houses during the war, it was placed at the disposal of the war effort. The new Lord Wimborne and his wife, with their baby son (the present Viscount), moved into the front part of the building overlooking Arlington Street, and the main rooms were given over to the British Red Cross Society.

Wimborne House became the centre of the 'Invalid Comforts Section of the Prisoners-of-War Department', which had been established by the Red Cross in 1939. Here were collected, packed and despatched to prisoner-of-war camps parcels of invalid foods, as well as medical, surgical and dental supplies and equipment. According to the official *History of the War Organisation of the British Red Cross Society and Order of St John of Jerusalem*, the Section sent out 185,428 parcels for the wounded and sick between the 1 September 1940 and 31 August 1941.

They comprised standard parcels for a reserve at Geneva – milk, invalid foods, medical and surgical dressings, soap and disinfectant; special parcels based on requests from RAMC Officers at the camps, and from camp Captains; supplies to lazarets also based upon special requests; parcels for individual prisoners requiring a special diet; and parcels of urgently needed surgical appliances, spectacles and so on for individual prisoners. The Section was divided into two branches – one dealing with standard parcels, and the other with individual parcels.'

Wimborne House became a centre for the despatch of individual parcels. It was from here, for instance, that a set of artificial limbs was sent to Wing-Commander Douglas Bader after he had damaged his own while trying to make an escape.

During the War, the house was shaken on a number

1 *The British Red Cross Society packing medical comforts at Wimborne House during the War.* 2 *The 1947 Auction Particulars.*

of occasions by bombs which burst nearby. Nonetheless it survived with little more than surface damage. But, as for so many houses which had been given over to the War Effort, continuity had been broken, and change became inevitable. Other great houses in London had succumbed to change even before the start of the War. On the sites of Grosvenor House and Dorchester House, there now stood hotels. Devonshire House and Northumberland House had given way to groups of smaller buildings and office blocks. The valuable central sites of such houses made their development for more intensive and profitable use increasingly tempting to their owners.

The nature of politics and society had changed too. During the early part of the century, when politics were almost exclusively the pursuit of a social elite, there were political gains to be had through social contacts, even for the small number of Trades Unionists and Labour leaders whom Society managed to embrace. After the War, the enormous increase in the number of working class representatives, whose attachment to working class culture formed their primary tie with

their constituents, resulted in the growth of a powerful group who rejected social integration with the upper classes. Those who, like Ramsay MacDonald, did not, paid heavily for their political 'treachery' and gained little in return. The great London house, as a setting in which political business could be conducted under the guise of social intercourse, had become a thing of the past.

Wimborne House was never re-occupied by the Guest family. Lord Wimborne and his family moved to a more modest house in Chesterfield Street, and in 1946 22 Arlington Street was put on the market. Predictably it did not find a private buyer. The house was bought by Eagle Star Insurance Company with an eye to redeveloping the valuable site; its days appeared to be numbered. The survival of the house, and indeed its recent lavish refurbishment, is testimony to its remarkable character. 22 Arlington Street has shown itself capable once again of adapting to changing circumstances and has, by its own special qualities, engendered in its present owners the necessary commitment and enthusiasm to effect its revival.

By direction of the Right Honourable Viscount Wimborne.

Plans, Particulars and Conditions of Sale

of the

𝔥𝔦𝔰𝔱𝔬𝔯𝔦𝔠 𝔐𝔞𝔫𝔰𝔦𝔬𝔫

known as

Wimborne House

22, ARLINGTON STREET, S.W.1

Situated in a

CENTRAL POSITION ADJOINING PICCADILLY AND OVERLOOKING THE GREEN PARK

The accommodation comprises : Eight spacious Reception Rooms, 26 Bed and Dressing Rooms, and Seven Bathrooms, giving the

EXTENSIVE FLOOR SPACE OF 21,000 SQ. FT. APPROXIMATELY.

With the prospect of **FUTURE DEVELOPMENT OF THE SITE,** having an area of approximately **22,000** sq. ft.

Partial Central Heating.   Electric Passenger Lift.

FREEHOLD

(except for the small Garden adjoining Green Park, which is held on lease from the Commissioners of Crown Lands at a Ground Rent of £60 per annum (temporarily reduced to £10 per annum) for a term of about 28 years unexpired.)

VACANT POSSESSION UPON COMPLETION

To be offered for Sale by Auction by Messrs.

COLLINS & COLLINS

In conjunction with Messrs.

ALFRED SAVILL & SONS

at WINCHESTER HOUSE, Old Broad Street, E.C.2

on WEDNESDAY, the 19th day of NOVEMBER, 1947

at 2.30 p.m. (unless previously sold by Private Treaty).

Solicitors :
Messrs. MONIER-WILLIAMS & MILROY
38, King William Street, London, E.C.4
Mansion House 3868

Inspection by appointment with the Auctioneers : Messrs. COLLINS & COLLINS, 50, Brook Street, Mayfair, W.1 (Telephone : Mayfair 6248), or Messrs. ALFRED SAVILL & SONS, 51a, Lincoln's Inn Fields, W.C.2 (Telephone : Holborn 8741) ; and at Guildford, Woking and Bournemouth.

2

An aerial view, taken shortly after Eagle Star acquired Wimborne House (arrowed). Below chapter title: the Entrance Porch in 1975.

6

JOHN MILLS

FOR SALE BY AUCTION

Eagle Star's association with Wimborne House can conveniently and precisely be said to begin on Wednesday 19 November 1947. This was the date fixed for the *Sale by Auction* in particulars issued 'by Messrs. Collins & Collins in conjunction with Messrs. Alfred Savill & Sons by direction of the Right Honourable Viscount Wimborne'. The title page is reproduced on p. 157 and the preamble to the particulars was as follows:

PARTICULARS

THE HISTORIC MANSION

KNOWN AS

WIMBORNE HOUSE

22, ARLINGTON STREET, S.W.1

Situated in a central position, daily becoming more favoured for Head Offices of important concerns. A few yards from Piccadilly and St James's Street and adjoining the Ritz Hotel, it occupies a valuable site of about 22,000sq ft with frontages of approximately 78ft to Green Park and approximately 77ft to Arlington Street. It is substantially built in brick with slated and leaded roofs. The Arlington Street elevation shows a handsome pillared portico, masonry corners and window jambs. The Green Park façade is relieved by bay windows and stone balconies with ornamental iron balustrades at ground and first floor levels.

Internally the accommodation is laid out on a grand scale giving a total nett usable floor space of approximately 21,096sq ft as follows:

	sq ft approx.
Basement	5,251
Ground Floor	7,505
First Floor, West Wing	2,739
First Floor, East Wing	955
Second Floor, West Wing	2,694
Second Floor, East Wing	427
Third Floor, West Wing	1,525
TOTAL NETT FLOOR SPACE	21,096

(excluding corridors, staircases, landings, bathrooms, cloakrooms and cellars under front courtyard).

The Ballroom, in the 1950s. COLOUR: *The main staircase rises to the first floor only. The balcony below the barrel vault is reached by a back staircase.*

Above the Ground Floor the house is planned in two wings each approached by separate staircases. The East (front) Wing is self-contained and designed to operate as a separate apartment, if required. Most of the rooms in the West (rear) Wing overlook Green Park.

Reception and principal Bedrooms are lavishly decorated in French, Italian and Georgian styles. There are many fine carved stone and marble mantelpieces and some very valuable original panelling.

The Main Entrance is from Arlington Street with a semi-circular drive approach paved in stone setts; two pairs of Portland stone entrance gate posts and railings enclose a gravelled Forecourt.

The particulars incidentally, did not notice that a substantial part of the house was the work of William Kent. The auction duly took place, but bidding, which opened at £150,000 and rose by way of £175,000, £200,000, £210,000, £220,000 to £225,000 did not reach the reserve. The house was accordingly bought in at £230,000.

On 21 November 1947 it was sold by private treaty to Eagle Star for £250,000 with completion arranged for 1 January 1948. Many tales are told of what went on

behind closed doors during these few days, but tempting though it is to reproduce them here, they are almost certainly largely apocryphal. Even though the facts about the purchase are of less obvious moment, and negotiations over the development of the site during the next thirty years are perhaps of greater interest to the student of town planning legislation than the reader of this book, the story of the house would be incomplete were we to pass over them entirely. The next few pages record the salient facts and main events.

Late in 1947 and during the first week of 1948 desultory discussions took place as to the future of the House. Not the least interesting proposal was the possibility of using it for officials and guests attending the forthcoming Olympic Games: this idea came to nought largely, one suspects, because of the condition of the House which had, like most London property at that time, suffered from lack of maintenance since 1939. Between April and June 1948 negotiations took place with a view to obtaining planning consent for office use

The Music Room

The Boudoir

The Green Drawing Room

COLOUR: *Henry Pelham's Room. The 1961 proposals. The scheme consisted of two tall blocks facing Arlington Street and the Park.*

and this was finally granted, initially for seven years, on 11 June.

A contract for basic refurbishment in the sum of £26,065 was awarded to Holland, Hannen & Cubitts in late 1948 and for the next three decades workmen were hardly ever absent from the house. On 8 August 1949 the *Star*, then one of London's three evening newspapers, reported the following:

HISTORY HOUSE

Scaffolding is up at historic Wimborne House, one of London's last great houses, in Arlington Street next to the Ritz. By autumn it will be opened as a West End office by the Eagle Star Insurance Company.

The mansion, 200 years old and containing 26 bedrooms, was bought by the Company for £250,000 from Lord Wimborne. Sir Brian Mountain, 49-year-old chairman and managing director, tells me the main rooms will not be altered. His firm had two properties damaged in the war and the Treasury are still occupying a third of their Threadneedle Street premises.

Between 1906 and 1916 Wimborne House, looking out on to Green Park, was a great official and social centre of the Liberal Party.

During the war the house was used by the Red Cross department, which traced people missing all over Europe.

Sufficient work to render the House usable as an office was completed in time for Eagle Star's Life Department to move in in mid-1950, the contract having been virtually completed by July of that year. The final account was agreed in June 1951 at £40,963.13s.6d. Scarce resources of labour and materials and a strict system of building licences limited what could be done and any attempt to carry out a thorough restoration would have been quite impossible. The difficulties are epitomised by a letter from the Ministry of Works dated 9 February 1950 saying that no allocation of scarce gold leaf could be made because 'although each room is good of its kind their decorative schemes are all different and do not present an outstanding uniform architectural composition'.

The Life Department continued to occupy the premises in varying degrees of austerity alleviated by a programme of works of improvement which went on until the building was finally vacated in 1977 to enable the present development to take place.

In July 1957 a scheme was submitted to the London County Council for a complete redevelopment of the site as offices totalling about 80,000 square feet and costing about £400,000 (an interesting side light on current building costs which are more than ten times greater).

The Planning Officers of the LCC were alarmed at this uncompromising proposal which, only a month later was watered down to a 'mixed' scheme including fourteen four-roomed flats and a penthouse overlooking the park and 25,000 square feet of offices on the Arlington Street frontage. This was followed in February 1958 by a more grandiose, and scarcely practical, scheme for comprehensive redevelopment of Wimborne House, the Ritz and 21 Arlington Street, consisting of a new hotel of 163 bedrooms and 81,000 square feet of offices. The LCC responded to this flurry of activity by making a proposal under Section 30 of the Town and Country Planning Act 1947 to include Wimborne House in the list of buildings of special architectural or historical interest. It was at this stage that they drew Eagle Star's attention to the previously unsuspected fact of Kent's involvement in the design of the original building. Such proposals have never been popular with property owners who tend to equate them with indefinite sterilisation and, this being no exception, formal notice of objection was lodged with the Minister in May 1958. This was followed by a Public Inquiry on 6 May 1959. On 1 December 1959 came the news that the Preservation Order had not been confirmed. It is interesting to speculate what would have happened if it had been. The feeling at the time might very well have been that the Order would have had such a serious effect on the value of the site that (unless an appeal against the decision could be won) a sale was the only sensible course to take. In the event, of course, the house was not sold and so the Minister's decision was a crucial event in its history which led, if not directly, at least eventually, to the decision to restore.

The next year was taken up with long and complex discussions with the planners resulting in the submission of a further scheme in December 1960. This and an earlier scheme came before the Town Planning Committee in June 1961 and both were refused. Eagle Star

appealed and a second Public Enquiry was held in March 1962. The decision, published in July 1962, was the somewhat unusual not to say frustrating one that, despite the Inspector's recommendation to permit the development, the Minister did not consider that there were sufficient exceptional circumstances to allow a new building in contravention of the LCC's 'strict policy of restricting the extension of office accommodation in Central London'. Significantly, perhaps, the Minister's refusal to permit the scheme made no mention of the desirability or otherwise of retaining the Georgian mansion. Notice of Appeal was lodged as a formality, but withdrawn in the face of almost certain failure, in October 1962.

What followed is rather curious and has to do with 'Third Schedule Rights'. Under Town and Country Planning legislation current at the time the owner of a property had the right to increase its size by 10 per cent and, if he were prevented from so doing by the refusal of planning consent, had a *prima facie* claim to compensation for the loss of those rights. Many months and indeed years were devoted to drawing up a claim under this heading, a procedure of almost impenetrable complexity, involving for example such arcane matters as methods of measuring the cubic content of a subterranean vault. Many discussions were held with eminent counsel, expert witnesses and the officers of the Greater London Council and Westminster City Council. The outcome of these – and this is to abridge the actual events to an almost dangerous degree – was that, subject to testing public opinion, it seemed that there was a good chance that planning consent might be granted for the demolition of the front part of the building only, its replacement by a new office building and the restoration of the Georgian building to something approaching its former glory. To encourage public participation an exhibition advertised in the local and national press was held in Wimborne House in December 1974 where full details complete with plans, model, artist's impressions and photographs were displayed. Visitors, who numbered 596, were invited to record their views under conditions of secrecy and the sealed ballot-box was collected daily by an official of the City of Westminster. Only 63 visitors expressed any objections to the scheme and Planning Permission was finally granted in July 1976. Work began on 18 April 1977.

1 The new building, Eagle Star House, at the front of the site. The rebuilt arcade (2) links it to the restored house at the rear.

The Great Room as it was in the 1950s. Below the title: One of the experiments made while finding a colour for the surround of the ceiling.

JOHN MILLS

THE RESTORATION

The options facing the restorers may be summed up as follows. They could restore the house to as near its original appearance as research and competent advice could ascertain; they could recognise that the house reflected the changing tastes of its various owners, that it was an historical document in three dimensions and should be preserved as such; or they could compromise and try the dangerous expedient of getting the best of both worlds. The first option means that most decisions follow quite simply from answers to the basic question, 'What did Pelham's house look like?' Even the most thorough documentary research and examination on the site may leave some matters open to question – but the principle is clear. The second option involves little more than necessary structural and maintenance work and redecoration in the existing style. Compromise on the other hand involves endless decisions which depend on personal judgement and taste – one must ask what is appropriate and what is worth keeping – not just 'what was here?' or 'what is here?'

Whatever is decided, the project leader must assemble a team in whom he reposes complete trust and then steel himself to take their advice. He will be beset by well-meaning and very often well-informed advice from experts and others who are only sporadically involved: his involvement must be continuous and his commitment total. He must be prepared to be judged by the result.

At 22 Arlington Street, despite its difficulties, the compromise method seemed most appropriate. Following the demolition of the front block we were left with Pelham's original house, on the northern part of the site, albeit without the long corridor. To the south

The house, after demolition and clearance down to basement level of the front of the site. The Dining Room, later burnt out, is on the left.

was Stephen Wright's Great Room, the Oval Room and what is now known as the Music Room. Everything to the east had gone. It seemed best to approach the problem almost on a room by room basis, retaining only those rooms which were good in themselves. A study of the plan suggested we might achieve the Palladian ideal of a circuit of interconnecting rooms without passages, something which neither Kent's original house, nor the house in any of its later stages had managed.

The documented history of the House tells us that the oldest rooms, and therefore the only ones which can be attributed to Kent, are those comprised in the original three bay[1] house. Pelham's acquisition of the adjoining property permitted the house to be extended in various directions. The major addition, the Great Room, was started by Kent and finished after his death by his pupil, Stephen Wright. The Oval Room adjoining this and the Dining Room,[2] were certainly added much later. On the basis of this chronology it is easy to put the first and second floors into a fairly accurate

historical sequence. The restoration has been as faithful as possible to Kent and Wright in those rooms and elevations which can reasonably be ascribed to them. Elsewhere individual rooms have been treated on their merits and restored as sympathetically as possible with the minimum of alteration.

As the restoration was undertaken on a room by room basis we will describe the house in the same way, taking the visitor on a Palladian progress. This will avoid the retracing of steps, but will not avoid jumps from period to period.

During the course of the work certain events and discoveries proved to be of crucial significance and these are discussed under the section where their impact was greatest. Thus the *fire* is dealt with mainly in the section devoted to the Music Room and the

1. 'Three bay' refers to the pattern of the front elevation, i.e. three openings on each floor, and not to the bay windows on the rear elevation, of which the original house had two per floor. See plan on page 9
2. Now called the Music Room.

Tuck pointing: Lines of pale mortar are ruled over the irregular brickwork which will be tinted to disguise the original joints.

discovery of original ceilings in the section dealing with the room in which the first discovery was made.

The house, after many vicissitudes, is now several decades into its third century and is alive and well. Alive because although the restoration was in many ways its own reward, what has been produced is no mere museum. The house provides an incomparable venue for business and social functions of all kinds and a day hardly passes when some of the rooms are not in use. Well because the health of the fabric has been painstakingly restored and strengthened to help it withstand whatever rigours are in store over the next two hundred and fifty years.

EXTERIOR

THE APPROACH FROM ARLINGTON STREET

Very little of Kent's original façade was visible until the structures to the east were demolished although the corridor has been rebuilt to match the original design.

Although the brickwork above was in sound structural condition, it was necessary virtually to rebuild below first floor level. This permitted a return to what clues on site and documentary evidence suggested was the pattern of fenestration at Ground Floor level. Attention was also given to a small but vital matter, namely the unification of the glazing pattern.

Unfortunately, countless repairs carried out to varying degrees of competence over two centuries had left the brickwork in a state of pock-marked and multi-coloured disharmony. Resort was had to 'tuck pointing'. Until the seventeenth century, bricks tended to be irregular in shape, requiring thick beds of mortar when being laid. The resulting texture is found pleasing today but when, under the early Stuarts, brick dimensions became more regular, permitting more geometrically perfect work to be produced, the taste for 'gauged' brickwork spread. It was, however, expensive both in labour and materials and led quickly to the evolution of tuck pointing, in which less regular and cheaper bricks

The arches of the arcade, shown with the centering still in place. 2 The park side of the house, under scaffolding, and with the roof off.

far more rapidly laid were used. The joints were well raked out and pointed flush with mortar coloured to blend with the bricks. A thin, slightly proud, pattern of pointing in a mixture of silver sand and lime[1] was superimposed on these broad bands while the coloured mortar was still 'green'. The effect is quite startling, if somewhat overwrought, and the method soon became popular in works of repair, because of its almost magical ability to pull together and homogenise a messy area of brickwork such as faced us here. Tuck pointing makes adjoining brickwork not so treated look rustic, an appearance to be avoided in this context so it was decided to adopt the same method in pointing the new work and the very badly weathered flank of 21 Arlington Street. Certain areas of original brickwork, in particular the back wall of the long corridor, were uncovered and were found to have been built to a very high standard indeed without the use of tuck pointing.

Repairs to the remainder of the original façade (i.e. above band course) consisted of making good the stucco dressings to the window openings and cornices. The blind balustrade beneath the first floor windows has been continued to form the parapet to the rebuilt Arcade and a stone balustrade to a similar pattern has been used to contain the basement area.

1. Sometimes, but not before 1796, compounded of Roman cement and lamp black. In fact certain areas of the elevation had at some time been treated in this way.

THE 'COCKPIT'

The 1947 Auction Particulars make mention of the Cockpit, 'which is situated under Arlington Street and is approached through the cellars which are under the forecourt'. It is a pity to cast doubt upon this romantic and rather raffish notion but it is extremely doubtful if this part of the cellars was ever put to this use. The cockpit (which no longer exists) consisted of a small rectangular chamber of about ten feet by thirteen feet within which an elliptical wall about four feet six inches high had been built. This would certainly suggest a cockpit if the awkward fact that there was no room whatever for spectators did not stand in the way of that thesis. Close examination of the elliptical internal wall showed that great care had been taken to isolate it from the main enclosing walls of the chamber. This attempt at insulation leads to the mundane but more tenable explanation that it was in fact an icehouse.

THE VIEW FROM THE PARK

Apart from the fenestration which was altered in the nineteenth century, this appears in much the same form today as in Daye's view dated 1797. It presents an uncompromising domestic secondary elevation which does not attempt to compete with its neighbours

3 *Attic, showing hip rafters.* 4 *The roof covering – lead coping and guttering, with a stretch of Welsh slates, the main roof covering, beyond.*

further down Queen's Walk, many of which (Vardy's Spencer House for example) are very splendid. It is unassumingly well-mannered and apart from essential repairs and painting no changes have been made.

THE ROOF

The roof could well form the basis of a chapter on eighteenth century building construction. Covered in traditional materials – Welsh slates and lead – and built using time honoured techniques, it is an exemplar of all a roof should be. Few changes were made to it, apart from the removal of a number of dormers, traps and other excrescences. The structural timbers were surprisingly sound and no attempt has been made to straighten out the slightly sagging hips which are merely displaying their honourable longevity.

The student of building construction will be interested to note that the hip rafters are independent of the main roof structure and of a relatively modest section (6in by 4in). They are supported by massive members of 12in by 4in which are framed to the other main timbers with stout wrought iron bolts.

Confirmation of at least two stages of building was given when, at the point at which the two parts of the L-shaped plan now meet, the original slating battens of what was once the external slope of the northern portion were discovered.

INTERIOR
THE ENTRANCE LOBBY AND
THE ENTRANCE HALL

Of all the rooms in the house these gave the least clue as to their original appearance. At the time of the auction the Entrance Hall and the adjoining Entrance Lobby were not subdivided as now but had been thrown into one room by Lord Wimborne. Known as the Ante-Room this was described as follows:

(about 34ft 9in by 23ft 6in); lighted by two french windows (North); plain ceiling; walls panelled and decorated in white and gilt, with modillion cornice; panels fitted with oil paintings in red monochrome on white ground; oak parquet floor; no mantelpiece, hob grate; two Central Heating radiators. On the East wall two sets of large glazed folding doors divide the Ante Room from the Winter Garden.

It was reinstated as two rooms in the early years of Eagle Star's ownership and this plan has been retained, largely in order to provide adequate toilet accommodation on this floor.

The Entrance Hall must originally have had two windows facing the Courtyard but these were removed when the Winter Garden was built and only the enlarged openings remained. The entire room had subsequently been stripped of all architectural detail and was no more than a plastered shell. The doorway to the Staircase Hall was in a different position and that now giving access to the Music Room had been

The Music Room (or dining room) as it looked when in use as an office. The double doors in the far wall led merely to a cupboard.

blocked up. The Entrance Hall is now almost perfectly square on plan and this has enabled a fine new ceiling with a circular motif based on one in 44 Berkeley Square to be installed. The window openings onto the Courtyard have been rebuilt and fitted with sash windows with semi-circular heads. The doorway to the Music Room has been reinstated and that to the Staircase Hall re-positioned on the axis of the Blue Drawing Room, providing an interesting enfilade, to be compared with that connecting the Music Room, Oval Room and Great Room.

There was a chimney piece in Lord Wimborne's Ante-room and consideration was given to installing it in the Entrance Hall on the partition wall. Support for such an action is given by earlier drawings, but as it is impossible to provide a workable flue, any fireplace in such a position must have been false. To install a false fireplace would have been out of step with what we were trying to achieve and as no other wall in the room would accept it, it was installed in the Staircase Hall.

THE MUSIC ROOM

This nineteenth-century room, described as the Dining Room in the Auction Particulars had, by the time of Eagle Star's acquisition, been completely redecorated three times. The walls were panelled in plaster (each panel featuring a decorative motif in low relief). The removal of the Ballroom and other structures to the east made the room very much lighter – they had obscured three tall and graceful casements which originally admitted its natural light. An attempt to mitigate this had been made by the construction of an additional window in the south wall and an elaborate laylight in the ceiling, lit in turn by a large light in the pitched roof above. All the surfaces in the roof void above the laylight were white-washed in an attempt to obtain every particle of available light and although this scheme had met with qualified success, the room was always rather gloomy.

The adjacent demolition had not only lightened the

The results of the Music Room fire. 2 From above, looking south west. 3 Detail of the damage. The room, beyond restoration, was rebuilt.

room; it had brought to our notice the deplorable condition of the structure, particularly the front wall. This like much brickwork of the time, was a mere 4½in skin behind which was virtual rubble. The inherent strength of even poor brickwork is so great that such structures, left undisturbed, can last for centuries. Once they are disturbed however, something has to be done and the intention in this case was to stabilise it by injecting a cement grout and building a new brick skin against it to harmonise with the main façade.

The problem was exacerbated by the discovery of extensive dry rot. This had attacked the grounds supporting the ornate panelling, the bonding timbers of the front and return walls and some of the structural timbers of the roof. A scheme of remedial works which would have preserved the room unaltered, was evolved, but it seemed certain that much of the panelling was affected and it was not known how much would eventually be saved.

Then fate took a hand in solving the problem. In the

early hours of 18 August 1978, a severe fire, the cause of which is still unknown, gutted this part of the building. The innocent remark that this would 'sort out the dry rot', the classic cure for which is the blow lamp, has led certain cynical persons to suggest that the author might, as a last desperate throw, have resorted to arson. That such accusations are the blackest calumnies need hardly be said, but it must be admitted that fate had, at a stroke, solved a number of problems. The dry rot had been cured, the front wall now had to be rebuilt, and the panelling was damaged beyond redemption. The necessity to consider this entire area from scratch now faced us. The question of what to do was partly answered by investigations carried out in the roof space before the fire. These showed that at some time the ceiling had been in the form of a shallow vault with the springing about twenty feet above floor level. The opportunity to return it to this style was grasped and the present room is the result. Externally the rebuilt façade shows three tall window openings filled with

The Oval Room, built in the 1920s, smoke stained after the Music Room fire. A chimney piece from the old Entrance Hall was inserted here.

double-hung sashes with narrow glazing bars and finished with flat gauged arches. Above these are blind recesses to relieve the expanse of plain brickwork. The shape of the new roof was the subject of much discussion; its form before the fire was a simple double pitched affair with the gables abutting our neighbour's flank wall to the south and the flank of the original three-bay house to the north. It was suggested that the opportunity should be taken to alter this and construct a hipped roof which, it was claimed, would visually separate the building from its neighbours. An equally strong body of opinion insisted that the original simple roof should be recreated. A compromise solution of a simple pitch with a shallow hipped front slope is the result.

Internally a style of decoration in keeping with 1790, its original building date, was decided on. The window to the south was filled in so that a chimney piece,

formerly in the Ballroom, might be installed. The opening linking the room with the Entrance Hall to the north was reformed thereby enabling a room by room progression to be achieved. The result is a room of considerable splendour ideal for use in the manner suggested by its name.

THE OVAL ROOM

The latest addition to the house was built in the 1920s and consists of a beautifully proportioned room based on an oval plan with four deep semi-circular niches. A new ceiling centre and a chimney piece from the original front Entrance Hall have been installed. Apart from redecoration no other changes have been made.

The Great Room stripped down. The ceiling and the cornice below are the great legacy from the second phase of the house's development.

THE GREAT ROOM

It is a continuing source of pleasure to observe the varying reactions of visitors seeing this room for the first time. Hyperbole is rarely absent although some reactions might be a paraphrase of 'C'est magnifique, mais . . .!' Approbation is not universal but all seem to be, momentarily at least, searching for the apposite phrase with which to sum up their astonishment. Its scale, its grandiose conception, its overpowering magnificence seem to be at odds with the rest of the house and indeed they are. Isaac Ware, eighteenth-century architect and faithful adherent of the Palladian theory, had strong views on the 'Great Room,' forcibly expressed in his *Complete Body of Architecture.*

In houses which have been some time built and which have not an out of proportion room the common practice is to build one on to them . . . the custom of routs has introduced this absurd practice.

Our forefathers were pleased with seeing their friends as they chanced to come and with entertaining them when they were there. The present custom is to see them all at once, and to entertain none of them; this brings in the necessity of a great room, which is opened up only on occasions and which loads and generally discredits the rest of the edifice . . . this is the reigning taste of the present time in London, a taste which tends to the discouragement of all good and regular architecture, but which the builder will be often under a necessity to comply with, for he must follow the fancy of the proprietor, not his own judgement . . .
(Quoted by Dan Cruickshank and Peter Wylde, in their wholly delightful *London: The Art of Georgian Building.*)

It is conventional to describe a room ceiling first but in this case one has little choice. The complicated plan has been superbly rationalised into a system of ribs and coves into which *grisaille* paintings on grounds of red, blue and green have been inserted to form a pattern which, embellished by the gilded enrichments, is like the roof of Aladdin's cave. The subject matter is virtually a classical pantheon. Each picture was originally

painted on canvas in the usual way and then fixed to the ceiling. Where the ceiling was flat this was done stretchers and all; where a curved surface was involved the painting was removed from the stretchers and stuck directly to the plaster. The notion of an eighteenth-century Michelangelo, lying on his back within a stone's throw of Green Park is unfortunately just fancy. The similarity between the treatment of this ceiling and that in the first floor saloon in 44 Berkeley Square is striking. Although temporal, if not aesthetic superiority must be ceded to Berkeley Square, there can be no question that some single design, though not perhaps one hand, is parent to both. Even after the many restorations both have suffered, differences of style seem to be discernible in each case. The latest restoration followed the near disastrous fire of 1978, the smoke from which applied an evil patina over the whole room. Removal of this necessitated partial repainting of parts of the ceiling, this is not now detectable except by the closest inspection.

Due to its importance and impact the decorative scheme of the room offers more scope for controversy than any other in the house and this may be a good point at which to discuss the sources generally at our disposal in dealing with questions of decoration. Our advisor on decoration was Ian Bristow who is pre-eminent in his subject. In his researches he explored three avenues. First it was possible, by taking minute samples and examining them microscopically, to ascertain the colour of every coat of paint ever applied. It seems that our forebears were not over-zealous in stripping paintwork before redecoration because in the case of the Great Room four separate decorative schemes could be inferred from the samples taken from the background areas of the ceiling. Second physical examination of the building could be compared with documentary evidence. The original building accounts still survive and are in the Library of the Royal Institute of British Architects. They make fascinating reading and yielded up a great deal of useful information. Third Ian Bristow's own knowledge of the taste of the age and of the pigments available ensured that we could never stray too far from the correct path. The result is as near authentic as may be.

It may be remembered that a shortage of gold leaf had an inhibiting effect on the partial restoration carried out in the 1950s. Ironically there is now no shortage as such but we had chosen a time to do our work when the price of gold had reached record heights. Its use had to

3

3 *One of the grilles in the floor of the Great Room. The new heating grilles, throughout the house, were copied from those at Holkham Hall.*

be very carefully restricted for reasons of cost alone, although this necessary economy was easier to accept in the knowledge that Kent himself had not used a great deal of gold in his original decorative scheme. Gold has therefore been used only in this room, on the balustrade of the great staircase, the ceiling of the first floor Saloon and in the restoration of the 'discovered' ceiling in Henry Pelham's Room. This need for economy imposed a discipline which was probably healthy. The unrestrained use of gold can easily appear meretricious and actually obscure good detailing which is more subtly displayed by the interaction of light and shade. But there are no cheap alternatives; a sample area carried out in gold paint confirmed that there is no substitute for the real thing.

The damask wall hangings and curtains were specially woven using authentic cards and dyes. The colours were based on Pelham's inventory post mortem.

Accepting, as seemed inevitable, that the ceiling of the Great Room must be the predominant factor, it had to be faced that other elements in the room were totally at variance with it. Doors and door-cases imported by Lord Wimborne had a mediaeval appearance. The two main sets of doors replacing them are based on proto-

types at Holkham Hall, themselves superb examples of eighteenth-century joinery. The two smaller openings, leading to the closets have now withdrawn discreetly into the background having been replaced by jib doors. The compartment behind the right-hand one, which was almost certainly a urinoir, has a *trompe l'oeil* trellis decoration in the style of an arbour and a tiny south facing window of which the curvilinear glazing bars add an amusing *art nouveau* flavour. The Auction Particulars somewhat coyly state that this 'partitioned corner piece is fitted with two stone console basins'. The geography of great houses often meant that the provision of such a convenience was very necessary if a long walk to the nether regions was not to interrupt a good dinner. It is interesting to compare this one with that in the dining room at Holkham Hall where, behind a splendid door exactly matching the others in that magnificent room, lies a cupboard only a few inches deep with a shelf for the appropriate receptacles. The twin cupboard to the urinoir in the Great Room, originally a passage, and later a closet, now houses, behind its jib door, the nerve centre of the house's audio system.

The chimney-piece, is of particular interest. Its outstandingly fine design and execution make it a work of

The similarity between the ceiling in the Great Room and that in the first floor saloon at 44 Berkeley Square has already been noted. In the latter case the theme is the loves of the gods and goddesses; in Kent House the artist has not chosen a particular theme, satisfying himself with depicting them in characteristic situations. The ceiling can be rationalized into seventeen panels (see plan on page 177) and the descriptions which follow are similarly numbered.

PANEL 1

Encircling the supporting boss of the chandelier are Zeus (Jupiter) and Hera (Juno) with their two messengers Hermes (Mercury) and Iris.

Zeus is bearded and crowned. He holds a sceptre in one hand and a thunderbolt in the other. He is accompanied by an eagle. Opposite him is Hera, his wife and sister who also wears a crown and holds a sceptre. She is accompanied by a peacock.

Hermes is immediately recognised with his winged feet and helmet, the petasus. He holds the caduceus, a magic wand with entwined snakes. Iris, the goddess of the dawn is shown with butterfly wings and her symbol, the rainbow.

PANEL 2

This shows the conventional portrayal of Apollo and Daphne. She is turning into a laurel tree, her fingers are sprouting leaves and her feet have become roots. The figure on the left with the palm, the symbol of victory, is Perseus or Theseus. On the right is Demeter (Ceres) seated at the foot of a tree holding the traditional cornucopia.

Narcissus is shown with his spear on the ground gazing at his reflection in the water. Artemis (Diana) with a dog and a hunting horn is next to him.

Below, Lethe the river god reclines beside an urn and Prometheus, chained to Mount Caucasus is condemned until the end of time to the grisly cycle of having his liver preyed upon by an eagle all day, the liver being renewed at night.

PANEL 3

Heracles (Hercules) is seated in the centre wearing a lion's skin and being served by Hebe the goddess of youth. Deianeira, his earthly wife stands by a broken pillar in a mournful attitude. On the right of Heracles his friend and servant Hylas stands with a pitcher.

PANEL 4

Daedalus and his son Icarus occupy the centre of this panel. Icarus is shown at the apogee of his flight with his wings about to part from his shoulders.

Actaeon is on the left; his head is that of a stag, into which he was transformed as a punishment for watching Artemis (Diana) bathing. On the right is Athene (Minerva) holding a spear and a shield upon which can be seen the Medusa's head. An owl, the symbol of wisdom, perches on her head. The two pictures below depict Alpheus and Arethusa. Alpheus the river god is shown clutching at a cloud into which Arethusa was transformed in order to escape him. She is seen in the adjacent picture emerging from the cloud.

PANEL 5

Hephaestus (Vulcan) in his forge, assisted by a cyclops is working at an anvil. A helmet and shield lie at his feet. On the right is Pandora whom Hephaestus formed from clay. She is holding the box, which, as is often the case, is shown as an urn, from which the evils were released. On the left an alchemist holds a crucible over a fire, the gift of Hephaestus.

PANELS 6 AND 7

Ganymede and the eagle are on one side of the window and Leda and the swan on the other.

PANEL 8

Apollo and the nine Muses occupy the semi-dome above the window.

PANEL 9

Poseidon (Neptune) crowned and holding a trident, is in a chariot with a dolphin's head. It is being drawn by a hippocampus, a creature with the head of a horse and the tail of a fish. A putto with a sheaf of corn is behind him.

Below, flanked by a dolphin and a group of tridents is Triton, half man half fish, blowing a conch shell.

PANEL 10

Hades (Pluto) is seen abducting Persephone (Proserpine) on his chariot. An amoretto with bat-like wings leads the way while one of Persephone's companions raises her hand in alarm. The two headed dog Cerberus is chained to a post below.

PANEL 11

Dionysus (Bacchus) is seated on a chariot drawn by a leopard. There are vine leaves in his hair and he holds a thyrsus, a wand surmounted with a pine cone. Beside him drinking from a jar, is a satyr with goat's legs. On the right, in flowing drapery and beating a tambourine is a maenad, one of the followers of Dionysus. Ariadne is on the other side. She was rescued from Naxus where she had been abandoned by Theseus after their escape from Crete.

Aphrodite (Venus) is below with a dove and Eros (Cupid) has his familiar bow and quiver.

(continued p. 177)

COLOUR: *Top: The Great Room (door to the Oval Room on the left). Bottom: semi-dome over the window. Overleaf: the ceiling (see plan on p. 177).*

PANELS 12 TO 15

The figures in the four corners of the ceiling represent the four seasons. Spring with flowers, Summer with vines, Autumn with the harvest and Winter with fire.

PANELS 16 AND 17

The four Cardinal Virtues flank the door opposite the windows. Justice with a sword and scales, Prudence with a snake and a looking-glass, Fortitude with a broken column, Temperance with a vessel of water.

COLOUR. *Top: The Blue Drawing Room. Bottom: The Octagonal Room. The bay is matched by one glazed with mirror glass at the other end of the room.*

The Yellow Drawing Room, about 1905. Comparison with an earlier photograph (page 140) shows how taste in furnishings had changed.

art in its own right. It is remarkably similar (as has been noted) to one depicted in the second print in Hogarth's series, *Marriage à la mode* (see p. 44), first advertised in 1743. Hogarth is generally supposed to have based the room in his print upon the drawing room in Horace Walpole's house in Arlington Street, probably No 19 according to present street numbering. It seems unlikely that our chimney-piece is that very one, as its known history takes us some way from Arlington Street; in fact to Midgham House near Reading. Midgham House, which was demolished in 1965, was owned in the first part of the eighteenth century by the Hon. Stephen Poyntz, and the supporting caryatids on the chimney-piece are supposed to be based on his two daughters. He was tutor to the young Duke of Cumberland who resided at Midgham and for whom a wing, 'the Duke's Rooms' was added to the house in 1738–39.

Later he moved to the suite of rooms provided for him by George II at Hampton Court, which were decorated by Kent. The architect of 'the Duke's Rooms' at Midgham was Henry Flitcroft, 'Burlington Harry', who, like Kent, was a protégé of Lord Burlington. As an architect he is not commonly considered as the equal of Kent, although the two men were great friends. Flitcroft specialised in designing chimney-pieces in the style of Inigo Jones, and as it is known that the one under discussion was in the Dining Room of the 'Duke's Rooms' it may safely be presumed that it was by him. There is at least one other version of the design in existence in another Flitcroft house, Woburn Abbey. Such replication is only to be expected when we remember that eighteenth-century architects and master builders frequently produced pattern books of chimney-pieces, door-cases, mouldings and so on from which

The Blue Drawing Room. 1 The original cornice appearing as the later cove moulding is removed. 2,3 The room stripped down for redecoration.

their clients were invited to choose. The overmantel, which is modern, is based on one by Kent at Raynham Hall in Norfolk.

Putting modern services into historic buildings presents problems. The cast iron air conditioning grilles set into the walls and floor of this and other rooms in William Kent House are faithful copies of those installed in Holkham Hall, where they serve as outlets of what must be one of the oldest warm air heating systems still in use.

THE BLUE DRAWING ROOM

We know from Pelham's inventory post mortem that this room was hung with blue damask in 1754 and it has been redecorated with blue wall cloth and curtaining similar in design and manufacture to those in the Great

Room. The clues provided by the discovery of an original ceiling in Henry Pelham's Room, and an early photograph, led to investigations in this room, which were rewarded, when following the removal of the cornice, which consisted of a plain stepped cove surmounting a bold rope pattern feature, the Classical cornice we now see was discovered. This, though intrinsically sound, was most insecurely attached to the structure. Working from above and using wire stirrups it was possible to anchor the majority of it back into position and renew the remainder. The early twentieth-century photograph shows an enriched box member running parallel with the cornice and about 12in from it. Such is the quality of this early print that it has been possible to reproduce this feature in perfect detail. The fine marble chimney-piece was acquired recently but its history is not known.

1 The Green Drawing Room. 2–4 The renovation of the Staircase. 2 New plasterwork matched up to old on the frieze below the balcony.

THE GREEN DRAWING ROOM

In 1977 the ceiling in this room still had the familiar flat bed and large diameter cove which early photographs show painted as a skyscape. The walls were panelled in oak, in Louis XVI style, which displayed first class craftsmanship, a credit to Thornton Smith & Co who, it is thought, carried out the work in about 1917 when the lower ceiling was installed. Unfortunately the ravages of time aided by damp, had left the woodwork in a very friable condition and it was doubtful whether repair would have been successful. The relative heights of this and the adjoining rooms gave good reason to suppose that, once again, the plain ceiling might be hiding something of interest. It was; but this time the ceiling above had been brutally damaged when the timber supports to the later ceiling had been installed. It was much later than the mid-eighteenth century and possibly dated from the late nineteenth century. It certainly antedated the panelling with which it had no affinity. Had the ceiling and panelling been in repairable condition a severe problem would have presented

itself. To have retained both would have been unthinkable; they simply could not have lived together and in fact never had. To save one? Perhaps – but which? In the event the panelling was photographed, dismantled and sold, and a new Kentian ceiling installed. The chimney-piece is again a recent acquisition.

THE STAIRCASE HALL

Both here, and at 44 Berkeley Square, Kent astonishes us with his ingenuity in creating such spatial splendour within the confines of a modest town house. Before restoration much of this feeling had been lost, largely because the partitioning of part of the fireplace end of the Hall to form a lavatory had had a very unfortunate effect on the overall proportions. The space left between the columns and the end wall was cramped and mean. Providing toilets in the Entrance Lobby has made possible the restoration of this area to its original dimensions.

A great deal of the applied plasterwork was quite modern; in fact on the back of one moulding, removed

in an attempt to ascertain its date, the legend *Wimborne House* was found inscribed in pencil. This effectively dates the moulding as no earlier than 1880, when Sir Ivor Guest was created Baron Wimborne, and probably a good deal later, perhaps 1917 when a great deal of remodelling was done. Hardly a square inch of wall space had been spared some applied decoration and the engaged columns of the Ionic order at first floor level which lacked convincing bases or pedestals had a particularly uneasy and mawkish appearance. This work must have taken place at the same time as the filling-in of the First Floor Landing. It was not difficult to identify the earlier work and this was retained. This strict treatment has greatly ennobled the entire area.

The staircase itself has stone treads and leads to a stone paved landing, which has been renewed. The balustrade, which is original, is very similar to that at 44 Berkeley Square and Holkham Hall, but whereas the Staircase at 44 Berkeley Square, having progressed with an astonishing ebullience to first floor level, changes gear and in a more restrained but brilliantly inventive way continues upward, here in Arlington Street it stops at the first floor level. Further upward progress is by way of a secondary staircase.

FIRST FLOOR LANDING

When the house was acquired by Eagle Star there was, enclosing the space behind the present columns, a partition constructed to resemble glazing and then mirrored. The effect was far from happy and the landing was a poor climax after the splendid ascent. That this important area was once more sumptuous is borne out by Burn's drawings of alterations for the Duke of Hamilton showing the removal of a segmental apse to create the Duchess's Dressing Room. The screen was demolished and any qualms at the propriety of such an action were laid at rest by the discovery of the wooden cores of two columns standing immediately above those on the ground floor. The precise form of this area gave rise to much discussion and it was with some reluctance that a semi-circular apse and semi-dome had to be abandoned due to the difficulty of devising an architecturally satisfactory way of linking this with the staircase proper. The present scheme of a simple semi-circular compartment with columns as originally provided, flat bed ceiling and niches for statuary, is probably very close to Kent's original conception.

SECOND FLOOR GALLERY

As the Great Staircase does not extend beyond the first floor, access to the second floor is by means of a secondary stair. This emerges at second floor level onto a gallery surrounding the four sides of the stairwell. Soon after Eagle Star acquired the house the District Surveyor insisted upon the demolition of the gallery because of its unsafe condition. The connecting bridge that replaced it, while functionally adequate, was built with no regard to aesthetics, and the opportunity has been taken to replace it with a facsimile of the original gallery based on photographic records. The simple archways leading off the gallery have semi-circular heads, springing from bold imposts. The clue of further imposts to the north of these openings, was followed up and two arched recesses were discovered. These have been reinstated to restore the balance. That the recess in the south wall, originally a door, had no counterpart on the north side was established beyond any doubt when the plaster was removed for dry rot treatment. The roof light was restored to match the coffered treatment of the vaulting. The vault, the Diocletian window motif in the tympana and the almost bucolic quality of the mouldings give a feeling of simplicity and serenity which may owe something to the fact that this part of the house had received less attention from the long succession of owners than many more 'important' areas.

The view downwards is spectacular. It is worth noting here that several of the panels of the vault are hinged and must have given the servants (and perhaps the children) an exciting vantage point from which to watch their elders and betters regally ascending the Great Staircase.

HENRY PELHAM'S ROOM

The present splendid appearance of this and indeed other rooms in the house, is due to what was probably the most dramatic of all our discoveries.

In order to install services it was necessary to remove flooring throughout the building (in the principal rooms each board was numbered to facilitate reinstatement). Whilst examining the floor void on the second floor, above this room, it was noticed that, in certain areas, the plaster curls which form when wet plaster is forced through the spaces between the laths, giving such a

The Staircase, in 1950 after the first refurbishment. In 1979 the mirrored screen was replaced with a semicircular compartment.

Henry Pelham's Room. 1 The panelling in course of removal. 2 A detail of the carving – a trophy of globe, palette, square and rule.

ceiling its strength, were missing. These areas were not random, but seemed to form a regular pattern, suggesting that the ceiling in the room below had a rib pattern formed of boxes, covered in laths, and plastered. Yet what actually existed in the room below was a very simple plain plaster ceiling with a fairly large diameter cove at the junction with the wall. Perhaps when this later ceiling was constructed the original one had not been completely destroyed. An aperture was immediately formed in the ceiling, large enough to admit a head. Feeling like Sir Flinders Petrie when he gained the first glimpse of Tutankamun's tomb I peered into the void between old ceiling and new. It was no more than 18in deep, but it was obvious that the original work was almost entire and the gold leaf in mint condition.

It was a wonderful discovery, but immediately raised the question of what to do about the existing wall coverings. These were in a completely different style consisting of wooden panels with relief carvings in the style of Louis XVI, the whole being brush-grained in a greenish tint. The question of their intrinsic merit became secondary to the fact that they could not live

with the robust Kentian ceiling. There seemed only one answer; the panels were photographed, carefully removed and sold, making a small but welcome contribution to the overall cost. The room now contains what is possibly the best example of Kent's original work in the house. It has been further embellished by a fine chimney-piece for which the present owners of Mereworth House (Colen Campbell's near-replica of Palladio's Villa Rotonda) apparently had no further use. The fireback bears the Hamilton motto 'Through' surmounted by the ducal coronet.

FIRST FLOOR SALOON

The Saloon is perhaps the finest and most completely satisfying room in the house. Its counterpart at Berkeley Square has the ornate episodic ceiling which matches that in the Arlington Street ground floor Great Room. (At Berkeley Square the Saloon takes up two storeys and the second floor windows are blind.) The present appearance of the Arlington Street room owes much to its Kent ceiling. Lord Wimborne's restoration between

3

4

5

Henry Pelham's Room. *4 The first glimpse of the old work through the ceiling. 5 The plaster removed. 3 Only minor damage needed repair.*

1 The First Floor Saloon in 1965. 2 The Great Room at Marble Hill – casts of this plasterwork were used in the 1917 refurbishment.

The Octagonal Room, looking towards the internal bay, which completes the room's symmetry. As originally, it is now lined with mirror glass.

the wars complemented this and virtually no alterations have been made.

The chimney-piece is similar to that in the beautiful Great Room at Marble Hill but the putti which decorate the latter have not been repeated here. Thanks to the co-operation of the Dowager Viscountess Wimborne we can quote from Thornton Smith & Co's account for copying this overmantel on 12 January 1917.

To sending scaffold to Marble Hill Twickenham and plasterer's time and materials taking impressions of all ornaments in frieze and overmantel etc to be reproduced.

To supplying and delivering to the London County Council (the owners of the House) plaster casts of the ornament squeezes at Marble Hill in accordance with the provisions of their letter of permission.

The cost of this work was £13.10s.0d.

It is very probable that at one time there was another chimney-piece at the opposite end of the room; a flue is available and size and symmetry suggest it. The jib door, now leading to the lobby to the rear of the first floor landing, was probably once expressed because there is evidence that its counterpart, leading merely to a very shallow cupboard, lay to the right of the central entrance door. That this can only have been the shallowest of closets is obvious when it is realised that it was formed in the thickness of the partition, the other side of which is the Great Staircase. Although its presence was dictated by symmetry, it may have been put to

the same use as the small compartment in the Great Room on the ground floor. The elaborate doorcase does not appear in the nineteenth-century photograph and certainly formed part of the work carried out by Thornton Smith & Co.

The centre piece of the ceiling is new. It replaces one which was in poor condition, and was not contemporary with the rest of the plaster work.

THE OCTAGONAL ROOM

The bay window, a feature of English house building since the middle ages, is very difficult to adapt to a Palladian scheme. William Kent House offers a number of solutions to the problem of integrating it into a classical interior, as no less than five principal rooms have bay windows looking onto Green Park. In this room in particular the bay was not despised because, partly no doubt in the cause of symmetry, it is repeated at the opposing end. Investigations of the false work revealed that the conceit had originally been carried to the length of installing facsimile windows, glazed with mirror glass, and they have been restored to this pattern. The chimney-piece is probably original.

The room otherwise has been left as found, which probably means as left by Lord Lincoln who removed Kent's frieze and architraves. A jib door leads to the short flight of stairs rising into the space over the

The Boudoir, inserted in the space above the Great Room. In this form it dates from c1917, when alterations were made by Lord Wimborne.

ceiling of the Great Room. This space was for many years merely a void not having sufficient headroom to meet the custom of the time.

THE BOUDOIR

It was left to the Duke of Hamilton, or perhaps the Duchess, and their architect, the ingenious Mr Burn, to realise that a room could be inserted into this space. What we have now forms part of Lord Wimborne's alterations, the third in the history of the room. It consists of an oval chamber in the style of Louis XVI. The joinery in particular is of a very high standard and the attention to detail is most impressive. Very few alterations have been made; the uncompromising flat ceiling has been relieved by an oval centrepiece in sympathy with the room and the paintwork has been freshened. The slip rooms which flank the Boudoir are lined with cupboards – some glass fronted – superbly designed and finished.

THE SECOND FLOOR

The second floor originally housed the less important bedrooms and nurseries. As these were from the first, simple, and have not been substantially altered, they are a rich repository of everyday Georgian detailing.

THE THIRD FLOOR

The garrets provided accommodation for the servants, which was by the standards of the time, probably better than average; for example each room had a window, a fireplace and permitted a reasonably upright stance. By our more enlightened standards they are unusable, but far from lacking in interest.

on this and the following pages the inventory of the contents of 22 Arlington Street, made in March 1754 after the death of Henry Pelham is printed in full. Two pages of the original document are reproduced facing pp. 192 and 193.

An Inventory of all the Household Furn, Plate, Linnen China etc. of The Rt. Hon: Henry Pelham Deceased Taken at his House in Arlington Street May 1754

Garretts etc.

A large table with Drawers, a brass hall Lanthern. A spinning Wheel

Lumber Room

Cusheons belonging to a Sofa. 2 old mattrasses, 6 old Curtain Rods, 3 old Grates and some old Lumber   4.10.0

Maids Room and little Room adjoining

A 4 post bedstead and green printed Stuff Furniture: a featherbed bolster Mattrass 3 blanketts and a quilt. A Bedstead as before and blue Serge furn. A Bed bolster and mattrass, 4 Blanketts and a quilt. A piece of fruit and a picture of Mrs Pitt. A picture in a gilt frame – 2 Wains^t Chamber Tables. A Deal Do. A Wains^t. Desk and an old Glass. 3 matted and 2 Damask Chairs old. 2 small parcels of Down. A large persian Carpett. A smaller Do. another Do. Abt. 20 yards of narrow wilton Carpett 9 yards of french Do. and border – A small old Silk persian Carpett. An old list Carpett. Shovel tongs and fender. Old Cafoy hangings lin'd with linnen. A mahog Corner Cupboard A mahog small book shelf.

Little Room next Do.

A small bed^d. and Striped linnen furn. A feather bed bolster mattrass, 4 blankts and a quilt, a gilt picture frame 2 reading Desks   39.11.6

Miss Mary's Dressing Room, Bed Cha^b. & Servants Room

A small 4 post bedstead and blue Stuff furn to thro'over. A feath: bed bolster, 3 Blanketts a quilt and a mattrass. A wall Double Chest of Drawers 2 matted Chairs, a Copper Coal Skuttle. A Corner press. An old Crimson Couch beds^d. A small Wains^t. Chest of Draws. A table Do. A matted old Chair and Stool. A p^r. of tongs and fender. A small tin lanthorn on landing. 3 Check W Cur^s. A large turkey Carpett. 6 Mahog. Marlbro back Stools in Check Cases. A wall Dressing Stool. A toilett Table and glass. A small Indian Cabinett. A wall Couch Cover'd with Damask. A mahog reading Stand. A wall buroe Table and a small Escrutore (A Harpsicord a leather Chair – deleted). A pillar and Claw print Screen. A pillar & Claw mahog Table. A Do. with a Cutt rim. 2 small Mahog Cabinetts. A wire fender Shovel tongs poker fender beloows and brush. A picture of St Jno. the Baptist and Our Saviour in gilt frame. A Crayon and a small picture Do. A flowerpott with a black and gold frame. 2 small Landscapes no frames. A Head, A small 4 post Bed^d. with Ticken furn. A straw bed. 2 Check Mattrass. A bolster & pillow. 4 Blanketts & a quilt. A Slope lath field bedstead and Check thro'over furn. A feath: bed bolster & pillow, one Mattrass, 3 blanketts & a quilt. 3 Green Lindsey Curtains. A turkey Carpett. A wall Chest on Chest. 4 matted Chairs, a Wains^t. Close Stool and pan. A small Mahog Claw Table. A small Wains^t. table. A Deal Stool. A small Mahog. Bookshelf. Shovel tongs poker fender Bellows & brush. 2 Copper Coal Skuttles. One warming pan.   35.19.6

Chintz Bed Chr. Dressing Room & Serv^{ts}. Do.

A 4 post bed^d. with Scarlett Cloth thro'over furn. A feather bed bolster matt^s. 3 Blanketts & a quilt.

A matt^s. and a wood Chair. A mahog

Sidelanthern. A small 4 post bedstead and old Satten furn. A feath: bed bolster a mattrass, 4 blanketts and a quilt, a wood Chair, 2 old brass high fenders. An airing Horse.

Chintz Bed Chamber

2 4 post bedsteads with mahog. feet posts & Chintz furn. inside white. A feath: bed 2 bolsters, 4 pillows, 1 small Do. and a strawbed.

2 Check and 2 White mattrasses, & blanketts, 2 quilts & 2 Chintz drawing W Cur^s. a Wains^t. Toilett Table (a small Chest of Drawers – deleted) A mahog. breakfast table. 3 Marlbro Mahog Chairs and Check cases. One walln: Do.

2 matted Chairs and 1 Small Stool. 2 small bed Carpetts. A Wains^t. night Table. A mahog. Do. A pillar and Claw old Indian Screen. A table Clock and brackett. A shovel, tongs, poker & Iron hook. A mahog Cloaths Chest.

Closett adjoining etc.

(2 small Indian Cabinett for China – deleted)

A 4 leaved green Cloth Screen. A Deal toilett Table. 3 small Elbow Chairs and Check Cases. An Easy Chair and old Cotton Case. 2 matted Chairs, an Inlaid Cabinett on a Japan frame. A Do. less. A grate shov: tongs poker and fender, tea trivett, bellows & brush. A Copper Coal Skuttle. A persian and a Turkey Carpett.   63.5.6

Great Room & Landing to Do.

A 4 post iron bedstead and blue Serge thro' over furn. A feath: bed bolster. 1 pillow. A straw & a Check Mattrass. 4 blanketts and a quilt. A wall: Escrutore. An old Inlaid Cabinett. A wall Elb: Chair no case, a Japan Teatable. A mahog. tray on a high stand. 2 Candlestands Do. A Deal toilet a warming pan. A Wains^t. Chest on Chest. A single Do. A bronzed small figure. A blew paper horse Screen. A matted Chair. A small stool, a quilted Elbow Chair. A steel Grate Sho: tongs, poker and fender. A view of Greenwich in a gilt frame A Do. of Chelsea it's Compannion. A small landscape in gilt frame. A frame only. A wall Escrutore with folding doors. An old leather Square Trunk. A small stepladder. A mahog: close stool. 2 boxes and a backgammon Table. a coal

skuttle a grate shovel and brush. A Deal toilett table. A bell lamp with brass ornamts. & Shade.   32.16.6

Blew Dressing Room & Bed Chb^r.

3 Blue Marine W Curtains. A wilton carpett 8 Marlbro Wall Elbow Chairs & Check Cases. A 4 leaved India paper Screen. 3 matted Chairs. A mahog table. A writing Stand on a pillar and Claw. A wall chair with leather seat. A mahog Circular Table. A rosewood Strongbox. A small pillar and Claw table. A Japan box on a frame. A grate wire fender. Sho: tongs poker bellows & brush. 2 small book Shelves. A needlework Screen Mahog pillar and claw. A 4 post bedstead and blew marine furn. 2 thick matrasses pillow and bolster, 4 blanketts a white quilt. 3 Draw up W curtains 4 Elbow Chairs & Check Cases as above. A large couch feath: bed & bolster & pillow, a mattrass, 4 Blanketts & a quilt. A small 1/2 head laths & ticken furn. A mahog Do. & a Wains^t. flytable. A Wains^t Airing Horse. A wall. press with Draws under An old Small turkey Carpett, Shovel tongs poker tin fender Bellows & Brush and tea trivett. A blue paper 2 leaved Screen. K. Willm. on horseback over Chim: A mahog breakfast table, A small Dressing Glass. A Wains^t. Close Stool & pan.   62.4.6

Mr Pelhams Dressing Room

3 Green Lutstring window Curtains lin'd with Tammy Threadline and Cloakpins. A turkey Carpett. 6 small Elbow Chairs in Linnen & Check Case. A green mantel 2 Stools Cusheons and bolsters, a mahog: writing table. A mahog breakfast table. A Do. flytable with a Shelf. A small Canvas Screen. A Steel Grate wire fender furn. bellows and brush. (Glasses in pier pannels – deleted). A bronzed figure on book case and 2 Urns. One brass & 2 Small plaister figures 4 Crayons in black & Gold frames.   41.5.0

Blue Draw^g. Room & Closett

Blue mixt & Dam: hanging. 3 WCs Do. lin'd. A turkey Carpett. A mahog Buroe table Carved Therms. A marble table on a Carv'd and painted frame. A Glass over. Do. inlaid and part gilt frame. 11 large strait legg'd back stools. Damask & Cases. 2 Elbow Do. A steel Grate wire fender furn bellows & brush. (2 large pictures of a fish & Smiths Market. A Do. of

dead Game. A Do. of Fruit. –
deleted.) 5 Landscapes in gilt frames
over Doors, one Do. with frame over
the Chimney. 2 Indian paper 2 leaved
Screens. Glasses as above fixt in
piers.   291.8.0

Great Room & Closett & passage

Crimson Dam. hangings. 5 W Curtains
lin'd, Silk lines & tassells. 12
Mahog Carved & gilt Chairs cover'd
with Dam: & Cases. 3 Window Stools
Do. –

(A large persian Carpett. a bay Cover
to Do. – deleted)
A smaller. 2 Granate marble tables
with brass moulding Gilt frames. 2
Glasses over Do. in gilt frames. A
Glass lustre hung with Silk lines &
tassells & linnen Case. (2 fine India
Screens – deleted). A steel Grate &
high brass wire fender. Sho: tongs
poker bellows & brush. a picture over
the Chimney 2 whole length K.G. the
2nd & Q Caroline. 2 large History
pictures in Gilt frames [in the margin
is noted: P. Vandich & Castilione] A
marble Bauzo, a landscape & a gilt
frame. A head in Do. A Do. black and
Gold Frame. A tapistry Screen on a
strain'g frame. Another of plush
work. 2 Colour'd prints – one of Mr
Pelham in black and Gold frame a fruit
p. ᵛ p Mich. Ango. A mahog side
lanthern 2 picts Caniletto 2 heads and
two battles & 1 other Landscape.   865.11.0

Waiting Room

2 wall presses with brass mouldings.
An old Wainsᵗ. pillar & Claw table 4
wall. Matted Chairs. A Grate fender
furn. bellows & brush. A longhair
broom. A board Covᵈ. with Green
Cloth.   10.0.0

Dining Parlour

2 blue mixt Dam: WCs lined silk lines
etc. 12 Mahog leather Chairs nail'd.
A mahog Card table. A blue vein'd
Marble sideboard. Mahog frame with
Thin end feet. A marble Table Carved
& gilt frame –

A turkey Carpett. 2 large China
Cisterns and mahog frames. A mahog
pail. A pier Glass in a Carved and
part gilt frame very bad colour. A
night table. A steel Grate wire
fender bellows & brush. (A large
picture of the School of Athens –
(Kent) – deleted).

2 Whole lengths Duke & Dˢ. of
Newcastle, Duke of Richmond on

horseback. A Landscape Do. sʳ.
Rob't Walpole 2 oval Do. over 2
Doors. A bust of Lord Pembrooke over
the other. A Landscape over the
Chimney   125.16.6

Passage and foot of great StairCase

5 Mahog side lantherns 4 busts on deal
painted Therms. 5 plain and 2 carved
therms. A sett of mahog Dinᵍ.
Tables to join. 2 braziers. A group
of figures bronzed. A small square
Dinᵍ. Table. 3 wall. matted
Chairs. A Brass lanthern with line &
Balance weight. A Dumbwaiter. 2
large Chests. A wall: press. A
Copper Scuttle a long tin fender. A
piece of Oil Cloth, 2 bragg tables a
round and a hexagon. Small mahog
Table.   71.10.6

Porters Hall & bed Chamber

5 Wainsᵗ. Hall Chairs & a table. 1
Deal painted form. A parrott stand.
An 8 Day Clock.

A Hall Lanth: with balance Wᵗ.

Shovel tongs poker & fender. A Wood
Shutter & 2 Slates.

A Press bedstead, green Serge Curtains
& rod. A feath: bed bolster and Check
Covers a pillow a Check Mattrass. 3
Blanketts and a quilt. 2 Sedan
Chairs. An old brass Coalscuttle.   11.6.0

Mr Quinches Room

A mahog writing Desk a Do. Square
pill: & Claw table, an old Wainsᵗ.
Cham: table. 3 leather bottom Chairs
one wood stool. An old Dressᵍ.
Glass, a Copper Coal Scuttle Shov:
tongs poker fender and brush.   2.11.6

Mr Roberts's Room and Passage

2 old green Stuff Dam: W Curtains.
(An Indian Cabinett in a Japan frame.
A wall Chest on Chest – deleted).

A Mahog Breakfast Table. A pillar and
Claw Do. A Cloaths Chest Do. 5
wall. matted Chairs (An old Elbow and
– deleted) a windsor Chair. Shovel
tongs poker fender bellows and brush.
A Wainsᵗ. Close stool a CopperCoal
Scuttle (An old Spinnett and –
deleted) part of a marble Slabb broke.   9.14.6

Little Bed Chambʳ.

A Slope lath field bedstead and blue
Serge furn. A white Mattrass 4
blanketts & a quilt. A feather bed
bolster and pillow. 2 matted, 2
leather Chairs and a Wainsᵗ. Table.

A Copper Coal Scuttle, Shovel tongs poker bellows & brush.

Young Cook & Saxby

An Iron bedstead and old red stuff furn, A feath: bed bolster an old white mattrass. 4 blanketts, a quilt and a Cover lid & 3 wood chairs.

Black boy

A field bedstead and old yellow stuff. furn. A feather bed bolster and an old mattrass 3 blanketts a quilt and a wood Chair.   8.19.6

Pantry

5 plate and 2 knife basketts. 2 old Chairs and a Stool. Shovel Tongs poker and fender one Mahog tray. 3 Wains^t. Do. A Gun, a brass platewarmer a Do. pail A mahog Cistern. One old picture. *Glass* 2 doz of water Glasses 8 Decanters 56 water Drinking glasses. 70 wine Do. 6 Cruetts 2 Cups & Covers 4 small muggs 9 Lemmonade Do. Six Salts

Confectionary

A large Deal table. 6 Chairs with pincusheon Leather Seats an old Wains^t. Round Table an old wood Chair. A small beds^d. and yellow Serge thro' over furn. A feath: bed bolster and pillow. A white 3 blanketts & a quilt. A jelly frame, 2 high brass Candlesticks. A pr. of Snuffers. A Copper jelly Saucepan & Cover. A Do. smaller no Cover. One large preserving pan. 2 Do. less. 2 Do. with handles. 4 Copper plates 2 wire plates for Dry Sweetmeats. 2 Copper Scimmers and a ladle. A large brass Scimmer. 2 Copper spoons one Copper Chocolate pott lin'd with Silver. 1 Do. Common 5 Dutch Coffee potts.
7 Do. teakettles 2 Do. Copper. A tea trivett. 1 Copper & 1 brass Coal Scuttle. An Iron toasting frame. Shovel tongs poker fender and bellows. A Coffee mill. a sugar breaker and 2 Hatchetts. a mahog Cuttrim tea tray. 2 round small waiters. 1 large Japan Do. 5 smaller Do. 3 Do. for tea Kettles. 3 Square Small Japan tea waiters.

10 Sieves, 2 oval tea trays Wains^t. brass Hoops. a pr. of Scales no weights, 2 Stove trivetts. 2 tin Ice pails and 4 Sugar Canisters. 2 pewter moulds, 6 Do. Cheese moulds. A compleat Desert frame with french

plate rims consisting of 20 pss of Glass broke. Jelly Glasses, Sweatmeat Do. and pillars etc:–

China:– 25 Dishes of Different sizes, round & octagon painted. 24 long Dishes for Sides coll^d. 21 blue & wt. Soupplates. 28 Common Do. 7 octagon. 5 doz & 7 same of the first Dishes. 3 punch Bowles broke & mended some Chipt. 4 wash hand basons & a funnel 8 Comport Dishes 2 large Bowles & Covers. 1 Cover broke 2 burnt in China pint Muggs. 6 Sugar basons Do. 6 Do. Dragon China with Saucers. 2 Do. half pint Bow China 6 pint Do. Crackt 1 blue & wt. tea pott. 1 large brown Do. 1 smaller Silver Spout, 5 Staffordshire 5 Doz & 11 Saucers for water Glasses, 16 odd Cups of Different Sorts Some imperfect – One Sett:

12 blue & wt tea handled Cups & Saucers. 12 Do. smaller. 12 Do. less. 3 doz handled Coffee Cups & Saucers. Six blue & wt handled Cups & Saucers. 1 slopp bason & plate. 1 sugar Dish and Cover. 12 tea Cupps & Saucers. 6 Chocolate Cupps no Saucers. A Creampott & a Canister. A tea pott & Saucer. A boat for spoon 4 pint basons blue rims – 4 large Dishes Do. A Dragon Do. broke. 9 blue & wt breakfast Cupps & Saucers. 5 small blue & wt. Cups & Saucers 3 odd Cupps. *Stoneware* 7 tea potts, 2 quart Juggs, 4 large Cupps & 5 Saucers. 4 handled Cups. A silver marrow spoon 4 Teaspoons and a strainer –   85.14.0

Still Room

A large linnen press. A large Cedar Chest of Drawers. A large linnen Chest Do. A small Chest of Drawers. A mahog Claw table. 6 beech matted Chairs. A mahog Dumbwaiter. A parrott Stand. A copper Coalskuttle. A fender Shovel tongs poker bellows & brush. A Copper Saucepan one large and 3 small tinn ones. A tea trivett, a large matt –

Bed Chamber

A 4 post bed and Scarlett Cloth furn. A matt^s. feath: bed bolster & pillow. 3 Blanketts and a quilt. A small Glass.

A Wains^t. Chest of Drawers. a press & a tin lanthern in passage. A large old Chest 3 lantherns on back stairs. 28 Dam: table Cloths 19 Birds Eye Do. 5 Sideboard Draper Cloths. 21 Draper TableCloths 7 Draper Small Do. 8

An Inventory of all the Household Furn:
Plate Linnen China &c of The Rt Hon:ble
Henry Pelham Deceased Taken at
his House in Arlington Street May the 1764

Garretts &c
A large table with drawers. a brass Hall
Lanthern. A spinning Wheel ————

Lumber Room
Cushions belonging to a Sofa.
2 old Mattrasses. 6 old Curtain Rods
3 old Grates and some old Lumber

4. 10.—

Maids Room & little Room
adjoining
A 4 post bedstead and green printed Stuff
Furniture. a feather bed bolster Mattrass
3 blanketts and a quilt. A bedstead as
before and blue serge furn: a bed bolster
and mattrass 4 Blanketts and a quilt
a print of feet. and a picture of L.d
Pitt. A picture in a gilt frame ——
2 wainscot Chamber tables. A deal d.o
a wainscot Desk and an old Glass
3 matted and 2 Damask Chairs old
2 Small parcels of Down. A large Persian
Carpet. A smaller D.o another d.o
ab.t 20 yards of narrow wilton Carpet
9 yards of finch D.o and border ——
A small old Silk persian Carpet.
An old list Carpet. Shovel tongs and
fender. Old Callico hangings lin'd with
linnen. A mahog.y Corner Cupboard
A mahog.y Small book Shelf

Little Room next D°

A small bed D° and striped linnen fur̄d

A feather bed bolster. mattrass 4 blank:ts

and a quilt a gilt picture frame

2 reading Desks   39 . 11 . 6

Miss Mary's Dressing Room bed Ch̄d

& Servants Room

A small 4 post bedstead and blue stuff

fur̄d. to the over. a fath: bed bolster

3 Blanketts a quilt and a mattrass

A wall Double Chest of Drawers 6 matted

Chairs a copper coal Skuttle. A corner

press. An old crimson Couch bed D°

A small wains:t Chest of Draws. A table D°

A matted old Chair and Stool

A p:r of tongs and fender A small tin

lanthorn on Landing. 3 Check W Cur:t

A large turkey Carpett . 6 mahog:

marlbro back Stools in Check Cases

A wall Dressing Stool A toilett Table

and glass . A small Indian Cabinet

A wall Couch Cover'd with Damask

A mahog reading Stand . A wall

buroe table and a small Escrutore

~~A stuff seated 6 leather Chairs~~

A pillar and Claw print Screen

A pillar & Claw mahog. Table

A D° with a Cutt rim   a Small mahog.

Cabinet D°. A wire fender Shovel tongs

poker fender bellows S and brush

Damask Do. old. 45 Huccabuk table
Cloths. 13 Small Breakfast Do. 16
Stewards table Cloths. 10 Dimity
Cloths 12 Servants Cloths. 2 large
India Huccabuk Cloths. 23 napkins Do.
16 Doz of Dam: napkins 11 Doz. of
birds Eye Do. 7 Doz. of Draper Do.
13 Doz. of huccabuk Do. 2 Doz. & 7
Dam. waiting Napkins.

10 old Draper Do. 11 fine Russia
Draper Do. 27 Course Do. 36 tea
Napkins, 11 Draper waiting Do. 19 pr.
of fine holland sheets.

20 pr. of Course Do. 21 1/2 pr. of
second sheets. 30 Pr. of servantts
Sheets.

37 Com. pillow Cases, 80 holland Do.
6 Small Do. 19 Damask towells 16 old
Draper Do. 9 huccabuk Drink^s.
Cloths. 11 Jacktowells. 24 Rubbers.   131.3.0

*Stewards Room & Footman's Room &
passage and Servants Hall*

A 4 post bedstead & blue old Stuff. furn.
A feath: bed bolster, 2 old mattrasses,
4 Blanketts & a Rugg. Another press
bed old Crim: Stuff Curtains. feath:
bed bolster mattrass, 4 Blank^ts. & a
Coverlid.

Another Ironbed^d. & old linsey
furn. A featherbed bolster mattrass,
2 blanketts & 2 Coverletts. Shovel
fender and poker. A Coal tubb. 3 old
Chairs and a table a Copper and a
brass Coal Scuttle. An old bays
Case. 2 tin Side lantherns. A pss of
oil Cloth an old Tubb. A stepp
ladder. Old Curtains to Arch. A long
Deal table and form to Do. an old
Wains^t. small table. A stand to
brush Cloaths. 2 wood Chairs. a Coal
Tubb. a fender Sho: & poker –

A Wains^t. press, 11 leather Jacks.
A Din^g. table, a deal frame mahog
top. Sho: tongs poker fender and
bellows.

A small 4 leaved Wains^t. folding
Screen. A Copper Coal Skuttle, a wood
Chair. A form. 2 old Chairs without
Bottoms and some other Such lumber. A
small Range.   17.14.6

Kitchen & Laundry with Offices

A small table, a Do. pr. of stepps. A
small Stool and 2 Chairs. A meat
Screen lin'd with Tinn.

Copper: 4 large Broth potts and
Covers, 3 smaller Do. one Brazier pan
& Do. one fish kettle Cover and
plate. 2 Gravey pan and Covers, one

turbitt pan (plate only) 2 Cullenders
11 Large Stewpans 7 covers.

18 Small Do. and Covers. 3 Black
potts & 2 Covers one Dutch oven. 5
large Saucepans and 4 Covers. 4 small
Do. no Covers. 2 ovenplates one
poupton Mould & Cover.

A Cheese toaster 8 petty pans. 2 long
Do. 1 Dutch Kitchen Six bask^t. pans
& hand moulds. 20 tart pans 2 brass
Skilletts. 3 Copper lamps. 3 small
Turks Caps and Covers. 6 ladles. 7
Dresser Spoons, 3 large Scimmers. 5
Small Do. 1 broke. 24 petit patty
pans. A Drip^g pan & Iron Stand. A
basting ladle. A spice Box, a tea
kettle. A large Drinking pott. 3
frying pans. A multiplying Jack. 3
Chains, pullies & lead weights
compleat. 6 Ironwheel Spitts 11 lark
Spitts, a pr. of Standing Racks. 12
Iron Scewers one Iron Head^d. Do. 2
Cleavers. 2 mincing knives. 3
Gridirons. A fender Shov: & poker &
bellows. 1 trivett & 12 Stove
trivetts. A pr. of tongs poker & 3
Stove Shovells. a Charcoal Shovel. 2
tin Graters. A Bill mettle mortar &
pestle. A flower tubb. a Drudger, a
greenbaskett. 2 Iron frying pans. An
iron peal & raker to oven. A fire
Shovel. A Beeffork 2 Dishtubb 2 pails
one brass Candlestick. A small
Wains^t. Table. 3 leath:bottom
Chairs, 2 matted Do. Fender Sho:
tongs & poker. 2 powder tubbs lin'd
with lead.

Pewter: 28 Dishes, 3 fish plates & a
Ring, 5 Covers for Dishes, 15 Soup
plates. 43 Common Do. A large Copper
a Grate. An old linnen press. 12
washtubbs 12 flasketts, a wett horse 2
forms. A mangle. A large Drying
horse with pulleys. 3 large & 2 Small
Do. Horses. a Deal table. a small
Wains^t. Do. 6 wood Chairs. a
napkin form. A trivett fender 2
Shovels. tongs & poker. 13 flatt
Irons 4 Stands. 1 box Iron 2
heaters. 2 Japan beer Juggs. 4
Iron^g. Cloths, 9 round Cloaths
Basketts, 3 very old Beds at the
stables.   58.16.0

All the within named goods are valued
and Appraised to the sum of Ninteen
Hundred Sixty Nine pounds, Seventeen
Shillings & Sixpence.

£1969.17.6   Agents   Wm Bradshaw

May 1754   Paul Saunders